PAINTED REFLECTIONS

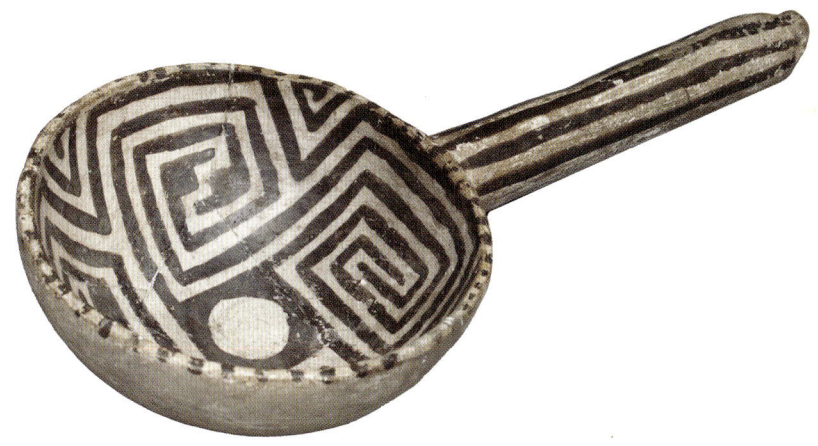

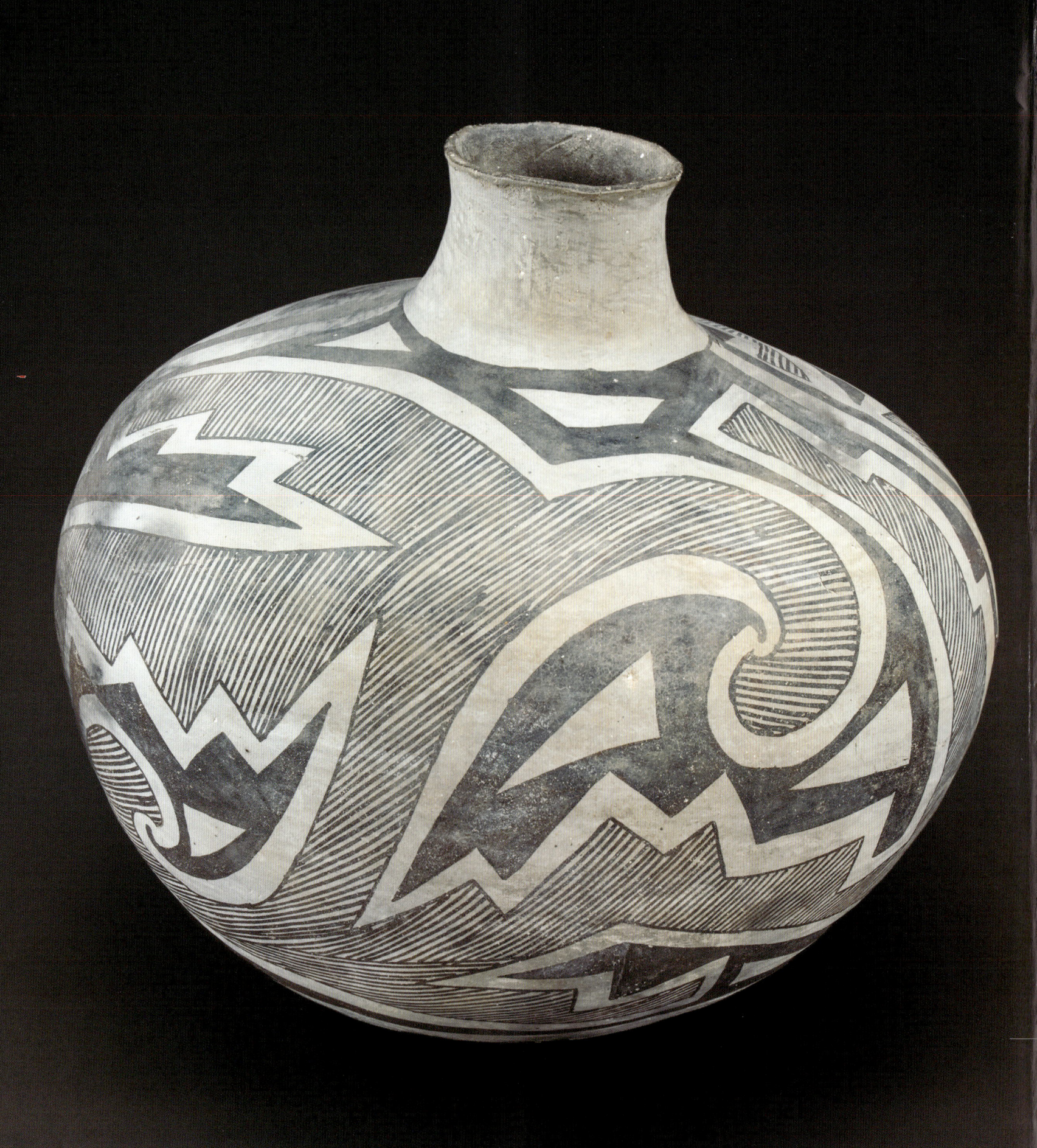

PAINTED REFLECTIONS

ISOMERIC DESIGN IN ANCESTRAL PUEBLO POTTERY

SCOTT G. ORTMAN | JOSEPH TRAUGOTT

MUSEUM OF NEW MEXICO PRESS | SANTA FE

© 2018 Museum of New Mexico Press. Text © Scott G. Ortman and Joseph Traugott. *All rights reserved.* No part of this book may be reproduced in any form or by any means whatsoever without the express written consent of the publisher. The Museum of New Mexico Press is a division of the New Mexico Department of Cultural Affairs.

Director: Anna Gallegos
Editorial director: Lisa Pacheco
Art director and production director: David Skolkin
Designed by Michael Motley
Composition: Set in Axiforma
Manufactured in China
10 9 8 7 6 5 4 3 2 1

Library of Congress Cataloging-in-Publication Data available from the publisher on request

ISBN 978-0-89013-637-9 hardcover

MUSEUM OF NEW MEXICO PRESS
PO Box 2087
Santa Fe, New Mexico 87504
mnmpress.org

CONTENTS

Foreword
Maxine McBrinn and Antonio R. Chavarria   7

Introduction   11
Abbreviations   15

1. Perceiving Isomeric Design   17
2. Isomeric Design Strategies   25
3. Relationships between Spiral and Stepped Elements   41
4. Isomeric Designs and Weaving   49
5. Isomeric Designs and Pueblo Philosophy   65
6. Isomers, Art, and Society   73

A Portfolio of Isomeric Designs   79
Further Reading   131
Acknowledgments   135
Index   137

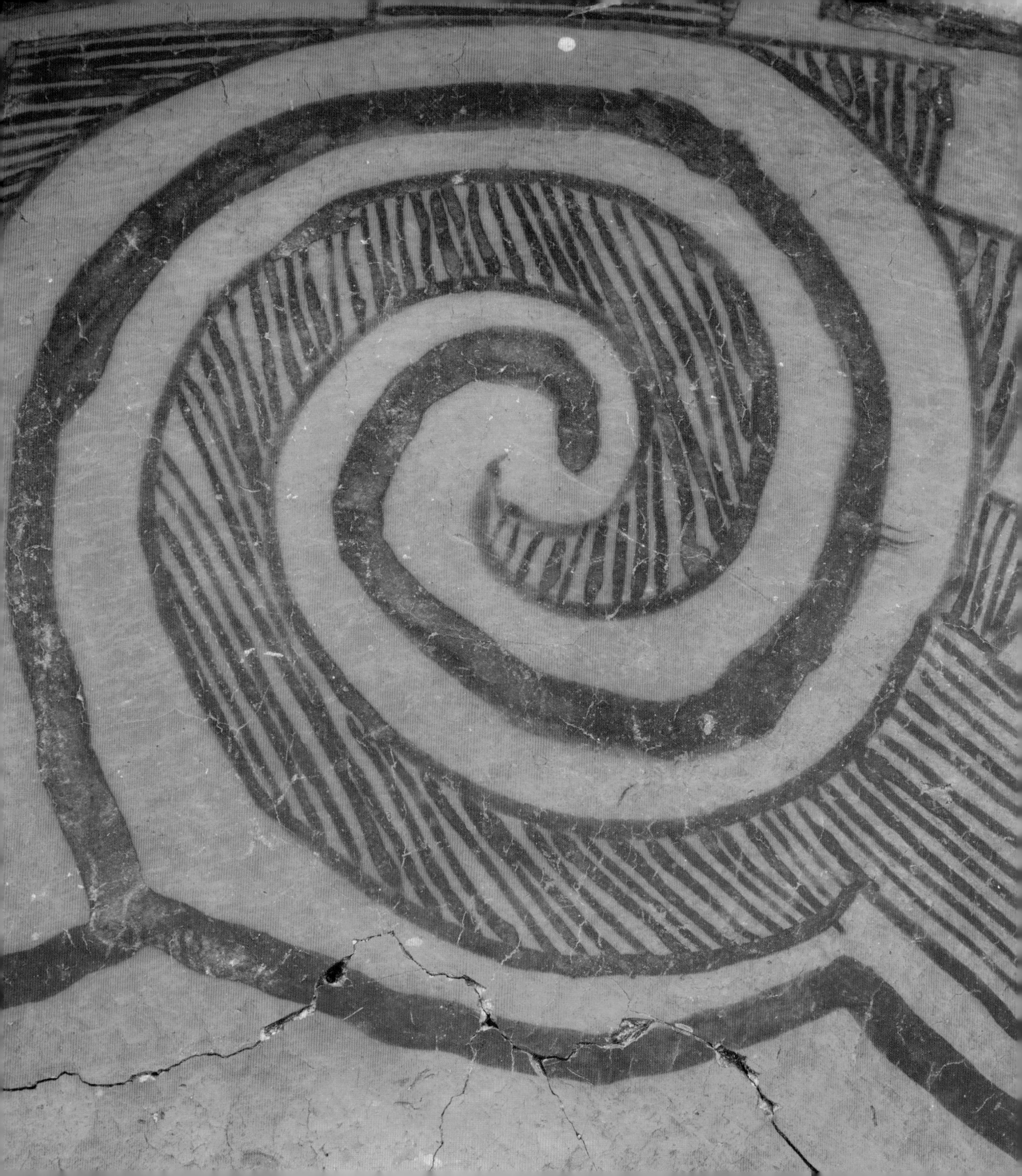

FOREWORD

Maxine McBrinn and Antonio R. Chavarria

We are honored to write this foreword and find that the topic touches nicely on our personal research, although in different ways. McBrinn is an archaeologist who works in the Southwest but primarily in the pre-pottery period. Among her interests, though, are textiles and social organization. Chavarria is a potter as well as a museum curator, and is a member of Santa Clara Pueblo. Each of us has known both authors for years. Joseph Traugott was a colleague in the Museum of New Mexico, which includes both the Museum of Indian Arts and Culture and the New Mexico Museum of Art. Scott G. Ortman's fieldwork is presently focused on Cuyamungue, an Ancestral Tewa Pueblo village just north of Santa Fe, and he has been active in Southwest archaeology for decades.

The genesis of this volume started in Joe's large and influential 2012 exhibition *It's About Time: 14,000 Years of New Mexico Art*, as part of which he showed several Ancestral Pueblo pots with isomeric designs. He had earlier consulted with Linda Cordell, the foremost synthesizer of Southwest archaeology, as well as a pottery specialist, about his discoveries. He even took Linda, who was notoriously susceptible to cold weather, out on a chilly winter morning to check whether the spiral rock art he found at Chaco Canyon was a winter solstice marker. Ever game, she accompanied him and reveled in the adventure.

It is rewarding to see Joe carry through his study of the isomeric-designed vessels and join forces with Scott, the leading voice for metaphorical analogy in the region and a researcher whose roots in the Mesa Verde region have extended into the northern Rio Grande. He is the perfect partner for this project. We have been fascinated to see them bringing their separate gifts to bear on building a richer understanding of the Great Pueblo Period pottery designs.

This book is a gratifying read from front to back; it is lavishly illustrated, and rich with intriguing ideas and connections in unexpected directions. Best of all, it makes sense. This volume provides a substantial stage for further debate and study of the Puebloan past. Even casual viewers cannot help but be struck by the importance of dualities in modern Pueblo life. Men and women play equal but distinct roles. The yearly ceremonial cycle has summer dances dedicated to bringing rain for a successful harvest; winter dances are more focused on hunting and the return of spring. Many villages have moieties, sometimes called turquoise or squash, or at other villages, winter and summer. Between them, these moieties divide administrative and ceremonial tasks, giving structure and a voice to the entire village's year.

Less obvious but also intuitively comfortable is the idea that the isomeric designs may reflect (pun intended) the complementary and consubstantial existence of the world we live in with the spiritual world. Use of these designs would have reminded every viewer of this reality. The vessels created centuries ago reveal artistic and cultural complexity, yet were also made to hold simple food such as mush and stews. Balance achieved through parallel opposition is an ideal place yet it is never constant, requiring physical and metaphysical maintenance. Along with this reinforcement is a reminder of the appropriate behavior expected of each individual.

One of the surprises is the sheer number and richness of isomeric designs on pottery dating from roughly 900 to 1300 CE. The four strategies outlined in chapter 2 are used singly and in various combinations so that the designs can be simple or very complex, and can be applied equally to bowls and to jars. Neither of us will be able to look at vessels from this time period again without looking for the existence of these strategies.

A wonderful addition to this book is the schematic diagrams that illustrate how the potter painted the designs, assertions bolstered by a few finished pieces where the framing lines are still visible. These diagrams allow the reader to see the mind of the artist at work, a connection that is immediate and visceral. Not only does this provide a greater appreciation for how the designs were produced, but also a greater appreciation for the brilliance of the artists. Discussions with Pueblo potters reveal that they also use this method to "unlock" the spacing and placement of designs. The fact that all of this was done using yucca leaf brushes makes it even more impressive.

That isomeric designs ceased to be created about the same time so many other social practices disappeared is an indication of profound social upheaval and the deliberate creation of new ways of doing things. Given that persistence and adaptation are constant necessities for living in the Southwest, the authors suggest that the underlying belief system persisted through this transition and still persists today. This is a hopeful vision for how a society can survive upheaval and emerge different yet still whole.

We are excited that more research might continue to illuminate Pueblo life in the past, as sketched in the last chapter of this volume, and encourage the authors or others to carry the work forward.

Maxine McBrinn is curator of archaeology and Antonio R. Chavarria is curator of ethnology at the Museum of Indian Arts and Culture in Santa Fe.

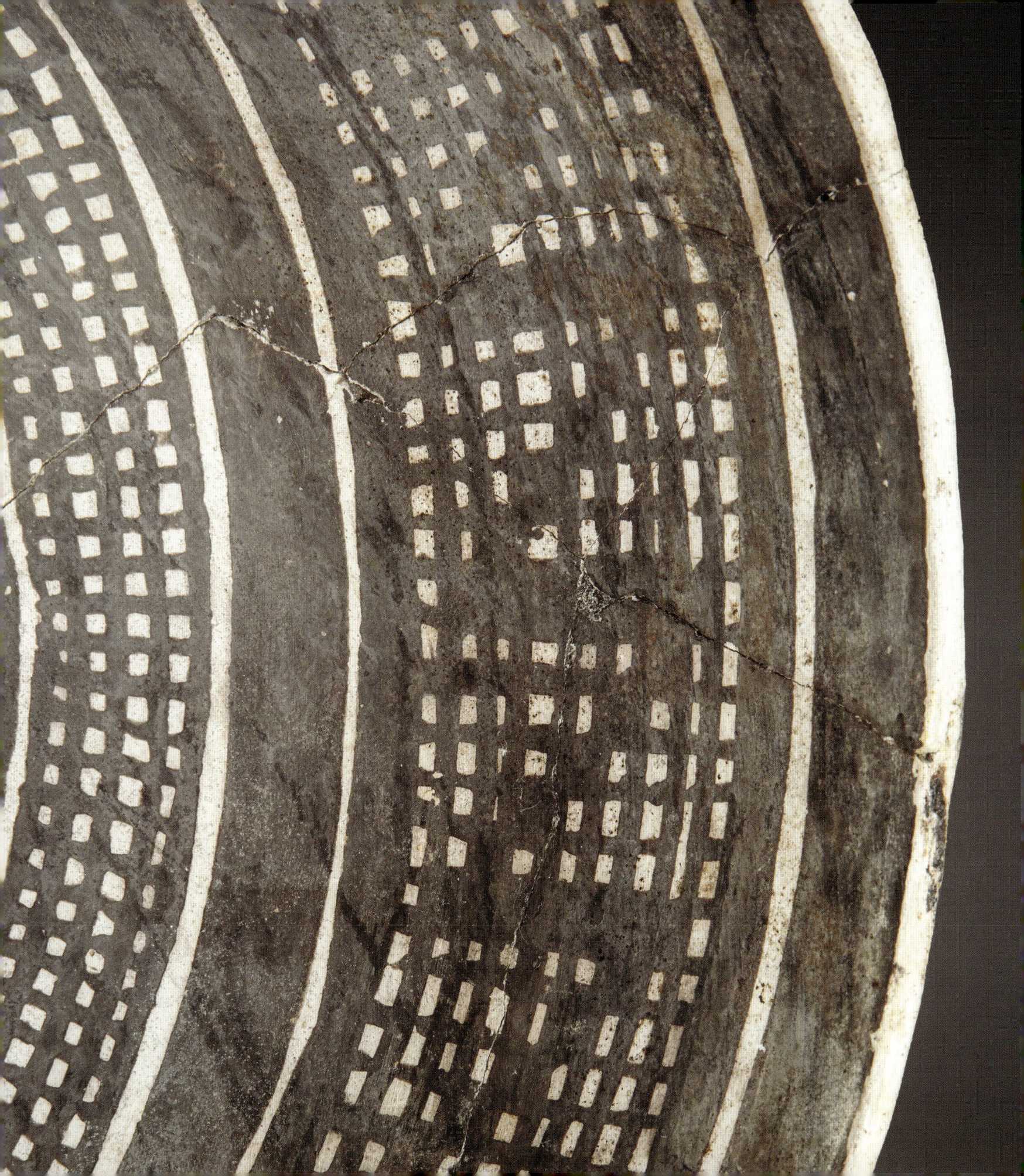

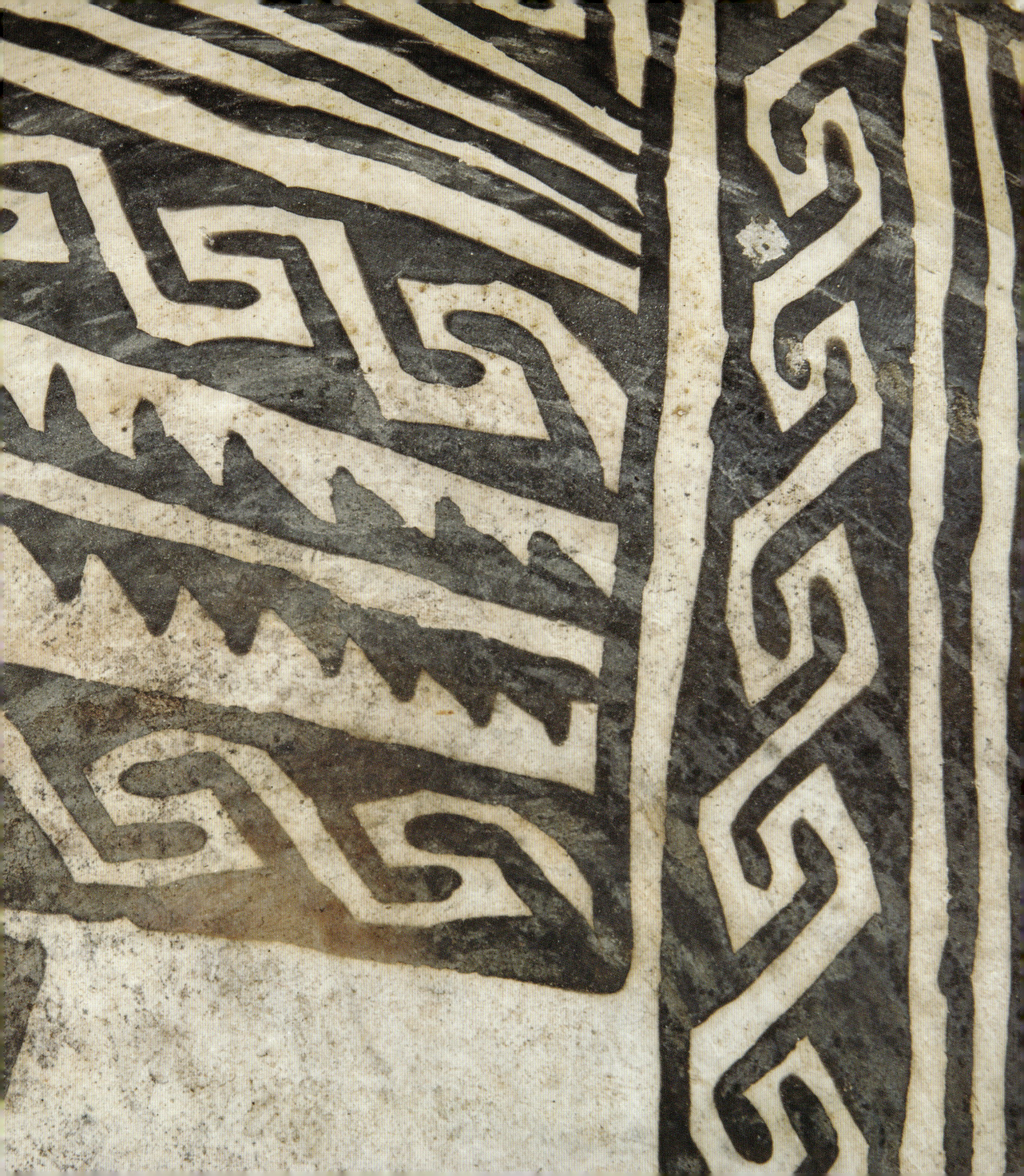

INTRODUCTION

For the past two millennia, the high desert mesas, plateaus, and river valleys of the American Southwest have been home to one of the most vibrant and compelling non-Western societies ever to have graced the earth. One can experience the vitality and distinctiveness of Pueblo communities today by visiting a museum, attending a feast day, or shopping at a trading post, but nowadays most people learn about Pueblo culture through its material legacy—perhaps the best-preserved, most precisely dated, and most intensively studied archaeological record of any society.

One of the most famous aspects of this material legacy is its intricate pottery style. Despite being based on simple geometric forms, the dynamic quality of the designs makes Ancestral Pueblo pottery distinctive and easy to recognize, even among people with only a passing knowledge of the American Southwest. Yet we have found that many who appreciate Ancestral Pueblo painted pottery as an art form have a difficult time describing the qualities that make it so interesting and pleasing to contemporary viewers. And we suspect even fewer have noticed what we view as a primary source of its appeal: spatial illusions and optical reversals that spring from the surfaces of these vessels into the minds of viewers. This book takes a closer look at the psychology, history, and cultural significance of this unique aspect of Ancestral Pueblo painting, and suggests it provides a window into the very foundations of Pueblo culture.

Most previous discussions of Pueblo pottery design have focused on the painted elements. Our study takes a different tack, investigating the perceptual relationships between painted and unpainted forms and emphasizing the importance of unpainted elements for understanding Pueblo design. We are not the first to discuss the perceptual phenomenology of Pueblo design or to explore its cultural significance. For example, art historian J.J. Brody and Pueblo scholar Rina Swentzell note in their book *To Touch the Past* that classic Mimbres pottery represents "a universe of balanced dualities and controlled ambiguities."

> These artists created shapes and masses that emphasized dark-light contrasts and were patterned to give positive visual value to unpainted negative spaces. By Classic times, the use of positive-negative imagery dominated, and painted dark forms and their negative by-products were equal, shifting images, each the product of the other. Planes also overlap, and painted forms can appear to move and shimmer in the three-dimensional space. These visual ambiguities are deliberate abstract visual puns, and the tensions become complex and spatially dynamic, loaded with perceptual uncertainties (Brody and Swentzell 1996:32).

We amplify this perspective here by exploring what we call *isomeric design*, one of the fundamental components of this painting tradition. The concept of isomeric design is based on an analogy with isomers in chemistry, which refer to compounds that are chemically identical but have mirror-image structures. In Ancestral Pueblo painting, isomeric design involves the use of paired forms that can be perceived as reversible spatial illusions. Isomeric design is first and foremost a series of techniques that connect painted compositions to properties of human visual perception. But we will show that, for Ancestral Pueblo people, it was much more than that. In fact, we suggest isomeric design provides a pathway to understanding the deepest notions of Pueblo philosophy and its historical development.

The archaeological literature is filled with studies of Ancestral Pueblo pottery that define a veritable periodic table of local styles and traditions, using these to distinguish groups and trace their interactions through time. This book, in contrast, focuses on the unity of Ancestral Pueblo design. Indeed, we see isomeric design as characteristic of the entire Ancestral Pueblo pottery tradition throughout the Great Pueblo Period, from the tenth into the fourteenth century CE. The arc of isomeric design thus accompanied many of the most important events in Pueblo history, from the formation of villages to the emergence of a regional center in Chaco Canyon to the depopulation of the Four Corners region in the late thirteenth century. We believe this correspondence is not a coincidence but reflects the emergence and transformation of threads that have remained central to Pueblo culture to this day. The way to see this is to focus on the principles that unified Ancestral Pueblo pottery painting across vast stretches of time and space. We suggest isomeric design is the basis of this unity.

In the first part of the book, we introduce four strategies for producing optical reversals through isomeric designs. These strategies are not mutually exclusive; hence some individual vessels simultaneously incorporate several strategies for producing visually active motifs. Then, after locating the characteristics of these designs visually, temporally, and geographically, the discussion turns to isomeric designs as reflections of Ancestral Pueblo society and philosophy. As Swentzell notes from her Santa Clara Pueblo perspective, "opposites such as light and dark, round and sharp, male and female" are essential concepts. She further clarifies that "modern Pueblo people consider opposites as essential to life. Because it is only through the interaction of opposites that regeneration and continuation—life itself—happen" (Brody and Swentzell 1996:32). Finally, we consider the decline of isomeric design following the dramatic population shifts and sociocultural reorganizations of the thirteenth century CE, arguing that although isomeric design faded from pottery the ideas expressed by it continued to be a part of Pueblo philosophy and remain central to Pueblo culture today. This discussion also leads us to consider the role of art in ancient societies more generally. The final section of the book presents sixty plates reproducing vessels displaying isomeric design. These vessels are organized by the dominant isomeric design strategy and arranged chronologically by strategy.

ANCESTRAL PUEBLO POTTERY AND ITS CULTURAL CONTEXT

Southwestern scholars have often suggested that pottery technology was introduced to Pueblo ancestors by people from the south. For example, archaeologists Dean Wilson and Eric Blinman (1995) note that a brown-paste pottery made from self-tempered alluvial clay was made in the Upper Gila area of southern New Mexico several centuries before the earliest pottery of the San Juan drainage in northern New Mexico, and they infer from this pattern that pottery technology spread northward through time. This may be true, but we think it is also important to note that the earliest clay containers in the Pueblo area emerged through a stepwise innovation process. This suggests the emergence of pottery was connected to the efforts of Pueblo ancestors to improve their lives, and this is important for understanding its eventual significance. The earliest clay containers were simply trays of a dried clay–juniper bark mixture molded inside coiled baskets. These trays appear to have been used as parching trays—they were heated over a fire and then seeds were toasted inside. People appear to have noticed that the clay hardened with repeated exposure to fire, to the point that it would no longer melt when wetted. From that point, it was a simple step to fire the clay intentionally—and pottery was born.

The earliest pottery appears to have been inspired by a desire to improve upon containers made of basketry or gourd. Thus there was a connection between weaving and pottery technology from the beginning, and this connection would be expressed symbolically through isomeric design in later periods. The development of true cooking pottery around 600 CE was an important innovation, as this made it possible for people to cook and eat beans, a good source of protein and a crop that adds nitrogen to the soil. During a period of rapid population growth in the centuries immediately following, Ancestral Pueblo society took on its distinctive character. In this way, pottery technology became associated in Pueblo consciousness with dramatic changes in the conditions of life. By the 800s CE, Pueblo people had begun creating villages and the ideas and institutions needed for settled communities to function. Pottery also became increasingly specialized by form and function and began to be decorated in increasingly elaborate ways. Isomeric designs first appeared during this period of rapid development in Pueblo culture and society.

OUR METHODOLOGY

Our approach to Ancestral Pueblo pottery design is based on a pair of methodologies that progress from descriptions of objects to their denoted meanings, and then to connotations providing broader, abstracted generalizations. In both approaches the analysis arrives at generalizations beyond the initial context of the objects under discussion. Together these approaches create a fusion of visual and cultural interpretations.

Traugott bases his visual approach on Erwin Panofsky's concept of iconology. He proceeds from description to iconographic analysis and concludes with iconology, the study of symbolic abstracted connotations in a broader cultural context. Iconology requires knowledge of the cultural context, hence the need for us to collaborate on this book. Ortman's conceptual metaphor approach borrows from the work of George Lakoff and emphasizes the way social meanings are constructed via analogy from bodily experience; it begins with description, then considers relationships between abstract concepts and concrete experiences, and concludes with metaphorical relationships and meanings.

Together we understand the visually active aspects of Ancestral Pueblo pottery designs as examples of Robert Plant Armstrong's concept of affecting presence. While it is not possible to understand the full range of meanings these designs had a thousand years ago, it is possible to make formal connections that stress their importance to the people who made and used them. Armstrong notes that affecting presence "is physically identical to what it presents" and is metaphorically "identical to the emotion which is transferred in the affecting transaction" (Armstrong 1971:55). Our goal is to reveal this presence through the combination of iconology and metaphor.

One final note: Josef Albers makes clear in *Interaction of Color* that placing two colors next to each other alters perceptions of both (Albers 1971). His point is that perception is not the same as a mechanical reproduction of physical forms. If you stare for a few moments at the plates in Albers's book and then close your eyes, an afterimage can appear. Afterimages reverse normal perception. The afterimage of a dark object on a white background appears as a glowing, indistinct white object on a dark background. Colors also produce afterimages, but they appear as a complement of the color: red becomes a blue-green version of turquoise.

Albers's discussion of changing color perceptions underscores a contradiction inherent in reproducing Pueblo pottery designs in a book. Presenting monochrome objects on a white background perceptually empowers the black elements, whereas staging them against a black background emphasizes unpainted passages. To combat this effect, most of the vessels reproduced in this study were photographed digitally in full color against a middle gray backdrop. This does not prevent perceptual changes to the objects, but it minimizes unconscious emphasis on the painted or unpainted areas by viewers.

The magic of flat designs painted on Pueblo pottery resides in their ability to produce spatial illusions, optical reversals, and intensified perceptions, and conceptually to complete incomplete designs. Perceptually isomeric pairs can flicker back and forth mentally like a neon sign. Although we can physically describe the marks the artists painted and illustrate their perceptual qualities, we can only infer how individuals understood these designs a thousand years ago. In addition, we can only describe these compositions as dualities of alternating perceptions and cannot know the full range of associations these designs connected in their original context of production and use.

Still, it is possible to identify forms that co-occur and make inferences about their past meanings. Through this investigation, we conclude that dual perceptions of Pueblo designs are both reflections of and metaphors for a distinctive philosophical system that first emerged during the Great Pueblo Period and remains a part of Pueblo culture to the present.

The isomeric designs created by these Ancestral Pueblo potters demonstrate exceptional perceptual abilities and painting skills, accomplished without the assistance of gridded paper and sharpened pencils. Clearly not all potters could take a lump of clay and a yucca brush and create an isomeric design. In the next chapter we explain how these artists incorporated organizational techniques that facilitated the creation of isomeric designs that produce optical illusions and figure-ground reversals.

The limited space in this book does not permit us to add "artist unidentified" to each reference to a specific piece of Ancestral Pueblo pottery. But it is important for readers to remember that, even though the pieces we illustrate are readily identified with regional and chronological styles the vessels were not made by a group. They were made by individual potters with great technical skill and aesthetic vision. As this study progressed we continued to be amazed by the sophistication of these works produced by unidentified, highly skilled artists. We hope you will, too.

ABBREVIATIONS

Institutions noted in the identifications of the objects reproduced in this book.

AMNH	American Museum of Natural History, Division of Anthropology, New York, New York
CSRSC	Center for Southwest Research and Special Collections, University of New Mexico Libraries, Albuquerque, New Mexico
CHM	Colorado History Museum, Denver, Colorado
FM	Field Museum, Chicago, Illinois
MIAC/LOA	Museum of Indian Arts and Culture/Laboratory of Anthropology, Department of Cultural Affairs, Santa Fe, New Mexico
MMA	Maxwell Museum of Anthropology, University of New Mexico, Albuquerque, New Mexico
MNA	Museum of Northern Arizona, Flagstaff, Arizona
NAA	National Anthropology Archives, Smithsonian Institution, Washington, DC
NMMM	New Mexico Mining Museum, Grants, New Mexico
SAR	School for Advanced Research, Santa Fe, New Mexico
UCB	University of Colorado Museum of Natural History, Boulder, Colorado

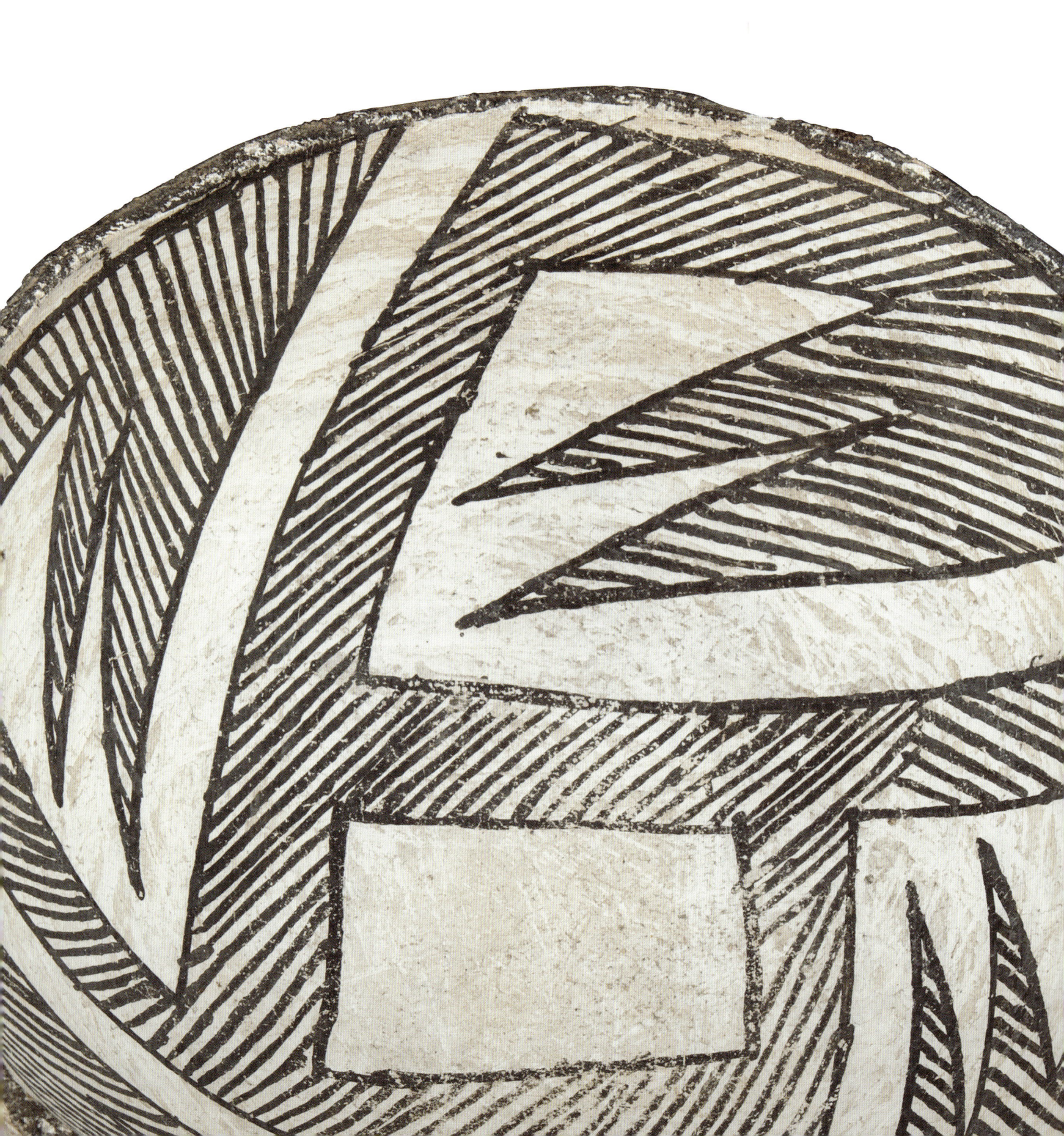

1 PERCEIVING ISOMERIC DESIGN

Carolyn M. Bloomer argues that poor visual training has promoted the fallacy that "the process of seeing is essentially objective and unlearned" (Bloomer 1976:7). In reality, visual perception is a synthesis of visual stimuli and clashing conceptual paradigms with culturally learned behavior. Human brains quickly sort through multiple perceptual paradigms with each visual stimulus and instantaneously produce an interpretive fusion that combines the current event with previous optical experiences.

This chapter investigates how perceptual processes in an observer's mind can interpret flat shapes as spatial relationships, even where none physically exists. By way of introduction, a small bowl from Chetro Ketl in Chaco Canyon (fig. 1.1) exemplifies the importance of looking closely. Stewart Peckham illustrated this particular vessel in his book *From This Earth,* but he didn't discuss it or its unique visual qualities. Instead, he explained that Gallup Black-on-white pottery vessels, like this one, were produced as part of the Chaco Phenomenon, the vast regional social system in northwest New Mexico dating to the tenth and eleventh centuries. Peckham viewed the participants in the Chaco Phenomenon as the "perpetuators of much of the Anasazi Mineral-Paint Tradition throughout the region" (Peckham 1990:72).

Looking closely, one will notice that the artist carefully painted four double-pronged forms radiating out from the rectangular center of the bowl. The painting of each double-pronged element left unpainted areas that mirror the pronged forms. These pairs of elements interlock physically and fuse visually into unified motifs. The pronged motifs also produce spatial illusions known as positive-and-negative spaces, also called figure-and-ground relationships.

What startles us is the ability of these motifs to reverse optically, allowing the original background to appear as the foreground and the painted designs to become the background of the design. However, most observers describe designs like these as black elements painted on a white background, a portrayal reinforced by the conventional terminology that labels this vessel as a Gallup *Black-on-white* bowl. This description locates the production of the vessel near Gallup, New Mexico, and notes the design was painted with pigments that turned black during firing, on clay fired a creamy white. Such nomenclature, typical of Ancestral Pueblo pottery classification, bolsters the assumed importance of the painted design and the insignificance of the background.

Figure 1.1. A close-up view of a pair of pronged isomers.

After painting the hachured form, a similar, unpainted, reciprocal shape remains. Gallup Black-on-white bowl, 950–1150 CE, 2 ¾ × 6 ⅛ in. dia., MIAC/LOA 43323/11.

Figure 1.2. An example of size creating spatial illusions.

Most people perceive the larger square to be closer and the smaller square to be farther away.

As a product of literacy, most modern observers have trained themselves to see dark shapes on light backgrounds. This works well for letters on paper, but not so well when the proportions between painted-and-unpainted shapes are equal. Such a situation creates visual ambiguity, which confuses normal perceptions and allows foregrounds to appear also as negative spaces, or backgrounds. Such spatial transformations are real perceptions but also products of seeing flat shapes painted on curved surfaces.

A basic knowledge of perceptual paradigms is essential to fully appreciate the complexity of the designs painted on Ancestral Pueblo pottery. Bloomer clarifies four concepts in *Principles of Visual Perception* that relate to Ancestral Pueblo design. The most basic perceptual concept, light and dark spatial illusions, posits that light objects appear closer to the observer than darker objects. A simple reason for this is that close objects reflect more light to an observer's eyes and inherently seem lighter, brighter, and more intense than objects that are farther away. A related concept, size-and-space illusions (fig. 1.2), concerns perceptions that larger objects seem closer to the observer than smaller objects. These two concepts work together as a size and intensity assumption that larger and brighter objects seem closer than smaller and darker forms.

Despite the seeming universality of this principle, it doesn't always work. The concept holds for nearby objects such as a Pueblo bowl but not for distant objects like a mountain range in the landscape. Viewing objects at a distance through air, dust, and heat waves alters their appearance. Known as aerial perspective (fig. 1.3), this phenomenon causes distant objects to look pale and indistinct, not focused and dark as predicted by the light-and-dark spatial paradigm. Similarly, closer objects in the landscape seem dark and sharply focused, not bright and intense. These contradictory experiences are so common we normally don't give them a second thought because our minds have been trained through experience to distinguish between these two varieties of distance perception.

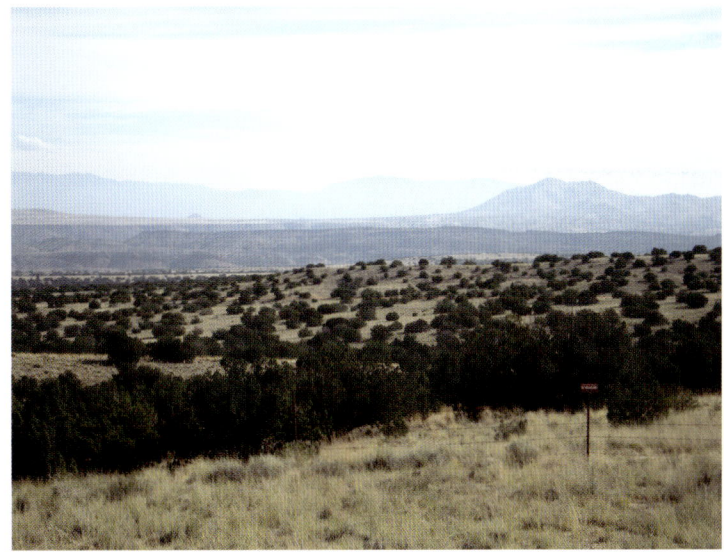

Figure 1.3. An example of aerial perspective.

The Sandia Mountains, photographed from south of Santa Fe, New Mexico. Objects in the landscape are dark and in focus close to the observer, but become less distinct as the distance from the observer increases. This contradicts the axiom that objects close to the observer appear well illuminated but darken as they recede in space. Photograph by Joseph Traugott.

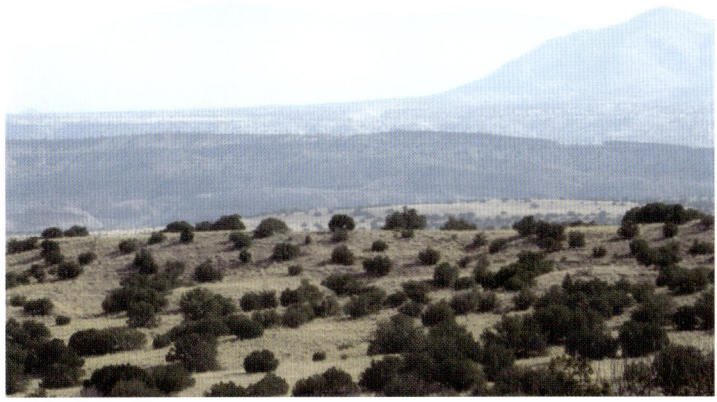

Figure 1.4. Border-contrast phenomena in a New Mexico landscape.

If you stare at this detail from figure 1.3 for a few seconds, an intense white band will appear in the sky at the juncture with the mountain. At the same time the edge of the mountain will seem darker. A second border-contrast phenomenon exists at the intersection of the two mountain forms, while a third example appears as an intense pale blue band separating trees in the foreground from the middle mountain.

A second perceptual paradigm involves border-contrast phenomena, an illusion occurring at the juncture of two forms in which light areas appear lighter and the dark shapes seem even darker. Experience reveals that the intensity of this phenomenon may seem to increase if the border is a zigzag rather than a straight line. That illusion enlivens designs in subtle ways that most observers do not recognize. Border-contrast phenomena at the juncture of land and sky might seem confusing because the tint of the sky intensifies at the juncture with a landform. This phenomenon is clearly visible in photographs of the intersection of land and sky (figs. 1.3 and 1.4).

Figure 1.5. Examples of designs understood through the law of simplicity.

Observers understand this sherd of a Tularosa Black on-white pitcher as a checkerboard design. However, a close view reveals the irregularities in the painting masked by the law of simplicity.

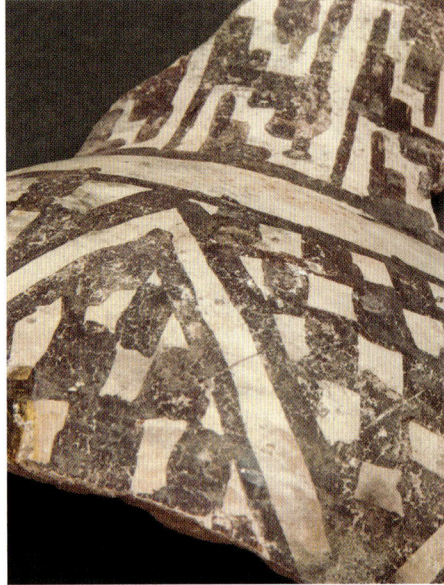
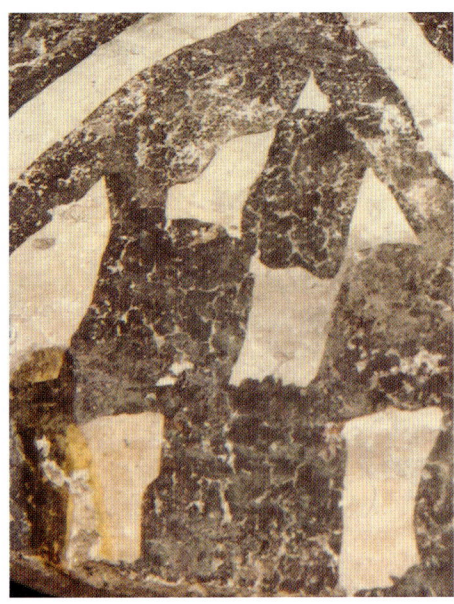

Experimental psychologist Tom Cornsweet investigated border-contrast perceptions in the 1960s, and his findings are now known as the Cornsweet illusion. His work dealt with pairs of equally toned gray rectangles that appear to just touch. Optically, however, the left shape appears to shift tonally darker until it meets the second shape, which appears a tint lighter. The importance of this research for our project is to underscore that the perception of border-contrast phenomena is well understood in psychology. Unconsciously, border-contrast phenomena and Cornsweet illusions are perceptual components of isomeric designs and are part of their affective presence.

The law of simplicity, a third optical principle related to Pueblo pottery, contends that the best solution to a perceptual problem is the simplest solution. This law explains in part why humans unconsciously correct mistakes in images. Humans, that is, do not see things as they are but employ past experience and cultural context to translate encounters into "the 'best' or most 'correct' possible form" (Bloomer 1976:15). A corollary to this idea asserts that we perceive general concepts before seeing the small details that may contradict aspects of the whole. When our minds encounter inconsistencies, they try to correct inaccuracies and achieve resolutions based on previous experiences.

The interpretation of a design painted on a Tularosa Black-on-white sherd affirms aspects of the law of simplicity associated with Pueblo pottery. From a distance, most viewers quickly perceive the frieze as a checkerboard design (fig. 1.5). The irregularities of the painting are not apparent to the viewer, who typically recognizes the general design through the law of simplicity. Further inquiry is not necessary; the design fits a well-established concept in the observer's mind.

Figure 1.6. Examples of figure-ground relationships.

When small shapes are positioned on larger forms, the larger form can be understood as a background. The white rectangle seems closer to the observer than the black shape, but both appear in front of the background.

However, a close-up view of this sherd reveals that the artist based the design on horizontal framing lines and then painted the "squares" freehand, sometimes misaligning the vertical edges and missing the framing lines. The law of simplicity explains the ability of humans to observe and quickly understand a specific form or concept, despite realities that may deviate from the preconception. This law also explains why Pueblo observers understand partial motifs, or abstractions of well-known designs, as holistic images.

A fourth perceptual illusion, figure-and-ground relationships, occurs when small shapes configured within larger ones create the illusion of space, even though the image is flat. The figures, or the smaller shapes (fig. 1.6), appear closer to the observer; the ground, the larger shape, seems farther away. Figure-ground illusions work for both light and dark objects, with both light and dark backgrounds, but they are most apparent when there is strong contrast between figure and ground. Spatial illusions associated with figure-and-ground relationships can contradict the spatial perceptions of both light-and-dark spatial illusions and size-and-space illusions.

Alex W. White describes three categories of spatial relationships in his book *The Elements of Graphic Design* (White 2002:19). Stable figure-and-ground relationships form unchanging spatial relationships where the subject is always perceived as the figure situated in front of the ground (as in Pueblo pottery painting before isomeric designs). Reversible figure-and-ground relationships present large variations in shape and size with small figures perceived in front of larger grounds (as in the "negative" designs on the Tusayan Black-on-white bowl in Plate 24). Ambiguous figure-and-ground relationships, the third category, allows the figure and ground relationships to reverse optically and be understood as both a figure and a ground (as in an Ancestral Pueblo isomeric design).

Figure 1.7. A Rubin diagram displays figure-ground reversibility.

Do you see a goblet? A pair of faces? Both? Neither?

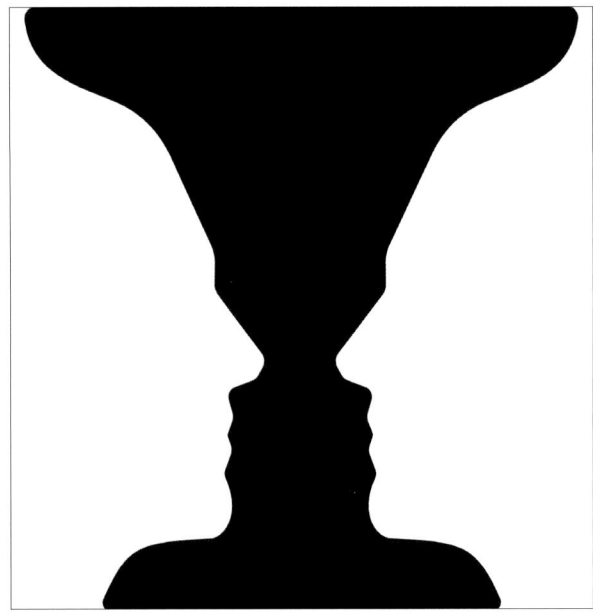

Figure-and-ground relationships are well known to youngsters who amaze and delight their friends with optical illusions. The most common involves a drawing of a wine goblet shape (fig. 1.7) that magically transforms into a pair of faces looking at each other. These optical illusions are associated with the work of gestalt psychologist Edgar Rubin. They occur because the equal-sized light and dark shapes create ambiguous figure-and-ground relationships, allowing the design to flip back and forth spatially and also conceptually with regard to the subject.

Ironically, when a Rubin diagram is turned from its normal orientation, the dual illusions are difficult to perceive (fig. 1.8). That failure suggests cultural knowledge, visual familiarity, and conventional contexts are preconditions for some optical illusions to work. Similarly, the lack of familiarity with the elements and motifs painted by Ancestral Pueblo artists may limit how contemporary viewers recognize conventional depictions and optical illusions in ancestral designs.

Some readers may initially have difficulty perceiving optical transformations in Pueblo pottery designs. If you consciously focus first on an unpainted area, rather than the painted forms, the reversal will appear because you are consciously working to reject your past training to attend primarily to black forms on white paper. Viewers also can change their gaze by allowing their eyes to unfocus, and this, too, will help reveal optical reversals, particularly border-contrast phenomena. It may take some time to retrain your visual skills to perceive both versions of Ancestral Pueblo designs simultaneously, but it can be done.

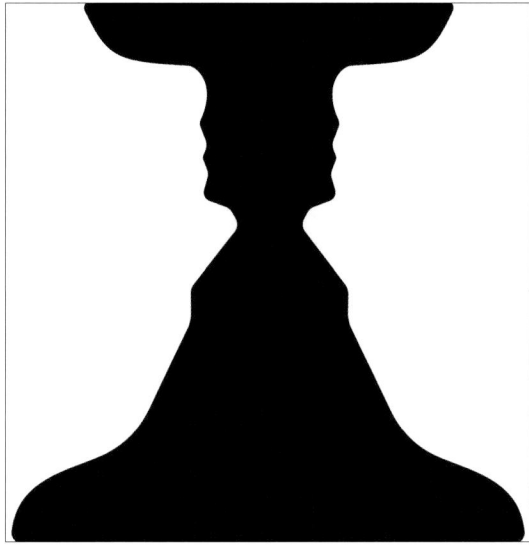

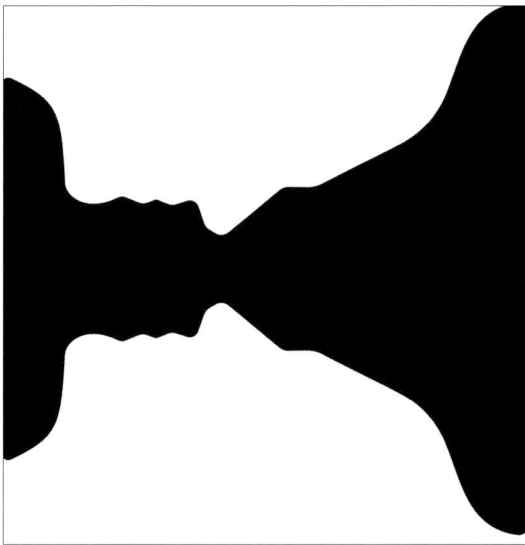

Figure 1.8. Inverted and sideways presentations of Rubin diagrams.

When recognizable forms are presented in unconventional orientations, they are difficult to perceive as recognizable forms and may not produce a reversible image. Rubin diagrams underscore the importance of cultural knowledge and conventional presentations for some optical transformations to occur.

Bloomer contends that "perception is ruthlessly parsimonious: we tune out, forget, or berate anything that lacks meaning for us" (Bloomer 1976:7). Yet she is deeply concerned with the relationships between visual perception and comprehension noting that "seeing is accomplished not in the eye—but in the mind" (Bloomer 1976:32). With this goal in mind, we present in the next chapter the visual perceptions that underpin our understanding of Ancestral Pueblo pottery designs.

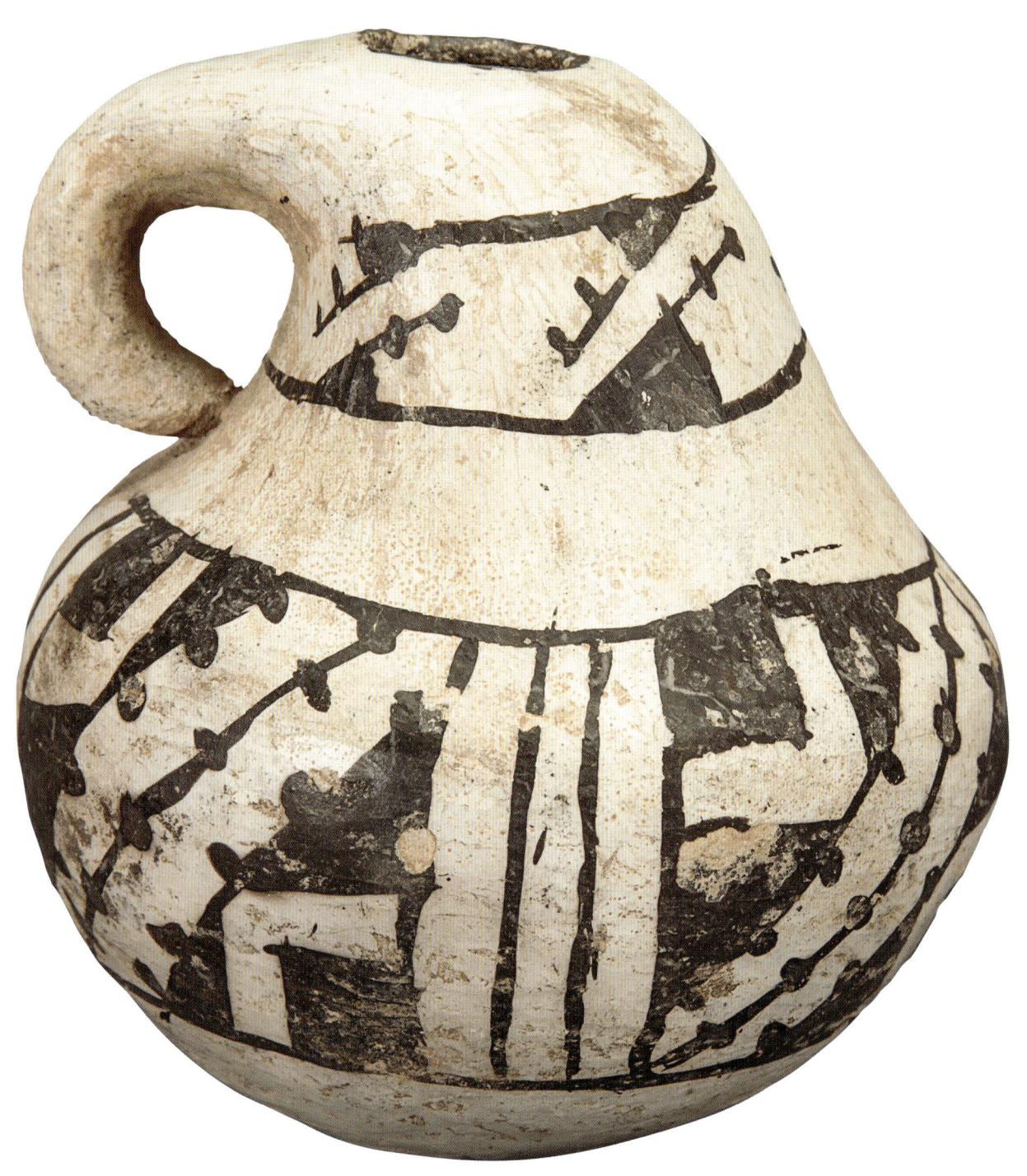

2 ISOMERIC DESIGN STRATEGIES

The smooth surface of unfired clay provided early Ancestral Pueblo artists the freedom to paint designs without the limitations of the warp and weft logic of woven designs. Pre-isomeric pottery designs in the Southwest exhibited a high degree of experimentation with materials, pigments, tools, firing processes, physical forms, and design strategies. With stable figure-ground relationships, these works did not produce spatial reversals or optical transformations, but they displayed a variety of experimental designs painted in a free-flowing manner.

A Kana-a Black-on-white pitcher molded in the shape of a gourd (fig. 2.1) exemplifies the experimentation of this period. The artist molded the complex form in at least three parts, merging the spherical base, conical neck, and closed top, which required great skill. The painting on this vessel gives the impression that the artist was uncertain how to meld design motifs with the sensuous curves of the gourdlike form. These design motifs may be prototypes of isomeric designs, but they do not produce optical reversals. Illusions do not occur because there is not an even balance between painted and unpainted shapes.

Around 900 CE, Pueblo potters began producing pottery designs that created spatial illusions through figure-ground relationships, dynamic visual qualities through border-contrast illusions, and recognizable simplifications through the law of simplicity. These changes seem to coincide with the beginning of the Great Pueblo Period, an era marked by the development of large, aggregated villages.

Painting curvilinear and rectilinear forms using a brush cut from a yucca plant leaf posed different physical and organizational problems. The artist chewed on the yucca stick, exposing the tough fibers on one end. Ancestral Pueblo artists did not scrub back and forth with the brush but pulled it toward them so the fibers would line up and stick together, producing a smooth line and eliminating wiggles. Long lines required reloading with the correct mixture of pigment and matching the end of a previously painted segment. Small curvilinear lines could be painted in the same manner as straight lines, but longer sweeping lines may have required turning the vessel in one direction while pulling the brush in the opposite direction.

Technically, painting curvilinear elements is more difficult than producing rectilinear forms. Painting a framing line at the center of a bowl, or tracking a straight line around the circumference of a large jar and having the ends meet, is not as easy as it might seem.

Figure 2.1. An example of a ceramic vessel imitating the shape of a functional object made from a gourd.

The painted elements may replicate designs painted on the gourds.
Kana-A Black-on-white pitcher, 725–1050 CE, MMA 66.93.10.

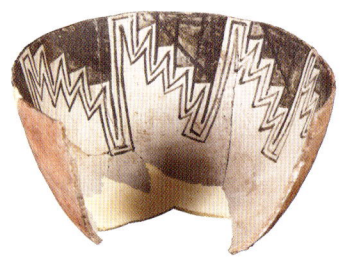

Figure 2.2. Fragment of a bowl revealing the development of both the organizational structure and the painted motifs.

La Plata Black-on-white bowl, 4 × 6 ¾ in. dia., MNA NA11355.PH1.10 A7849.

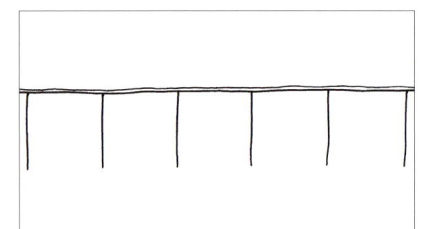

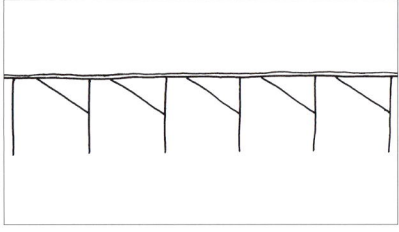 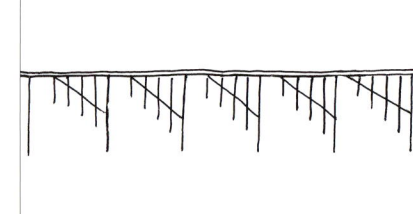

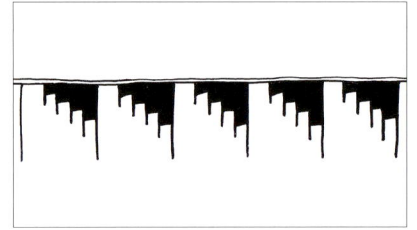 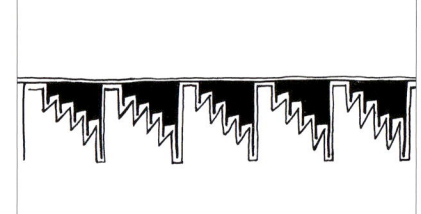

Painting a single element or motif is easy to understand, but how did Ancestral Pueblo artists paint complex designs that create optical illusions?

Artists began their designs by painting linear understructures that organized the spacing of motifs and defined the logic of complex designs. A fragment of a La Plata Black-on-white bowl (fig. 2.2) reveals the underlying grid the artist used to produce this isomeric design. The grid is clearly visible under the solid shapes because an inconsistent mix of pigment and water did not fire to a dense black. The exposed understructure demonstrates how quickly and freely the initial grid was painted, serving only to provide a rough outline. In this design the artist used multiple zigzag lines to define the painted stepped elements on an unpainted, implied stepped form.

A Mesa Verde Black-on-white bowl (fig. 2.3, *left*) provides an example of a Pueblo artist altering the organizing grid during the final painting of the design. A close look at this vessel reveals three organizational lines initially set at sharply raking angles that are still visible under the solid overpainting. In another example the artist abandoned the original structure during the final painting of a Reserve Black-on-white bowl (fig. 2.3, *right*). Small triangular outlines opposite the solid stepped elements show that the painter intended to produce unpainted areas within the hachured shapes, a popular design. A

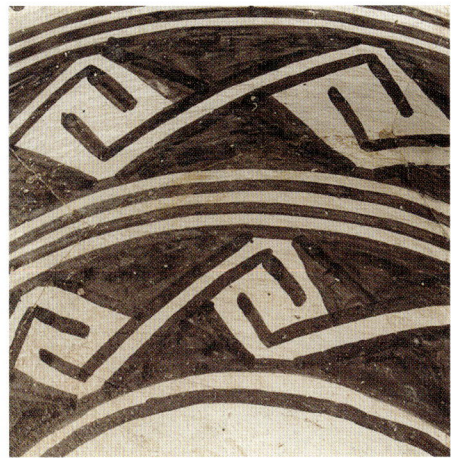 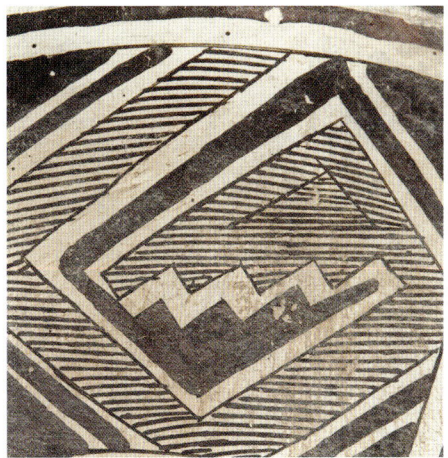

Figure 2.3. Examples showing deviations from the organizational structure.

The original organizational grid is still visible under the solid painting, revealing last-minute alterations, Mesa Verde Black-on-white bowl, 5 ½ × 8 ¾ in. dia., MMA 2010.168.41 (left). The right-angle triangle painted under the hachures (right) suggests that additional white shapes had been planned as isomeric pairs. Reserve Black-on-white bowl, 1000–1200 CE, 5 ½ × 12 in. dia., Honorable Daniel H. McMillan Collection, MIAC/LOA 8135/11.

close look at these triangles shows that they were inpainted after hachuring the design that butted against the unpainted shapes. The artist tried to match the original hachuring when filling in the triangle but was only partially successful. These three examples reveal the use of organizational understructures in Ancestral Pueblo pottery and how artists might alter their original plan during the final painting.

Ancestral Pueblo understructures function much like present-day contour drawings that artists can use to distinguish the subject from the background. Artists make contour drawings by "outlining" subjects in a manner that delineates the juncture between figure and ground. Art educator Betty Edwards has students use contour drawings to understand "the positive aspects of negative space," her version of spatial reversals (Edwards 1999:97). Edwards intends her exercises with contour drawings to improve her students' abilities to conceptualize a subject by drawing the surrounding negative spaces, not the subject itself.

Ancestral Pueblo artists employed linear understructures in a similar manner to Edwards's use of contour lines as a compositional device. Understanding the positive aspects of negative space constitutes an important component of the perceptual dualities inherent in isomeric design. The contour drawings in Pueblo pottery can be understood as delineations between positive and negative spaces, the juncture of figure-and-ground relationships, and the source of border-contrast phenomena.

FOUR ISOMERIC DESIGN STRATEGIES

Our observations suggest that Ancestral Pueblo artists devised four strategies for generating isomeric designs that yield optical dualities: painted-and-unpainted isomers paint shapes that simultaneously leave unpainted areas of the same shape; tessellated isomers repeat motifs that interlock into sequential chains; liminal-space isomers incorporate a space separating pairs of isomeric elements; and, finally, incomplete-element isomers

Figure 2.4. Examples of the four isomeric design strategies found on Ancestral Pueblo pottery during the Great Pueblo Period, roughly 950–1300 CE.

Gallup Black-on-white bowl, 950–1150 CE, 2 ¾ × 6 in. dia., MIAC/LOA 43323/11 (upper left). Gallup Black-on-white pitcher, 950–1150 CE, 7 ⅝ × 5 ½ in. dia., UCB 09501 (upper right). Escavada Black-on-white bowl, 950–1150 CE, 3 × 9 ¼ in. dia., MMA 76.68.51 (lower left). Mancos or McElmo Black-on-white bowl, 1200–1300 CE, 5 ½ × 8 ¾ in. dia., MMA 2010.168.41 (lower right).

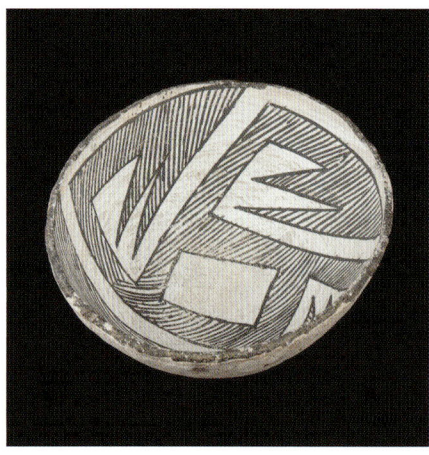

Painted-and-unpainted isomers

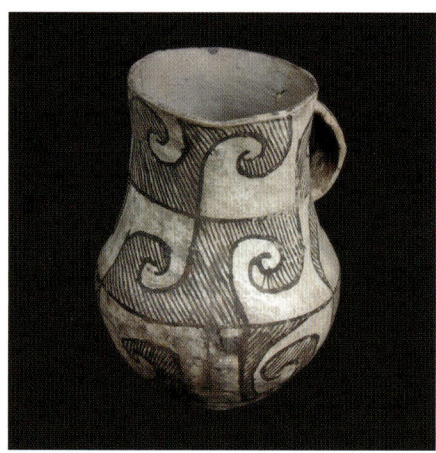

Tessellated isomers

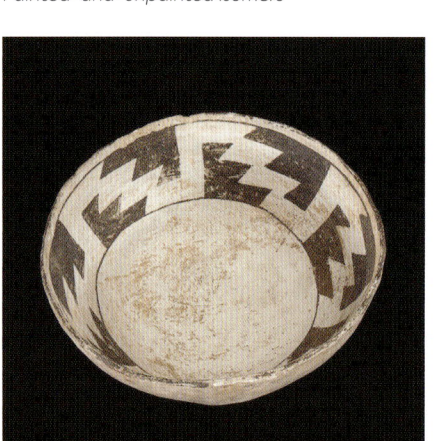

Liminal space isomers

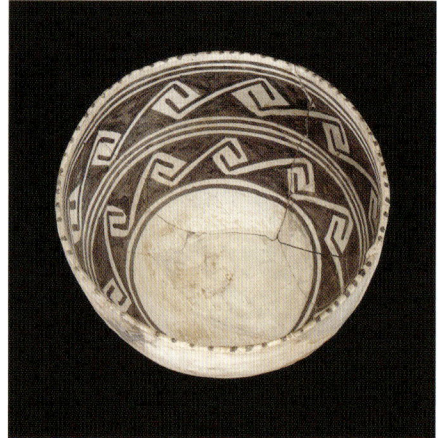

Incomplete-element isomers

present fragments or simplifications of common motifs that viewers perceive as whole forms. Examples of the four strategies are presented in figure 2.4. Each design strategy required similar but distinct organizational structures for adapting the intended design to the shape of the vessel. Artists completed their designs by inpainting areas of the organizational grid or by producing a combination of painted and unpainted forms.

Understanding Pueblo design strategies would be less complicated if these four approaches were mutually exclusive, but that is not the case. A single design often incorporated more than one strategy. Hence a design we offer as an example of one strategy also could be used to explain other design strategies. This is readily apparent in the Portfolio (pages 79 to 129) where the captions list relevant design strategies and their related perceptual phenomena.

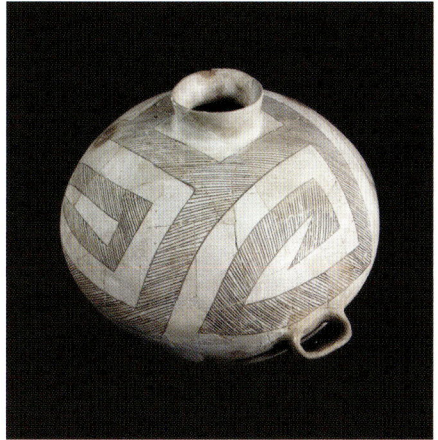 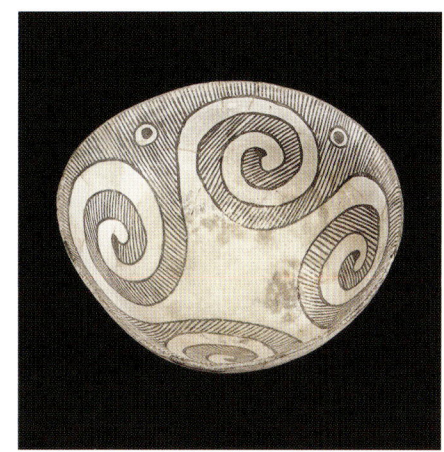
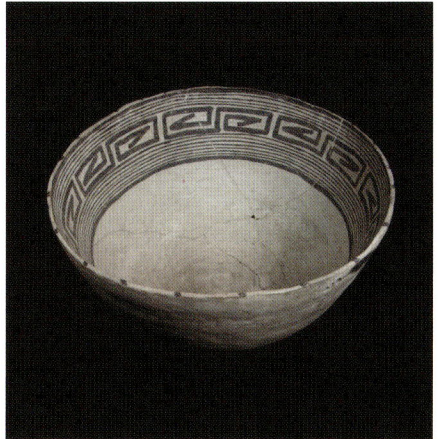 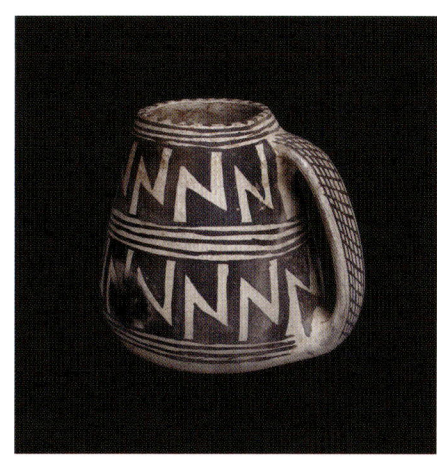

Figure 2.5. Examples of vessels displaying painted-and-unpainted isomeric designs arranged in chronological order, top left to lower right.

Gallup Black-on-white jar, 950–1150 CE, 14 ⅝ × 15 ⅝ in. dia., UCB 04032 (top left). *Chuska Black-on-white bowl, 1000–1125 CE, 4 ⅞ × 11 ¾ in. dia., MMA 42.12.131* (top right). *Mesa Verde Black-on-white bowl, 1150–1280 CE, 5 ⅞ × 12 ⅛ in. dia., UCB 09324* (lower left). *Mesa Verde Black-on-white mug, 1200–1300, 3 ⅞ × 4 ⅜ in., dia., courtesy of the SAR, IAF.2387, photograph by Jennifer Day* (lower right).

Painted-and-unpainted isomers may be the most difficult designs to create but perhaps the easiest to understand as isomeric pairs (see examples in fig. 2.5). With this design strategy the artists painted shapes that simultaneously left similar, unpainted, reciprocal forms that produced dynamic optical reversals. The motifs appear as painted figures against unpainted backgrounds but also as unpainted shapes in front of painted grounds. A sophisticated organizational structure is required to produce isomeric pairs by this reciprocal painting method.

The previously discussed Gallup Black-on-white bowl (see fig. 1.1) exemplifies this design strategy. It would be difficult—virtually impossible—to paint such a design without first producing an organizational grid to establish the spacing and produce motifs based on equal pairs of pronged elements. The underlying grid used to produce this bowl may

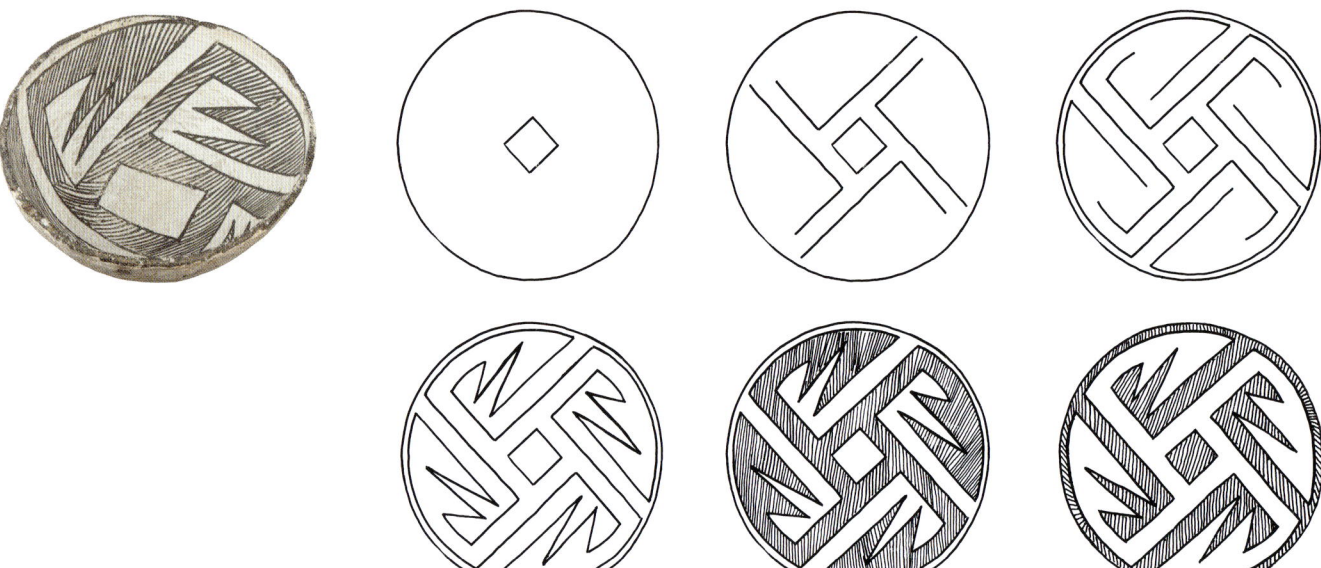

Figure 2.6. Diagrams showing the developing the organizational structure of a bowl displaying painted-and-unpainted isomers.

The first four diagrams depict the process for producing the organizational structure. The last two diagrams demonstrating the hachuring to either side of the organizational structure display the reversibility of the design. Gallup Black-on-white bowl, 950–1100 CE, 2 ¾ × 6 in. dia., MIAC/LOA 43323/11.

seem complex (fig. 2.6), but it is simply a process for dividing and subdividing the interior space of the bowl. Lines radiating out from the center of the bowl divide the interior into two separate areas. The division of the spaces is almost complete in the third diagram when all that remains is connecting the loose ends of the organizational grid. The artist completed the underlying structure by using four Z-shaped lines to make those connections, as shown in the fourth diagram.

The last two diagrams in figure 2.6 show the addition of hachures to either side of the organizational grid. In the fifth diagram, the hachures produce motifs replicating the design on the Gallup Black-on-white bowl, while the hachures in the last diagram replicate the *unpainted* space of the original vessel. This figure demonstrates the logic of an isomeric design and its ability to generate two reciprocal designs that can be understood as both figure and ground.

The visual balance between these light and dark forms allows viewers to perceive the composition as an ambiguous figure-and-ground relationship, a dual perception. Border-contrast phenomena associated with these angular prongs and the uneven hachures energize the unpainted elements. From our experience, the more familiar one becomes with isomeric reversal, the more the unpainted elements become the optically dominant perceptions.

To most present-day viewers, the painted elements of a painted-and-unpainted design first appear as positive forms spatially situated in front of an unpainted background (an example of White's stable figure-and-ground relationship). But as the vessel demon-

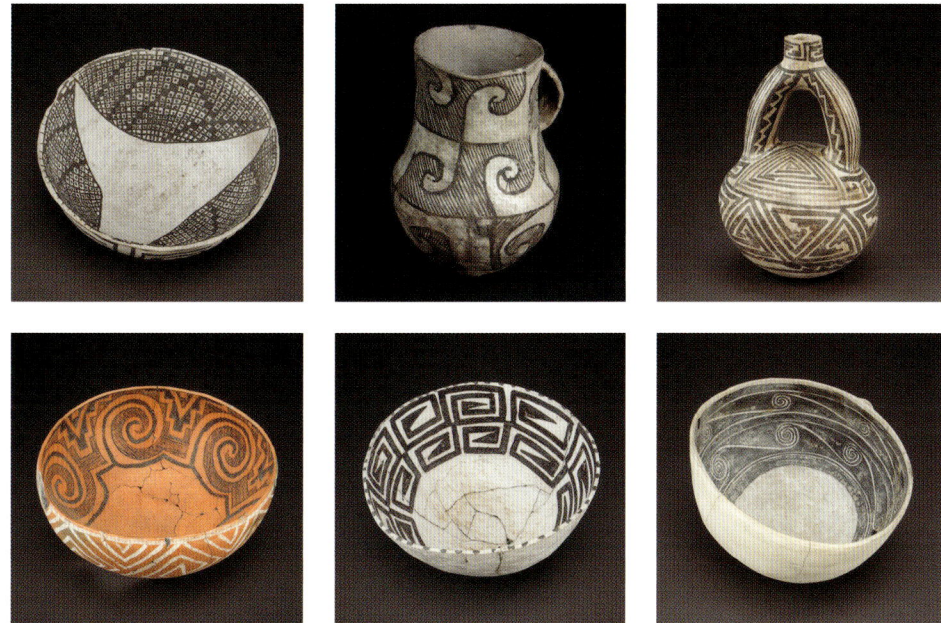

Figure 2.7. Examples of vessels displaying tessellated isomeric designs arranged chronologically, top left to lower right.

Tusayan/Betatakin Black-on-white bowl, 980–1150 CE, 3 ⅜ × 7 ½ in. dia., MIAC/LOA 43326/11 (top left). *Gallup Black-on-white pitcher, 950–1125 CE, 7 ⅝ × 5 ½ in. dia., UCB 09501* (top middle). *Klagetoh Black-on-white canteen, 1125–1300 CE, 6 ¾ × 6 ⅛ in. dia., courtesy the John and Linda Comstock and the Abigail Van Fleck Charitable Trust, MIAC/LOA 43341/11* (top right). *St. Johns Polychrome bowl, 1150–1300 CE, 5 ¼ × 12 in. dia., MIAC/LOA 46361/11, LA 4988, Collections from the Gila National Forest at MIAC* (lower left). *McElmo Black-on-white bowl, 1100–1300 CE, 4 ⅞ × 11 ⅛ in. dia., MIAC/LOA 19640/11* (lower middle). *Tusayan/Betatakin Black-on-white bowl, 1200–1300 CE, 5 1/16 × 10 ⅝ in. dia., MIAC/LOA 46588/11* (lower right).

strates (and as is confirmed by these diagrams), the unpainted shapes also can be perceived as the intended image and appear as a figure floating spatially in front of a hachured background. As this diagram affirms, the organizational grid produced an equal division of the space, creating ambiguous figure-ground relationships.

Tessellated isomers repeat elements to create a design resembling a tiled floor (see examples in fig. 2.7). The best-known tessellations are jigsaw puzzles and checkerboard squares. Jigsaw pieces are created by adding a shape to one side of a rectangular form and then subtracting the same shape from the opposite side, before repeating this process on the remaining two sides. The added and subtracted areas act like locks and keys, allowing the forms to interlock seamlessly. Jigsaw-style tessellations are rare and difficult to conceive, but the simplest tessellated forms in Ancestral Pueblo design are checkerboard patterns.

Twentieth-century artist M. C. Escher incorporated tessellated elements in his work by altering the tile-based elements of his pictures. Through his process of adding and subtracting equal forms to a basic tessellated shape, his generic fish morph into birds and birds transform themselves into farm fields (Seckel 2004: 80–93). The subjects of Escher's works evolve visually for viewers, as if by magic. Non-art examples of tessellations include 1950s pop beads and the links of a bicycle chain. These repeated forms slip together and produce endlessly repeatable forms. The important point is that each element in such a tessellated chain is identical and repeated.

Figure 2.12. Examples of liminal-space isomeric designs arranged chronologically, from upper left to lower right.

Kiatuthlana Black-on-white gourd-shaped jar, 850–950 CE, 6 ¾ × 5 ¾ in. dia., MIAC/LOA 8280/11 (upper left). Escavada Black-on-white bowl 950–1150 CE, 3 × 9 ¼ in. dia., MMA 76.68.51 (upper middle). Puerco Black-on-red bowl, 1050–1175 CE, 4 ⅛ × 9 ¼ in. dia., MIAC/LOA 43321/11 (upper right). Leupp Black-on-white jar, 4 ⅞ × 11 × 7 ¼ in. dia., 1100–1225 CE, MMA 73.43.160 (lower left). Mesa Verde Black-on-white bowl, 1150–1280 CE, 2 ¾ × 6 in. dia., MIAC/LOA 43345/11 (lower middle). Mesa Verde Black-on-white mug, 1200–1300 CE, 4 ½ × 5 in. dia., MIAC/LOA 43357/11 (lower right).

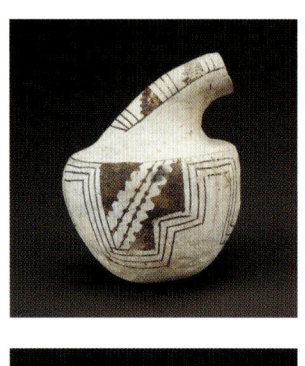
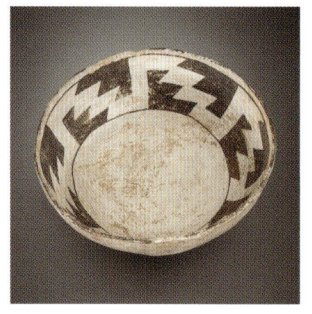
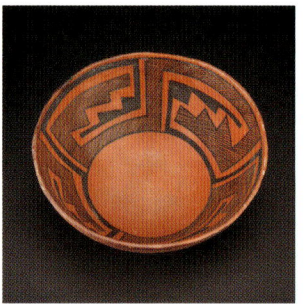
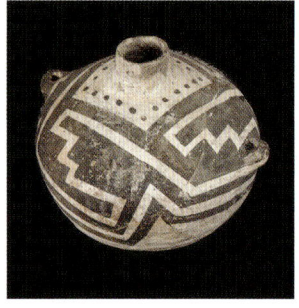
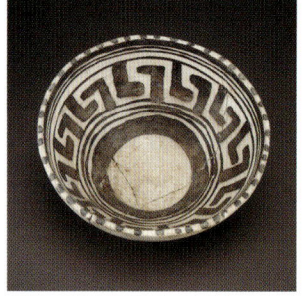
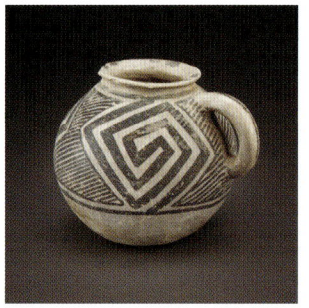

Figure 2.13. Diagrams showing the development of the organizational structure for a liminal-space isomeric design.

In the second diagram, pairs of straight lines set the spacing for the addition of Z shapes that complete the organizational structure. The last two diagrams demonstrate that the organizational structure can be used to create unpainted liminal spaces and painted liminal spaces. Escavada Black-on-white bowl, 950–1150 CE, 3 × 9 ¼ in. dia., MMA 76.68.

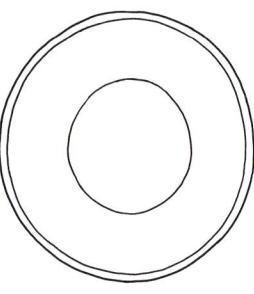
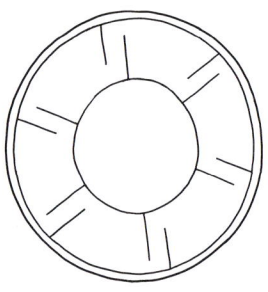
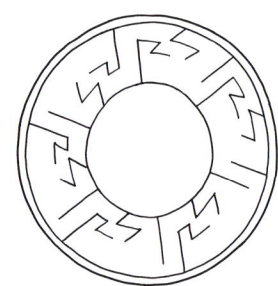
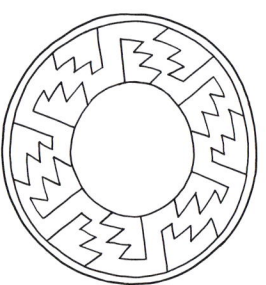
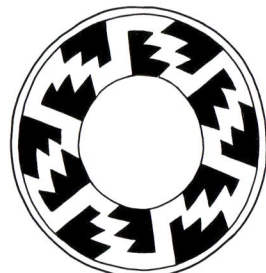
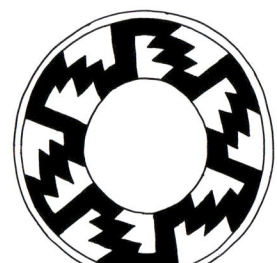

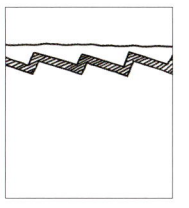 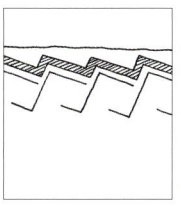 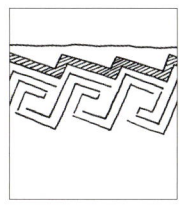 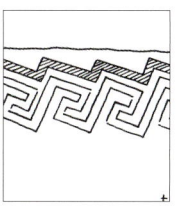 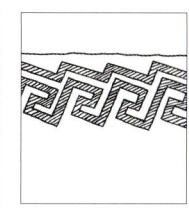

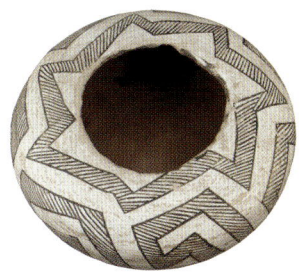

An Escavada Black-on-white bowl (fig. 2.13) presents a liminal-space design incorporating pairs of stepped elements divided by unpainted liminal spaces. Optically the design can be perceived as a meandering unpainted liminal space against a solid background or as stepped elements against an unpainted background. The diagram clarifying the creation of the underlying structure begins by painting pairs of lines separating the design frieze into equal parts. The stepped forms are outlined by pairs of Z-shaped lines that complete the underlying grid. The last two diagrams demonstrate that the understructure could be finished in two ways, either with painted isomers or a painted liminal space. But not all liminal-space designs are as simple as those on the Escavada bowl or the Gallup Black-on-white bowl (fig. 2.14).

A Puerco (Wingate) Black-on-red bowl (fig. 2.15) provides a complex design presenting a series of interlocked dual spirals painted as solid and hachured elements, separated by an unpainted liminal space. The intensity of the unpainted red slip accentuates the spaces between painted elements and produces the impression that the narrow bands of unpainted slip are the intended focus. The artist began the design with a pair of circles

Figure 2.14. Diagrams showing a liminal-space isomer design radiating out from the frieze at the center of the jar.

The frieze at the opening sets the spacing and the angle for Z-shaped lines that define the L-shaped isomers on the body of the jar.
Gallup Black-on-white jar, 950–1150 CE, 5 ½ × 9 ¼ in. dia., MIAC/LOA 8842/11.

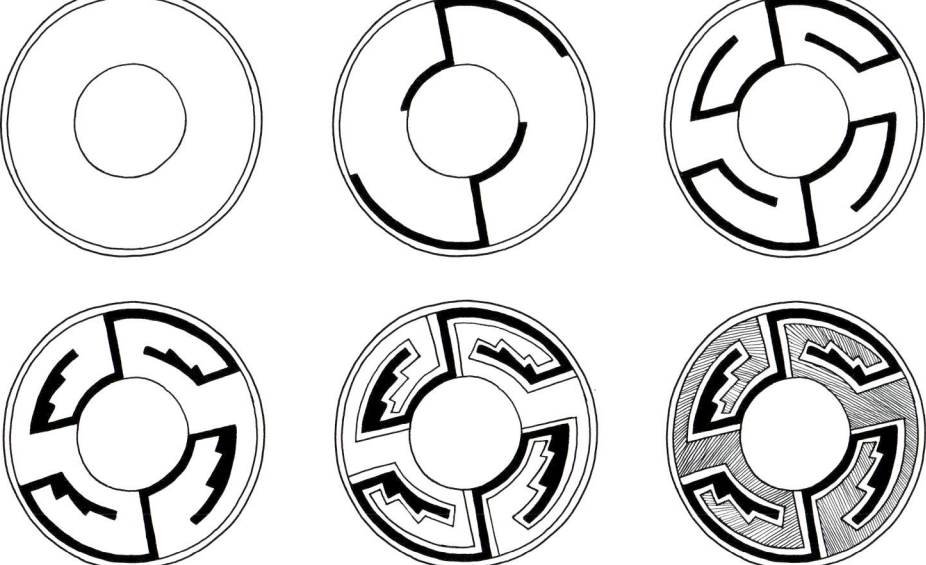

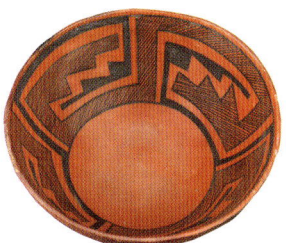

Figure 2.15. Diagrams showing the development of a liminal-space isomeric design with painted and hachured isomers.

Puerco Black-on-red bowl, 1050–1175 CE, 4 ⅛ × 9 ¼ in. dia., MIAC/LOA 43321/11.

Figure 2.16. Examples of vessels with incomplete-element isomeric motifs arranged chronologically from upper left to lower right.

Red Mesa Black-on-white pitcher, 875–1050 CE, 6 ½ × 6 in. dia., MIAC/LOA 8277/11 (upper left). Newcomb Black-on-white, 975–1050 CE, 4 ½ × 8 in. dia., MMA, 72.43.172 (upper right). Flagstaff Black-on-white bowl, 1125–1200 CE, 3 ¼ × 7 in. dia., MIAC/LOA 53295/11 (lower left). Mancos or McElmo Black-on-white bowl, 1200–1300 CE, 5 ½ × 8 ¾ in. dia., MMA 2010.168.41 lower right).

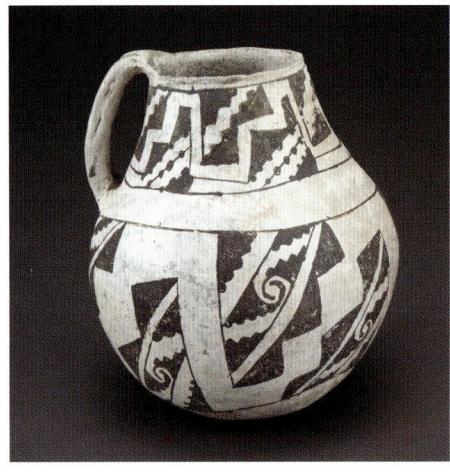
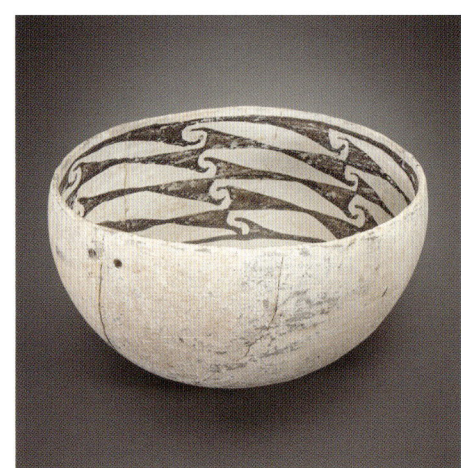
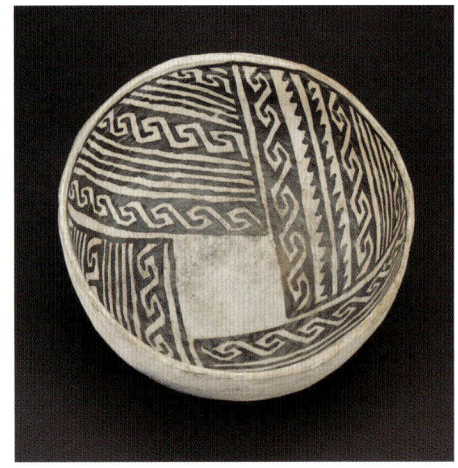
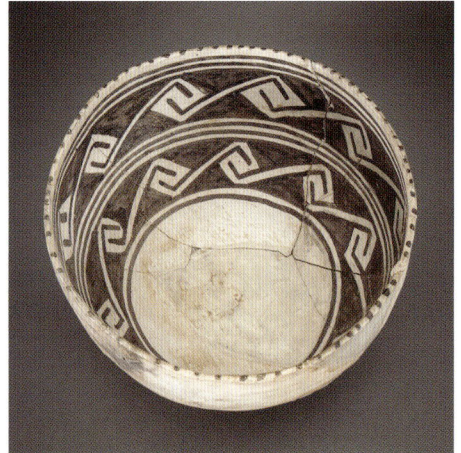

defining the upper and lower framing lines, and then subdivided the space with a pair of Z-shaped lines radiating from the framing lines that set the spacing for the design. The next move completed the organizational grid by further delineating the dual spirals. The addition of hachuring completes the design.

The perceptual ambiguity of this design produces two interpretive versions. One version perceives the painted forms as the intended figures in a figure-and-ground spatial illusion. The other perception understands the unpainted, intensely red slip as the positive figure against a background of painted forms. The jagged areas of the design produce border-contrast phenomena that intensify the spatial illusions, particularly when the unpainted elements appear as the positive elements, not negative spaces.

Incomplete-element isomers present partial versions of recognizable images that observers perceive as whole motifs based on the law of simplicity (fig. 2.16). This design

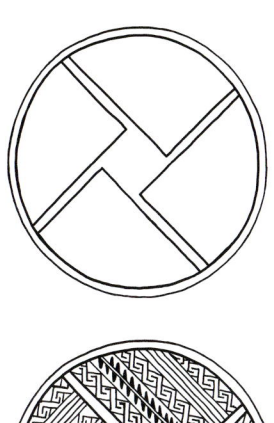
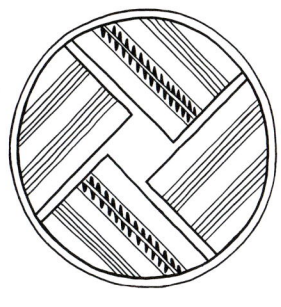
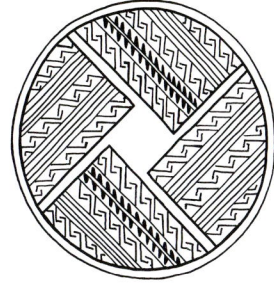
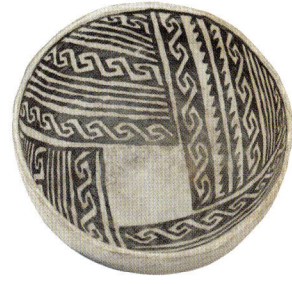
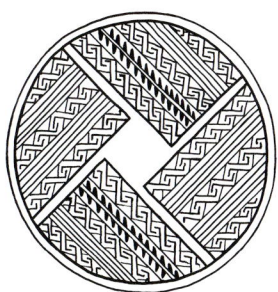
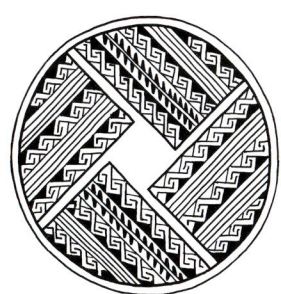

Figure 2.17. Diagrams describing of the development of an incomplete-isomer design based on Z-shaped lines.

Flagstaff Black-on-white bowl, 1125–1200 CE, 3 ¼ × 7 in. dia., MIAC/LOA 53295/11.

strategy usually involves simplifications of spiral forms that are understood through the law of simplicity, which seeks the simplest explanation for an event. Perceptions of incomplete-element isomers often appear as twisted cordage, reversals in which the liminal spaces dominate as unbroken chains, not a series of painted motifs. Examples of incomplete-element isomers produce strong figure-and-ground reversals in part through border-contrast phenomena.

Incomplete-element isomer designs often employ rectilinear versions of spiral forms, such as the Flagstaff Black-on-white bowl analyzed in figure 2.17. The artist began the organizational structure for these spirals by painting four triangular shapes arranged around an unpainted square at the center of the vessel. Each quadrant is segmented into panels of what will become alternating design friezes based on spirals, or patterns of painted-and-unpainted stripes, also of equal width.

The finished design appears as Z-shaped motifs but is painted with triangular forms and L-shaped elements. The artist created the rectilinear spiral elements from pairs of L-shaped lines attached to solid triangular forms. As these forms interlock, they produce abstractions of spiral forms that appear spatially in front of a dark background. These figure-and-ground relationships are intensified border-contrast phenomena caused in part by the angular shapes in the design. Viewers assume these forms are simplifications of interlocked spirals through the law of simplicity.

Adapting designs from bowls to jars required adjusting the organizational structure to fit each vessel shape and was not always successful. Three pairs of bowls and jars with similar

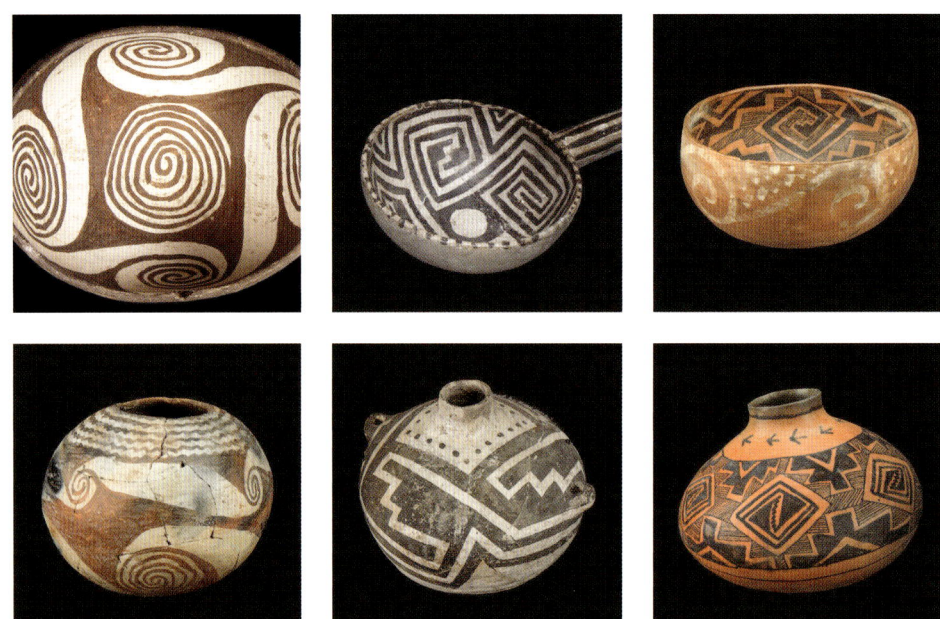

Figure 2.18. Examples of pairs of vessels showing the relationship between basic designs adapted to both bowl and jar forms.

Mangas Black-on-white bowl (upper left), *750–1000 CE, MNA A7849, and a similar Mimbres Black-on-white jar* (lower left), *750–1000 CE, MIAC/LOA 20224/11.*

Mesa Verde Black-on-white dipper (upper middle), *1150–1300 CE, courtesy of the SAR, IAF.2400, photograph by Jennifer Day, and a similar design painted on a Leupp Black-on-white jar* (lower middle), *1100–1225 CE, MMA 72.43.160.*

St. Johns Polychrome bowl (upper right), *1150–1300 CE, MIAC/LOA 54818/11 and a similar design painted on a Pinedale Black-on-red jar* (lower right), *1275–1325 CE, MIAC/LOA 8169/11.*

designs (fig. 2.18) demonstrate that the bowl versions are often simpler and technically more successful. This conclusion is most obvious with the pair of Mimbres vessels (*left*) where the bowl design is balanced and integrated, but the design fits awkwardly on the small seed jar.

This is to be expected. Painting bowl forms was easier because the artist could always see the whole design at a glance, and could easily adjust the organizational structure and proportions of painted motifs. Jars required the maker to paint an underlying grid when only part of the vessel was visible at a time. Starting framing lines on one view of a jar and having the two ends meet demanded conceptual and artistic skills. Certainly translating one design concept to multiple forms was not always a clear-cut process.

The optically ambiguous images discussed in this chapter disappeared at the end of the thirteenth century and corresponded with major population shifts in the Ancestral Pueblo world. A Pinedale Black-on-white jar (fig. 2.19) embodies the changing nature of isomeric design at the juncture of the thirteenth and fourteenth centuries. Bold framing lines on this vessel overpower the small diamond-shaped medallions presenting simplified stepped motifs painted as liminal-space isomers.

These diminished motifs are visually less important than the heavy framing lines and bold crosshatching, changes indicating a shifting design aesthetic. The composition on this vessel alludes to the impending disappearance of isomeric design early in the fourteenth century. Pairs of stepped elements continued to be painted as allusions to the past designs and design strategies, but these isomeric motifs became minor components of the compositions and do not produce strong optical transformations or border-contrast phenomena.

To summarize, fired clay containers offered functional advantages over woven baskets, but disadvantages as well. Pottery was waterproof, fireproof, and pest proof, but it was also heavier, more fragile, and more difficult to transport. Artists responded to the graphic freedom provided by pottery vessels by developing painted compositions that produced perceptual dualities, spatial illusions, and optical reversals based on isomeric design strategies. Vessels from this period demonstrate that not all ancestral potters produced fully realized isomeric designs.

In this chapter we described the process of creating isomeric designs through the use of underlying organizational structures, grids that facilitated the process of creating a balance between painted and unpainted elements. Artists often utilized straight lines for setting the spacing of an isomeric design but often used Z-shaped structures to ensure an even, dynamic division of space that clearly created pairs of isomeric relationships.

Our observations indicate that artists created perceptually ambiguous motifs by utilizing four design strategies: liminal-space isomers, painted-and-unpainted isomers, incomplete-element isomers, and tessellated isomers—friezes composed of chains of motifs. Artists often combined multiple strategies on an individual vessel because these strategies were not mutually exclusive. Isomeric designs integrate contradictory aspects of human perception to produce visual ambiguities that observers can perceive as figure-and-ground relationships, border-contrast phenomena, and simplifications through the abstraction of common images.

Figure 2.19. An example displaying the declining importance of isomeric elements at the end of the Great Pueblo Period.

The isomeric elements, the pairs of stepped forms, have become minor parts of the design and are subordinated visually to the bold framing lines. Pinedale Black-on-white jar, 1250–1325 CE, 3 ¾ × 4 ½ in. dia., MIAC/LOA 21171/11.

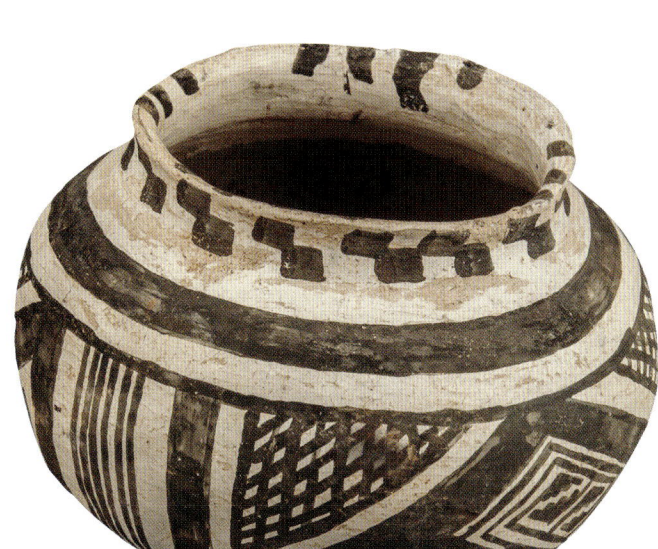

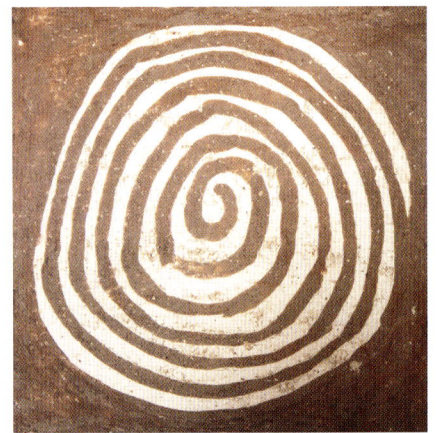
CURVILINEAR SPIRAL

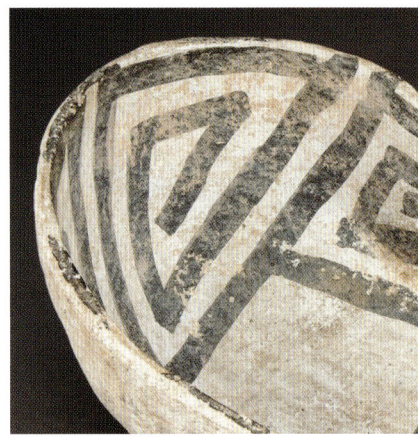
RECTILINEAR SPIRAL

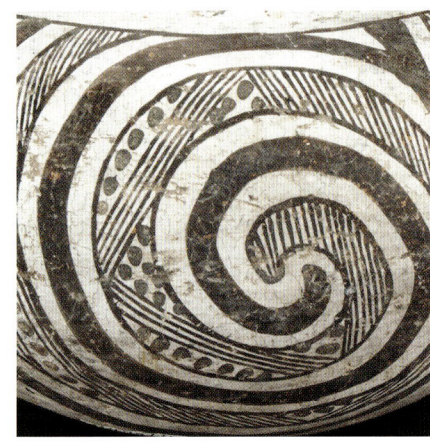
INTERLOCKED CURVILINEAR SPIRAL

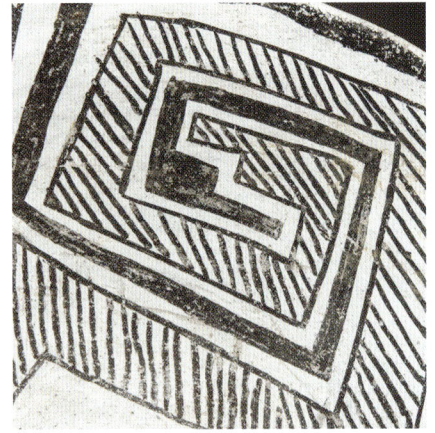
INTERLOCKED RECTILINEAR SPIRAL

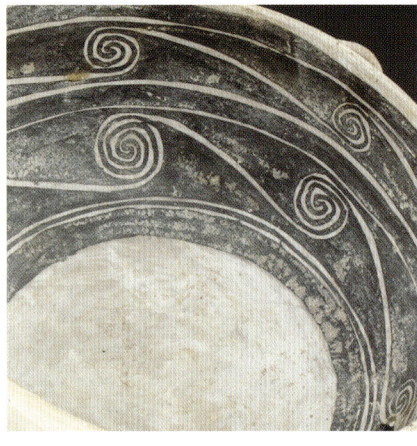
CURVILINEAR DUAL SPIRAL

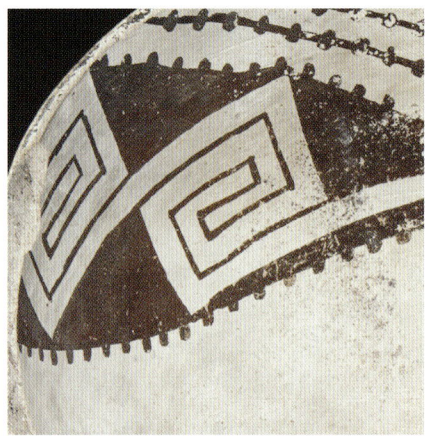
RECTILINEAR DUAL SPIRAL

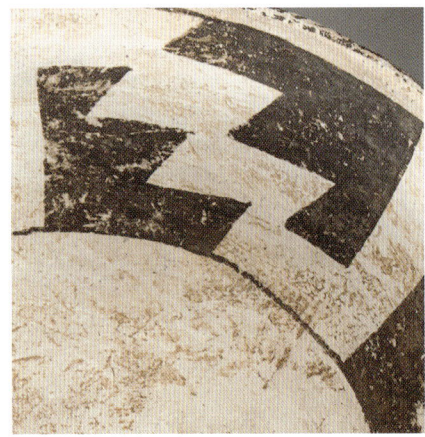
STEPPED ELEMENTS

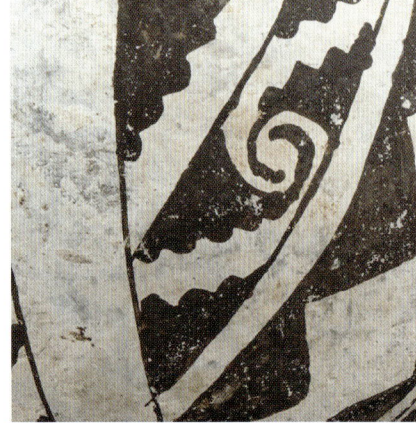
CURVILINEAR SPIRAL WITH STEPPED FORMS

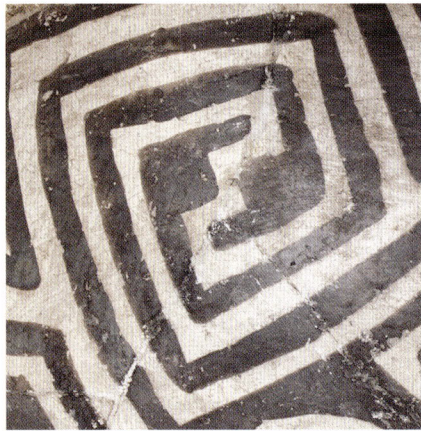
RECTILINEAR SPIRAL WITH STEPPED FORMS

3 RELATIONSHIPS BETWEEN SPIRAL AND STEPPED ELEMENTS

Spirals and stepped forms are the most common isomeric elements that create optical phenomena on Ancestral Pueblo pottery. This chapter investigates the formal interrelationships between them. We begin by presenting spiral and stepped forms as the building blocks of isomeric design strategies. Artists painted spirals as both curvilinear and rectilinear motifs, employing all four of the design strategies identified in chapter 2. Sometimes they painted both curvilinear and rectilinear spirals on single vessels, indicating formal similarities between the two methods of depicting spiral forms. Artists also merged spiral and stepped elements into single motifs, seemingly emphasizing their unity over their differences.

The basic elements of isomeric designs include spirals painted as both curvilinear and rectilinear forms and stepped elements painted only as rectilinear forms (fig. 3.1). Pueblo painters depicted spiral elements as a single line coiling out from a central point, while interlocked spiral elements were painted as a pair of spiral shapes coiled like a helix. Dual spirals are twin spirals connected together as a single element, but one spiral moves in a clockwise motion and the other counterclockwise. Stepped elements present blocklike forms divided diagonally with zigzag edges and are only produced as rectilinear elements. Presentations of spiral and stepped forms usually followed the basic postulate of Pueblo design that two dark, painted forms should not touch except at their corners, as in a checkerboard pattern. However, painters occasionally tweaked this prohibition by combining spiral and stepped shapes into conjoined elements, spirals with stepped forms. These combinations could incorporate stepped forms as shapes introducing versions of spirals, or as the centers of spiral motifs.

It is important to note that ancestral artists produced both curvilinear and rectilinear spirals using each of four design strategies discussed in the previous chapter. Figure 3.2 presents the relationship between spirals and isomeric design strategies. Curvilinear spirals are displayed on the left column while rectilinear spirals are illustrated on the right. The four isomeric strategies are presented from top to bottom. Painted-and-unpainted isomers are presented on the first line as simple spirals painted with a single line. Tessellated isomers with repeated spiral motifs are on the second line, while pairs of isomers separated by liminal space are on the third line. Finally, incomplete element isomers are presented on the last line.

It might appear that this presentation represents a chronological evolution. It does not; all four design strategies originated about the same time and were used throughout the Great Pueblo Period. The same is true for curvilinear and rectilinear spirals produced

Figure 3.1. Basic elements of isomeric motifs.

Curvilinear spiral, rectilinear spiral, interlocked curvilinear spiral, interlocked rectilinear spiral, interlocked curvilinear dual spiral, interlocked rectilinear dual spiral, stepped elements, curvilinear spiral with stepped elements, rectilinear spiral with stepped elements.

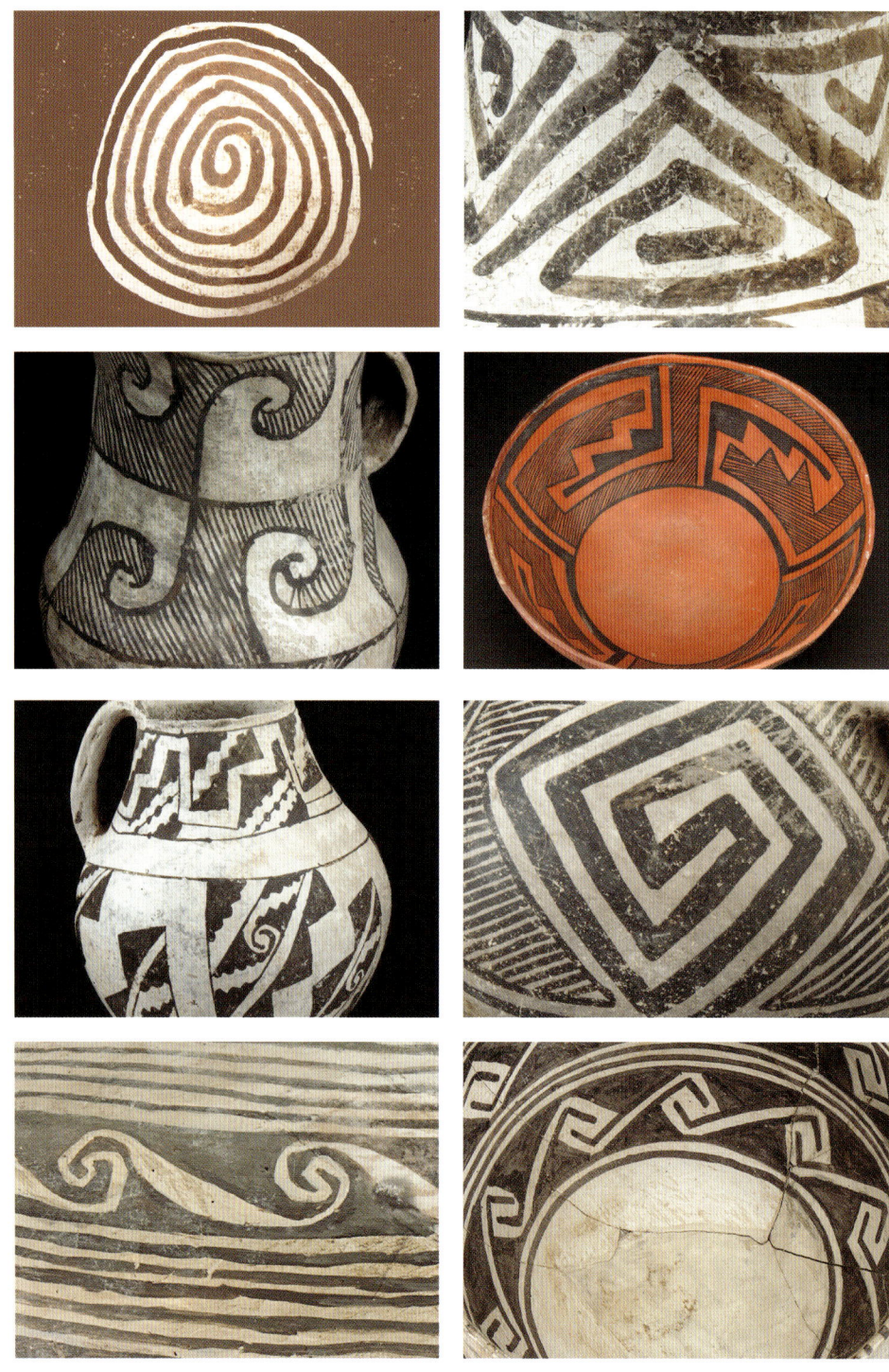

Figure 3.2. Spiral elements painted as examples of all four isomeric design strategies.

Curvilinear spirals are shown in the left column, with rectilinear spirals on the right. Isomeric design strategies are listed from top to bottom: painted-and-unpainted isomers, tessellated isomers, liminal-space isomers, and incomplete isomers.

42

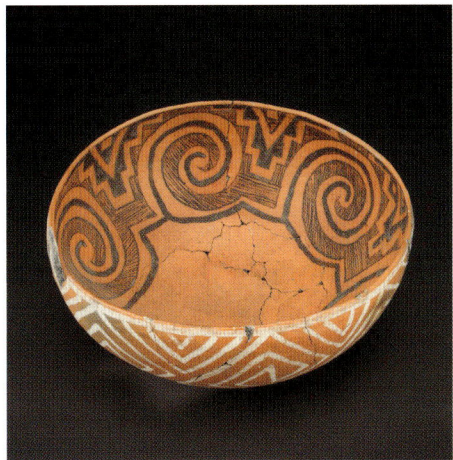 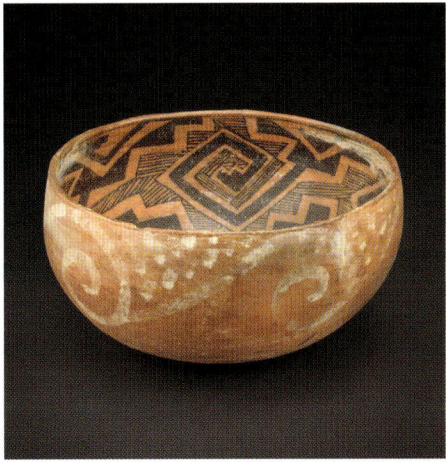

Figure 3.3. Examples of curvilinear spirals and rectilinear spirals painted on a single vessel.

St. Johns Polychrome, 1150–1300 CE, 5 ¼ × 12 in. dia., MIAC/LOA 46361/11, LA 4988, Collections from the Gila National Forest at MIAC (left). St. Johns Polychrome, 1150–1300 CE, 5 ¼ × 12 in., MIAC/LOA 54818/11 (right).

by the four design strategies. The diversity of design strategies and styles for depicting spirals underscores their centrality for isomeric design in the Southwest. Designs combining curvilinear and rectilinear spirals occur on individual vessels, and figure 3.2 presents examples combining rounded and straight-lined depictions of spirals.

The St. Johns Polychrome bowl (fig. 3.3, *left*) displays rectilinear spirals painted on the interior of the bowl, and each of these spirals includes stepped elements at its center. Dual spirals painted with white kaolin produce a tessellated frieze on the exterior. The second St. Johns Polychrome bowl (fig. 3.3, *right*) reverses this relationship, with curvilinear spirals painted on the interior and outlined interlocked spirals, painted with kaolin, on the exterior. The interior layout of these two bowls is the same: the design frieze incorporates repeated spiral forms, and the empty spaces between spirals are filled with stepped elements.

Several vessels combining both styles of spiral motifs were excluded from this study because they come from restricted contexts. Exceptional published examples include a Tularosa Black-on-white jar in *Generations in Clay* (Dittert and Plog 1980:86), a St. Johns Polychrome bowl in *Anasazi and Pueblo Painting* (Brody 1991:95), a Kayenta Black-on-white jar, Kiet Siel Polychrome canteen, and Showlow Glaze-on-white jar in *Re-creating the Word* (Moulard 2002:14, 15, 16, 119).

The terminology sometimes used to describe Pueblo pottery reflects subtle assumptions regarding common designs. Terms like *scroll* and *volute* describe curvilinear spirals but not rectilinear shapes that coil with straight lines and angular corners. The connotations of these terms imply that curvilinear and rectilinear shapes represent separate concepts. The vessels painted with both curvilinear and rectilinear motifs, shown in figure 3.3, counter this conventional view by suggesting a conceptual equivalence between the two styles for depicting spiral forms.

Figure 3.4. Examples of curvilinear spiral elements connected to versions of stepped elements.

Kiatuthlana/Red Mesa Black-on-white bowl, 860–950 CE, 3 ¼ × 7 ¾ in. dia., John and Linda Comstock and the Abigail Van Fleck Charitable Trust, MIAC/LOA 8224/11 (upper left). Red Mesa Black-on-white pitcher, 875–1050 CE, 6 ½ × 6 in. dia., MIAC/LOA 8277/11 (upper right). Tularosa Black-on-white pitcher, 1100–1200 CE, 6 ¾ × 7 in. dia., MIAC/LOA 19720/11 (lower left). Puerco Black-on-white bowl 900–1100 CE, 4 ⅞ × 9 ¼ in. dia., MMA 70.60.15 (lower right).

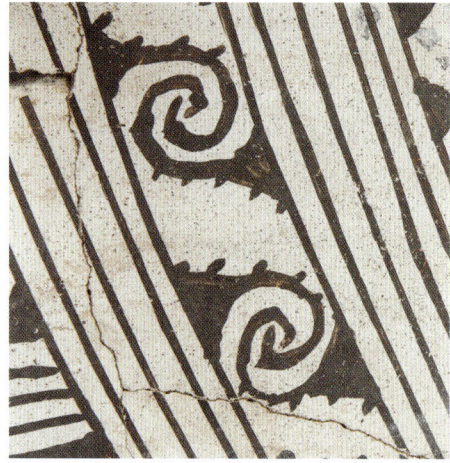
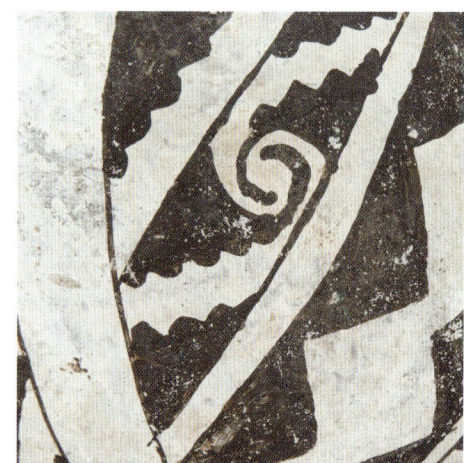
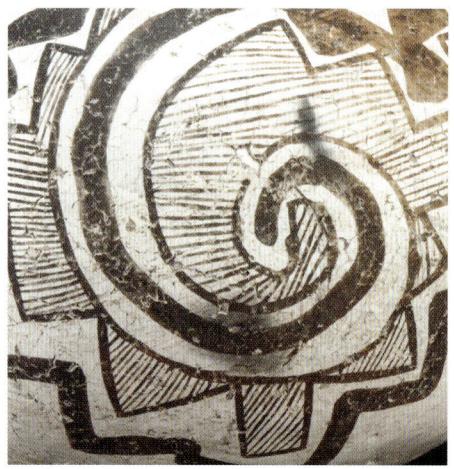
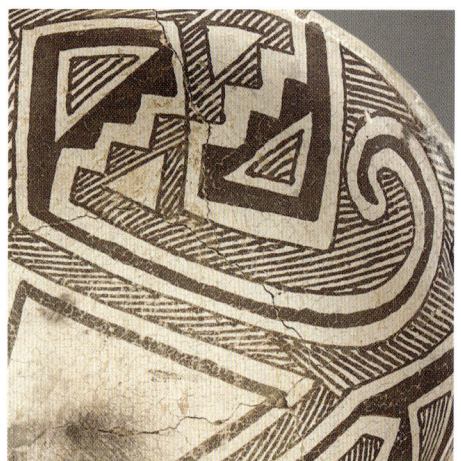

Ancestral artists often connected curvilinear spirals and stepped elements in a single motif. Frequently these combinations were painted as tessellated dual spirals (fig. 3.4, *upper left*) or as a single motif (fig. 3.4 *upper right*). Stepped elements also were painted to initiate spirals as incomplete-element isomers (fig. 3.4, *lower left*) or as components of interlocked complete spirals (fig. 3.4, *lower right*). In a similar manner, artists often added stepped elements to the centers of interlocked rectilinear spirals, and a series of vessels displaying this combination of elements is presented in figure 3.5. Ancestral artists painted rectilinear spirals with stepped elements on a wide variety of vessel forms, including bowls, dippers, jars, and mugs. This common motif was usually painted with liminal-space isomeric design strategies that seem highly energized through border-contrast phenomena and figure-ground reversals.

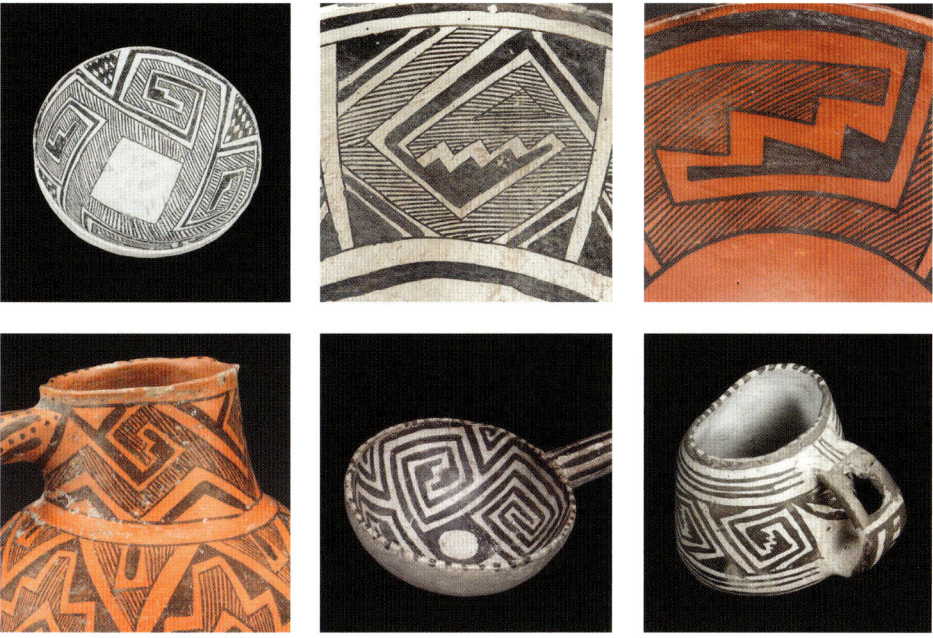

Figure 3.5. Examples of rectilinear spirals combined with stepped elements, presented in chronological order from upper left to lower right.

Gallup Black-on-white bowl, 950–1150 CE, 3 × 6 ⅛ in. dia., MIAC/LOA 18530/11 (upper left). Reserve Black-on-white bowl, 1000–1200, 5 ½ × 12 in. dia., MIAC/LOA 8135/11 (upper middle). Puerco Black-on-red bowl, 1050–1175 CE, 4 ⅛ × 9 ¼ in. dia., MIAC/LOA 43321/11 (upper right). St. Johns Black-on-red pitcher, 1150–1300 CE, 6 ½ × 7 in. dia., Honorable Dan H. McMillan Collection, MIAC/LOA 8871/11 (lower left). McElmo Black-on-white dipper, 1150–1300 CE, 2 ⅜ × 10 × 5 ¼ in. dia., courtesy of the SAR, IAF.2400, photograph by Jennifer Day (lower middle). Mesa Verde Black-on-white mug, 1200–1300 CE, 3 ⅜ × 4 ¼ in. dia., UCB 9332 (lower right).

A close look at rectilinear spirals reveals multiple methods of handling liminal spaces as they reach the center of the motifs. The inclusion of a pair of stepped elements allows the two liminal spaces to continue as a single element threading its way through the entire motif unimpeded (fig. 3.6, *left*). The second method of handling the center of rectilinear sprials (fig. 3.6, *right*) employs a Z-shaped line to connect the two liminal spaces. In both cases the viewer's eye can spiral in and out, unhindered, through pairs of isomers.

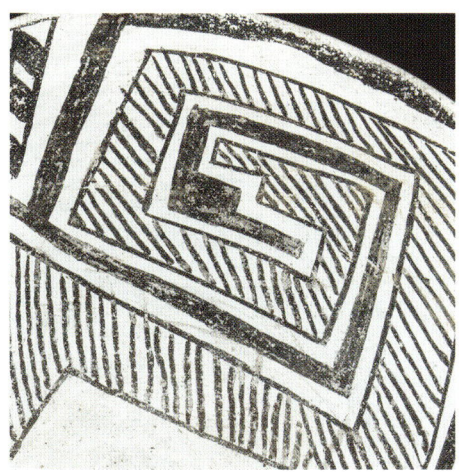 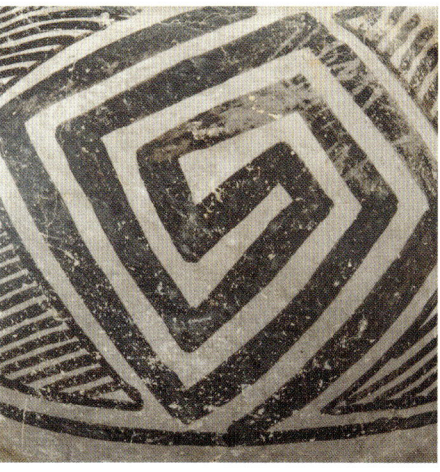

Figure 3.6. Examples of rectilinear spirals painted as liminal-space isomers.

A spiral with unpainted liminal spaces (left) *and painted liminal spaces* (right)*. Gallup Black-on-white bowl, 980–1150 CE, 3 × 6 ⅛ in. dia., MIAC/LOA 18530/11* (left)*. Mesa Verde Black-on-white mug, 1200–1300 CE, 4 ½ × 5 in. dia., MIAC/LOA 43357* (right)*.*

Figure 3.7. Stepped elements with rectilinear spirals (left) and simplified stepped elements as pronged elements (right).

McElmo Black-on-white dipper 1150–1300 CE, 2 ⅜ × 10 × 5 ¼ in. dia., courtesy of the SAR, IAF.2400, photograph by Jennifer Day (left; see plate 36). Escavada Black-on-white jar, 950–1150 CE, 11 ⅞ × 12 ¼ in. dia., MIAC/LOA 20175/11 (right).

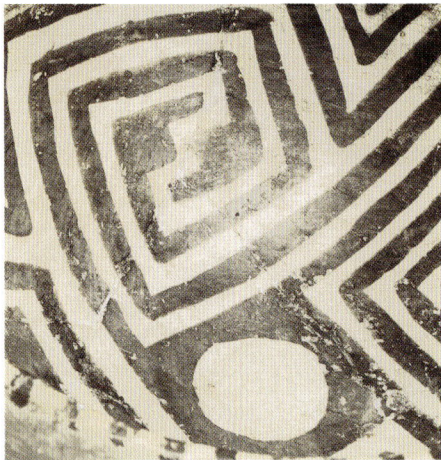 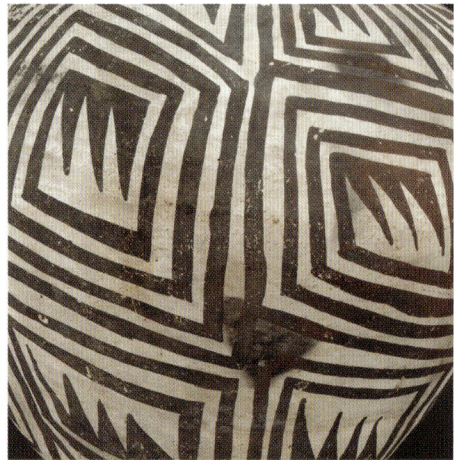

Pronged forms appear to represent simplified versions of stepped elements, particularly at the center of small rectilinear spirals. Beginning in the tenth century and continuing into the thirteenth century, pronged forms seem to have developed concurrently with stepped elements. Production of this variation of stepped forms may have been concentrated in the Chaco/Cibola region of western New Mexico and in the Mesa Verde region of southwestern Colorado. Figure 3.7 shows the relationship between a dual spiral painted as a complex motif and the simplification of the motif as a linear painting employing pronged forms. From an artist's perspective, painting pronged forms instead of stepped elements is simpler and quicker yet still understandable.

Pronged forms also offer optical advantages because their elongated isosceles triangles seem to generate stronger border-contrast phenomena, intensifying the spatial ambiguity of the design's figure-ground relationships. Vessels painted with the most acute triangular elements also seem to be the easiest to reverse perceptually, while the least dynamic motifs have the shortest prongs. This can be understood by comparing the prongs on four vessels in figure 3.8. The most dynamic pronged elements occur in the first version, a Gallup Black-on-white bowl (*upper left*), and the least vibrant prongs are the most simplified elements (*lower left and right*).

This chapter illustrates the formal connections between spiral and stepped elements painted as both rectilinear and curvilinear forms. Molded clay forms allowed artists the freedom to create curvilinear and rectilinear designs that transcended the constraints of the warp-and-weft structure of woven designs. Throughout the Great Pueblo Period, Ancestral Pueblo artists fused these images into compound motifs. The flexibility of clay allowed artists to evolve shapes and designs concurrently.

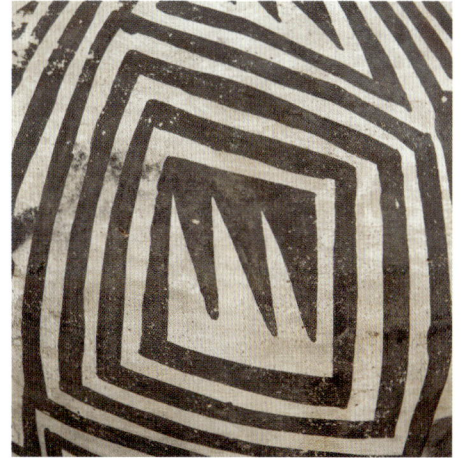

Figure 3.8. Examples of dual spirals incorporating pronged elements.

Escavada Black-on-white jar, 950–1150 CE, 11 ⅞ × 12 ¼ in. dia., MIAC/LOA 20175/11 (upper left). *Gallup Black-on-white bowl, 950–1150 CE, 3 ½ × 8 ½ in. dia., MMA 62.74.9* (upper right). *McElmo Black-on-white bowl, 1100–1300 CE, 4 ⅞ × 11 ⅛ in. dia., MIAC/LOA 19640/11* (lower left). *Mesa Verde Black-on-white bowl, 5 ⅞ × 12 ⅛ in. dia., UCB 09324* (lower right).

Artists painted stepped shapes as introductory elements for curvilinear spirals but also as terminating elements at the center of rectilinear spirals. The production of motifs connecting stepped elements and spiral forms continued for more than three centuries across vast areas of the Southwest. These repeated combinations of elements imply an enduring relationship between spirals and stepped forms. Figure-and-ground reversals created by these designs present a duality between the physicality of painted physical forms and their visual perceptions that exists only in viewers' minds. In the next chapter, we consider the connotations of these designs as metaphors of astronomical, historical, and spiritual contexts within Pueblo society.

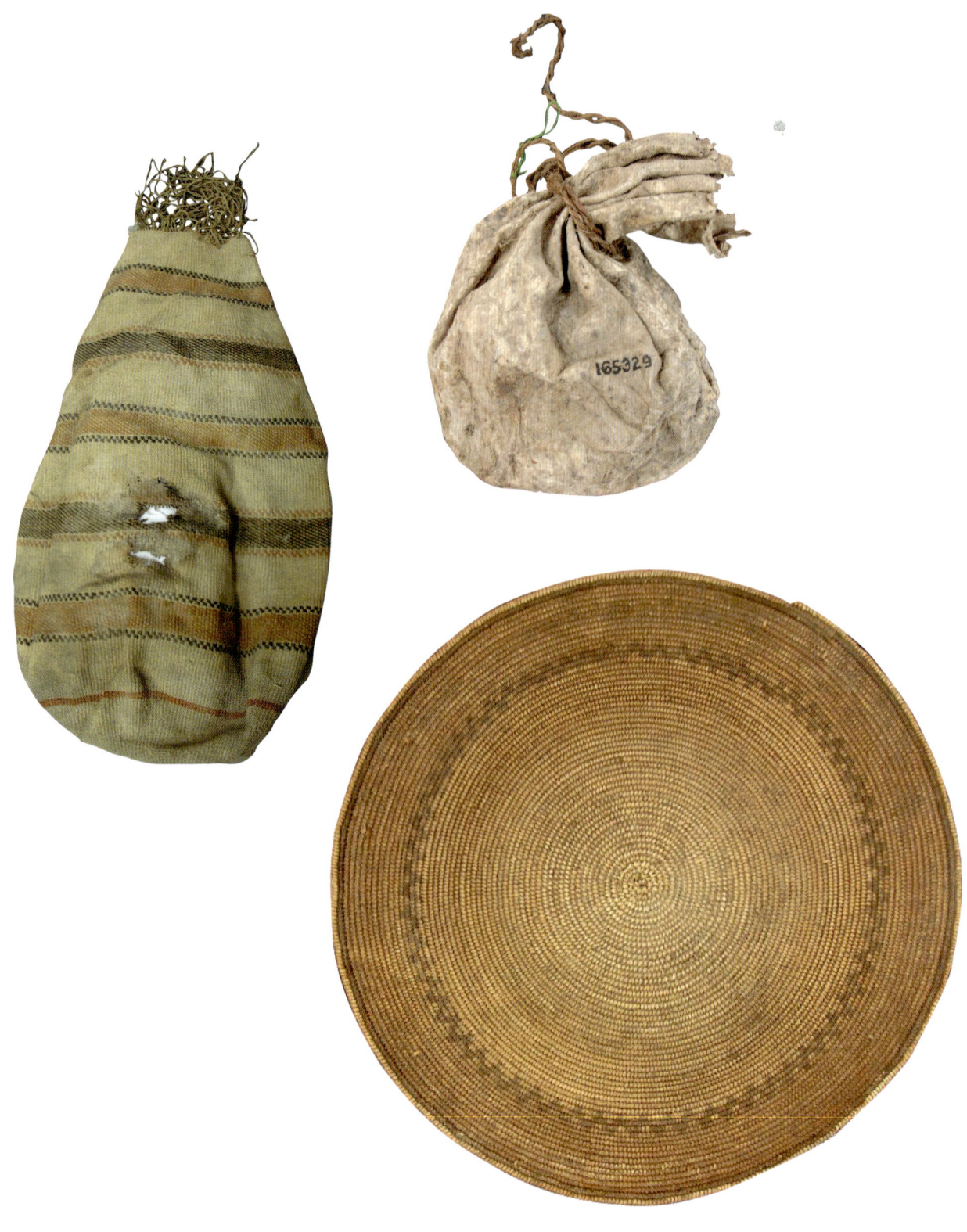

4 ISOMERIC DESIGNS AND WEAVING

At several points in the preceding discussion we have noted connections between elements of isomeric design and weaving imagery. These visual parallels provide an avenue for developing an interpretation of the broader significance of isomeric design. In this chapter we discuss the origins of isomeric design in weaving processes, the transfer of weaving imagery to painted pottery designs, and the significance of this relationship in Pueblo culture.

Today we use ceramics in daily life for cooking, eating and drinking, food storage, and as art objects, without giving them much thought. In order to understand the significance of pottery in Ancestral Pueblo life, one first needs to place oneself in a world in which pottery did not yet exist. In this world, Pueblo ancestors used a variety of organic materials as containers, from tanned skin bags to dried gourds to baskets of skunkbush stems, juniper bark, and yucca fiber (figs. 4.1, 4.2, and 4.3). These containers served many of the same purposes as later pottery vessels, and in certain ways they were functionally superior in that they were lighter and less brittle. However, these containers were not especially durable or watertight, and they were relatively limited as cooking utensils. Pitch-lined baskets could be used with heated rocks for toasting or boiling, but these techniques only worked for foods that cooked quickly. For foods that took a long time to cook, the only realistic option was roasting in a pit. There was no way to store large quantities of water or to cook foods that needed to simmer for several hours.

In this context, the emergence and development of pottery technology would have been revolutionary. Whereas earlier people had had to rely on pitch-lined baskets, dried gourds, and tightly sewn skins to store water, people could now make more permanent water-storage containers relatively easily. This made it much easier to live at some distance from a water source. Storing seeds inside sealed pottery vessels also provided much better protection from dampness, insects, and rodents than containers made of organic materials or storage bins resting on the ground. The use of harder-firing, shale-based clays mixed with crushed rock also created more "flexible" pots that were better able to withstand the thermal shock associated with cooking over an open fire. Thanks to these innovations, by 600 CE Pueblo households had reliable means of storing water and grain, and of cooking a wider range of more nutritious foods.

The ability to prepare beans was especially important for three reasons. First, as a good source of high-quality protein, beans allowed people to rely less on hunting. Second, cooked and mashed beans are much easier for toothless infants to eat than meat, and this probably led to earlier weaning, shorter birth spacing, and improved infant health overall. Third, beans actually add nutrients to the soil that other crops, such as maize, use as they

Figure 4.1. Small buckskin pouch from Allen Canyon, Utah.

Simple containers of perishable materials like this were used for millennia prior to the development of pottery. Courtesy of the FM, cat. no. 165329, photograph by Laurie Webster.

Figure 4.2. Twined bag of yucca fiber from Grand Gulch, Utah.

The colored decoration was created by inserting dyed cordage during construction of the bag. Courtesy of the AMNH, H/12521.

Figure 4.3. Coiled basketry tray from Allen Canyon, Utah.

Note the pattern of light and dark created by the texture of the coiling in combination with the use of colored stitching material. Courtesy of the FM, cat. no. 165295, photograph by Laurie Webster.

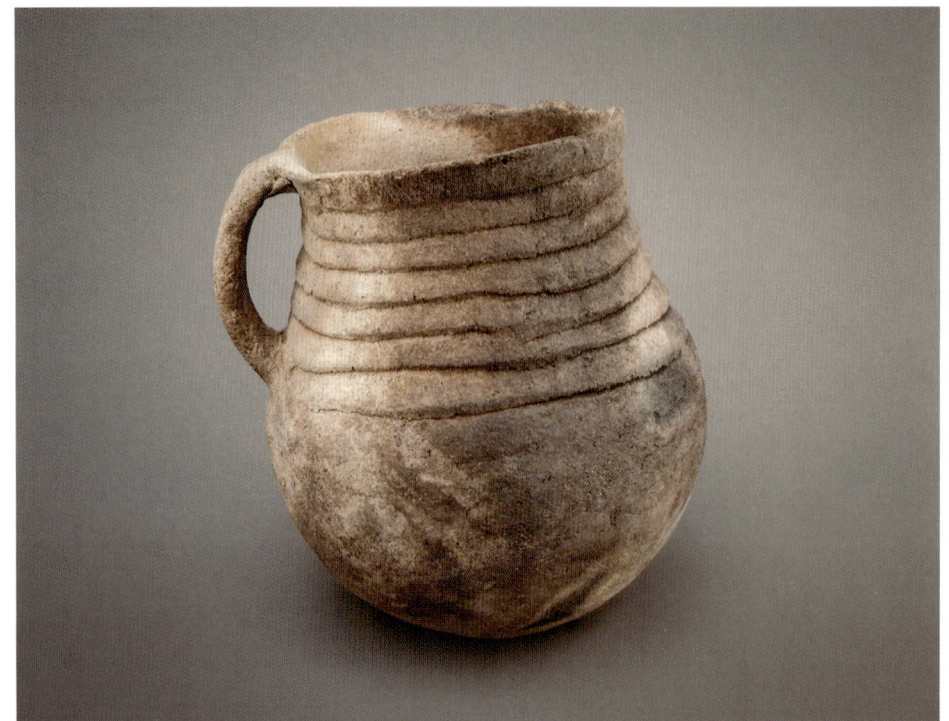

Figure 4.4. Pitcher with exposed coils above with smoothed coils on the bottom.

Kana-a Grayware pitcher, 750–1100 CE, 7 ¼ × 6 ¼ in. dia., MIAC/LOA 8284.

grow. Thus growing beans along with maize probably helped to maintain soil fertility over the long term. These important benefits, which people must have noticed, are traceable directly to the emergence of pottery.

The forms of the earliest pottery vessels mimic the shapes of earlier containers, including coiled baskets and bottle-gourd vessels. This correspondence in shape shows that, by and large, early experimentation with pottery was an attempt to improve upon existing containers of the time. Hence it is not surprising that the earliest painted pottery designs mimicked those that had been sewn into coiled basket walls for millennia. It is also not surprising that the earliest decoration appears primarily on serving vessels, as meals are perhaps the most common and important setting for social interaction among family and friends in all cultures.

Allusions to pre-pottery containers occurred throughout the Great Pueblo Period on both painted and unpainted pottery containers. The use of clay and paint gave ancestral artists the freedom to produce vessel forms and painted designs unencumbered by the structure of woven objects. Some artists created skeuomorphs of nonceramic vessel forms in clay, with painted designs mimicking the structure of woven containers. Obvious examples of earlier technology translated into ceramic forms include the previously discussed gourd-shaped Kana-a Black-on-white pitcher (see fig. 2.1). This vessel was produced before the

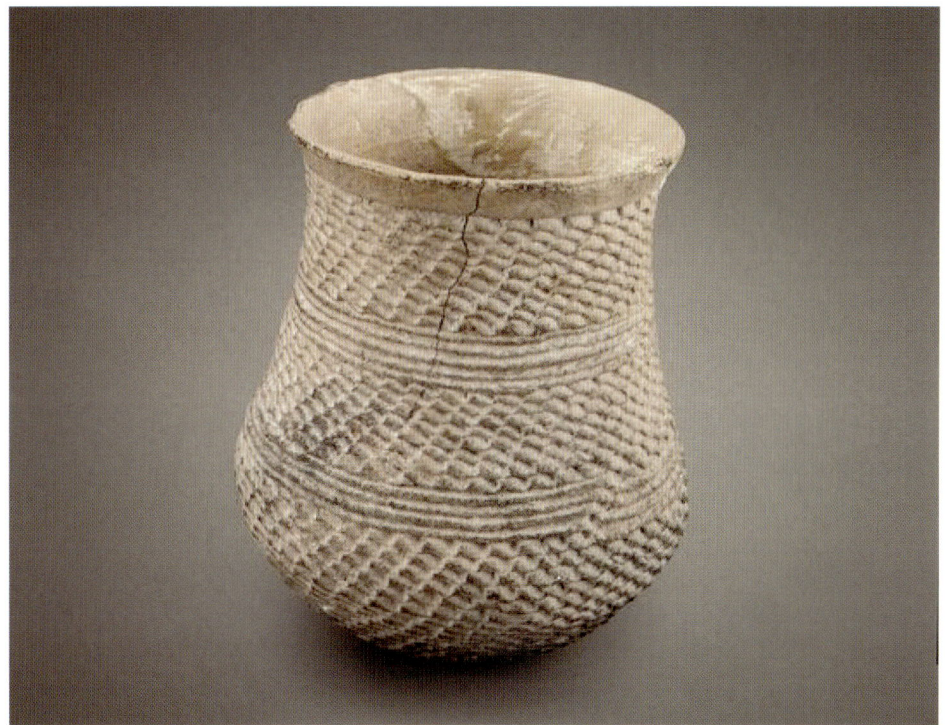

Figure 4.5. Corrugated jar showing a rough surface that imitates the surface of a plaited basket.

Coolidge corrugated jar, 1000–1075 CE, 8 ½ × 8 ¾ in. dia., MIAC/LOA, 20514/11.

development of reversible isomeric designs, and may allude to designs that had previously been painted or engraved on gourd vessels.

What is most important for our purposes, however, is that weaving technologies continued to influence pottery for centuries, and appear to have inspired a conceptual equivalence between pottery and weaving. A notable example is the development of textured surfaces on the exteriors of cooking pots. The earliest cooking pots were smoothed from rim to base. For some reason, in the ninth century CE potters started leaving the junctions between clay bands exposed and unobliterated on the exterior necks of cooking pots (fig. 4.4). Over time these "neck-bands" evolved from broad and flat to short and round, and from stacked bands to a continuous, spiraling coil. Then potters began making patterned indentations on the neck coils using a bone awl and/or their fingers. Finally, they began using this indented neck-coiling method to create entire cooking pots from a single coil of clay, from the base to the rim. The resulting cooking pots were made in a similar way to coiled baskets and looked like them, too (fig. 4.5).

The replacement of earlier cooking pot varieties with the new "corrugated" variety took place virtually overnight throughout the Ancestral Pueblo world during the tenth century CE, the early years of the Great Pueblo Period. Why did the new style of cooking pot spread so quickly? Experimental studies by archaeologist Christopher Pierce (2005) show that it was not because corrugated vessels were easier to make, stronger, or more durable. Instead, it was because corrugated pots worked better. The surface area of the exterior of a corrugated vessel is greater than that of its interior, and as a result such vessels dissipate heat from their contents faster than smooth-surfaced vessels. The somewhat counterintuitive advantage of this radiator effect is that cooking pots full of simmering posole, cornmeal, or beans would be less likely to boil over. As a result, more of the contents would find their way into a satisfied belly. Corrugation seemed to improve cooking control, and allowed vessel shapes with smaller throats and flared rims to further reduce spillage.

Ancestral Pueblo potters figured out that corrugated exteriors worked better on cooking pots made from the shale-based clays of the Colorado Plateau. And this technological innovation derived from mapping the process of sewing coiled basketry onto the process of making pottery. An engineer might explain why corrugated pottery worked better in terms of the thermal properties of differential surface area, but in cases of limited knowledge people tend to infer cause directly from correlation. So in this context it seems likely that Ancestral Pueblo people inferred that corrugated cooking pots worked better precisely because they were made like baskets. We think this was a crucial step in the emergence of isomeric design because it implied the advantages of pottery for Pueblo life derived from their relationship with weaving processes. Thus it was appropriate to think of pottery vessels as better baskets and to decorate them with weaving imagery. Indeed, this correspondence is reflected in a Tewa word for pottery, *nat'ú*, which combines a word for "earth" with a word for "basket." Apparently, when Tewa speakers coined this term long ago they were thinking of pots as baskets made of clay.

Any form of weaving that involves the interleaving of elements can produce an isomeric design as a byproduct of the weaving process. During late Basketmaker times, weavers began to notice this in their production of finger-woven tump bands, sandals, aprons, and twilled mats. Over time, weavers recognized that such patterns could also be intentionally incorporated into other types of weaving, such as coiled baskets and twined sandals. For example, the fine grid of the warp and weft of a basket could be woven with stitches that were either dyed red or black, or left undyed. Individual stitches produced colored forms with a slightly ragged edge, a style that was transferred to the "ticked" designs of early black-on-white pottery vessels.

Around 1000 CE, an especially important innovation set the stage for the proliferation of isomeric designs in pottery. One of the essential tasks in food preparation was the sifting of ground cornmeal through a twill-plaited ring basket in order to separate the meal from the fragments of grinding stone that became mixed with it during the grinding process. Typically, the meal was sifted through a twill-plaited basket into a large pottery bowl, after which it would be ready for cooking. The image of the fine meal falling through a woven vegetal object and settling on an earthen object is a natural symbol of rain falling to earth

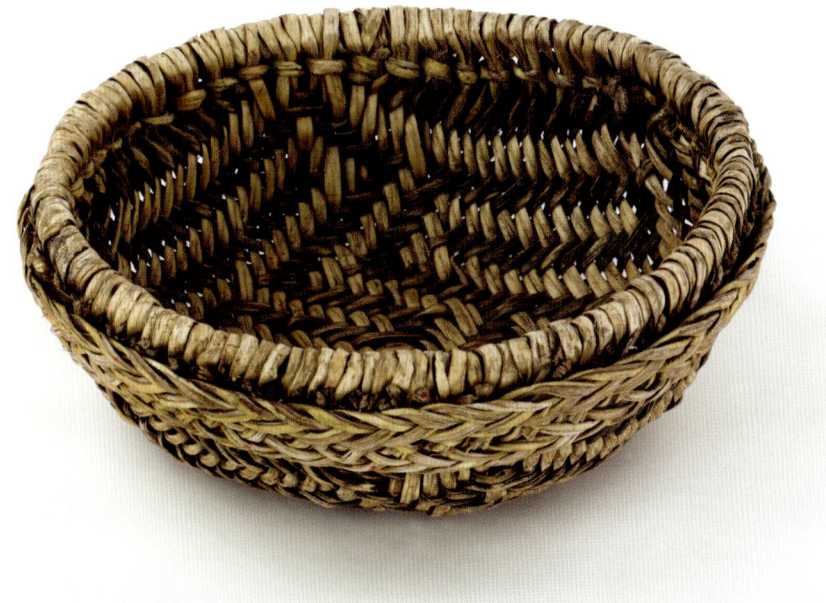

Figure 4.6. Twill-plaited basket of yucca with interval-shift designs from Mesa Verde, Colorado.

The isomeric pattern produced as a byproduct of the weaving method is revealed by the use of dyed yucca leaves for one set of the plaiting strips. Courtesy of the CHM, O.594.1.

to produce food, but for this discussion it is the specifics of the weaving process that are most important. Twill-plaited ring baskets were made by weaving a mat from strips of yucca and then fastening the ends to a ring of wood. To create a flexible fabric for sifting, weavers learned that weaving with an over-two-under-two or over-three-under-three pattern worked best. For such fabrics to hold together, the weaver also had to skip a leaf when starting the over-and-under pattern for each leaf she added to the growing mat. This imparted a characteristic twilled texture to the finished product.

Sifter baskets like these had been made for centuries, but around 1000 CE Ancestral Pueblo weavers noticed something interesting: if they shifted the skipping pattern when adding new yucca leaves to the growing mat, isomeric designs, including chevrons, nested diamonds, and interlocking scrolls would emerge as a byproduct (fig. 4.6 basket). The emergence of isomeric designs in a type of basketry that was used in conjunction with a pottery bowl must have encouraged potters to recognize the relationship between the two media and to begin formulating new isomeric forms of decoration on pottery. This was the origin of the most perceptually apparent form of isomeric design—painted-and-unpainted isomers.

In subsequent centuries, Ancestral Pueblo potters elaborated this connection, adapting aspects of both coiled and plaited basketry production and design strategy to pottery (see Ortman 2000). References to basketry are found in both the vessel forms and the

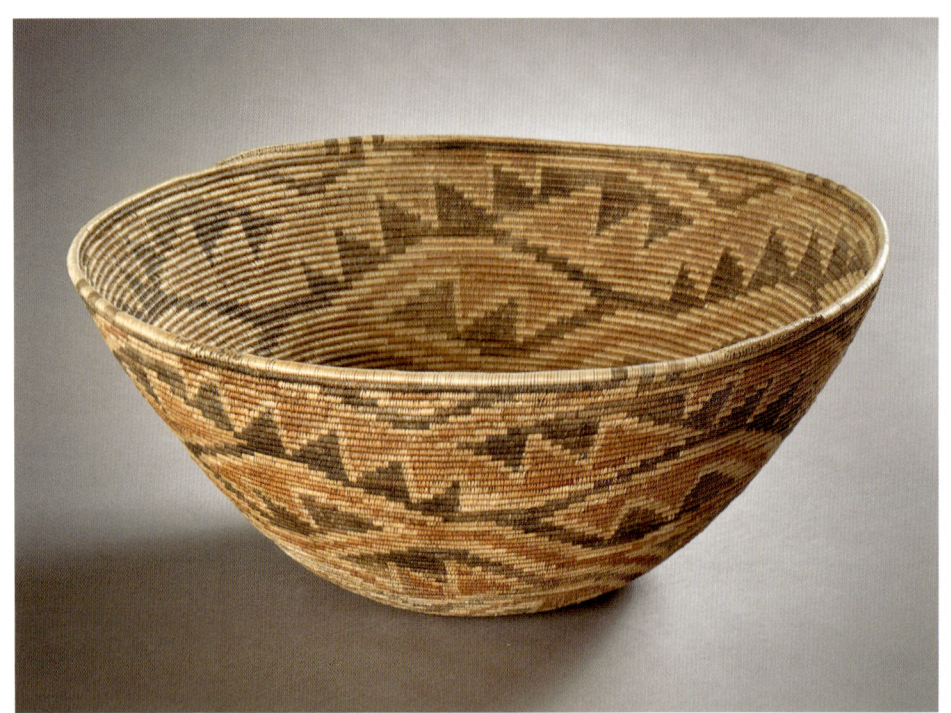

Figure 4.7. Pueblo III coiled basket with an interlocked pronged design.

The isomeric design is not a byproduct of the coiling method but was intentionally added during spiral weaving of the basket. Courtesy NMMM.

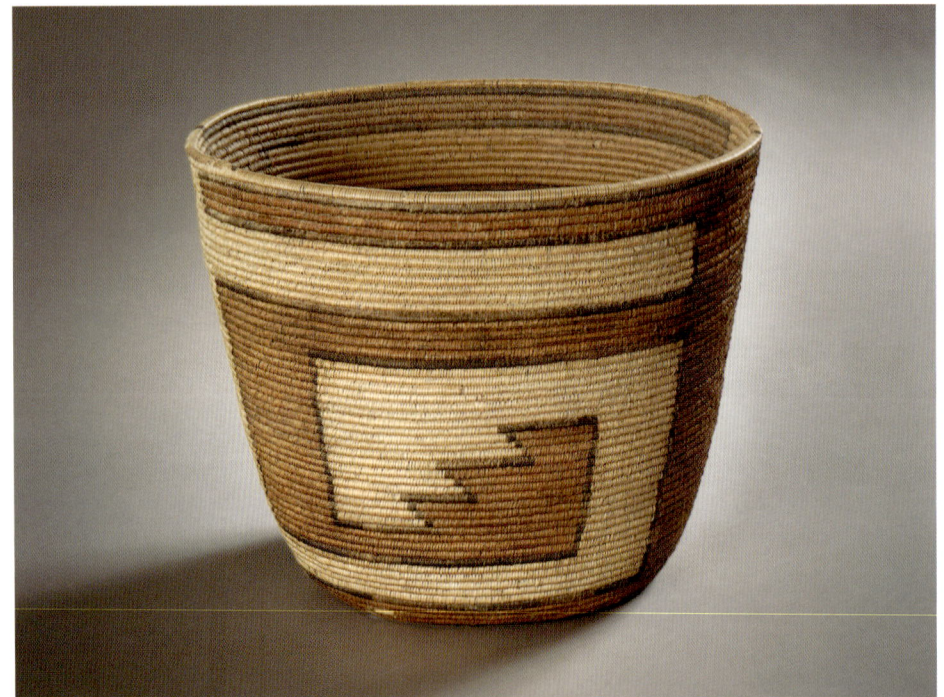

Figure 4.8. Pueblo III coiled basket with isomeric stepped motifs.

This remarkable basket illustrates the transfer of isomeric design principles that are a byproduct of loom-based weaving and pottery painting back onto coiled basketry. Courtesy NMMM.

painted designs. As painting skills and ceramic technology improved, ancestral artists began displaying the grid understructure for their designs and then inpainting the desired forms to create finished works. The best description for this style of design is a "woven painting." When the central element of a ceramic bowl is a circle, that sets up the structure for a tessellated design frieze around the rim of a bowl; but when the central motif is a square, the resulting four-part design radiates out from the center of the vessel and is divided into pie-shaped quadrants.

There is also a correspondence between these two types of layouts and the two primary basket-weaving methods, with banded friezes emerging naturally from coiling (figs. 4.7, 4.8), and centered, "draped" patterns emerging naturally from plaiting. Another important trend was the evolution of designs that drifted further and further from depictions of actual woven designs while maintaining the creative use of isomeric design principles.

Often the painting of spiral images bears a striking relationship to the process of coiling a woven basket and molding ceramic forms by coiling cylindrical ribbons of clay (fig. 4.9 *top*). The bottom image on the left displays the beginning of the coiling process. The artist smoothed the coils inside the vessel to lock them together structurally, but left the coils exposed on the exterior. A Mangas Black-on-white bowl decorated with a painted-and-unpainted spiral design (fig. 4.9 *bottom*) demonstrates a formal relationship to the initial coiling of a Pueblo jar.

A grouping of corrugated vessel starts (fig. 4.10) reveals slight differences in the starting of these ceramic objects but also affirms a strong relationship to basketry starts.

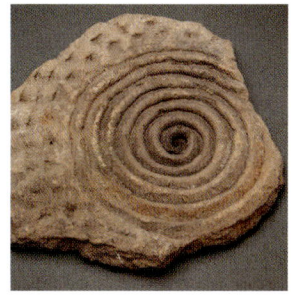

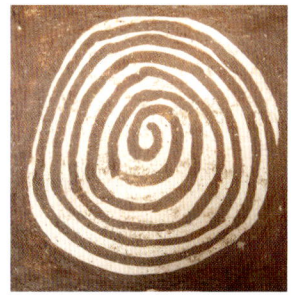

Figure 4.9. Coiling as cultural metaphor.

Both examples expand in a clockwise direction. The beginning coils of a corrugated jar (top) and a painted-and-unpainted isomer spiral on a Mangas Black-on-white bowl (bottom).

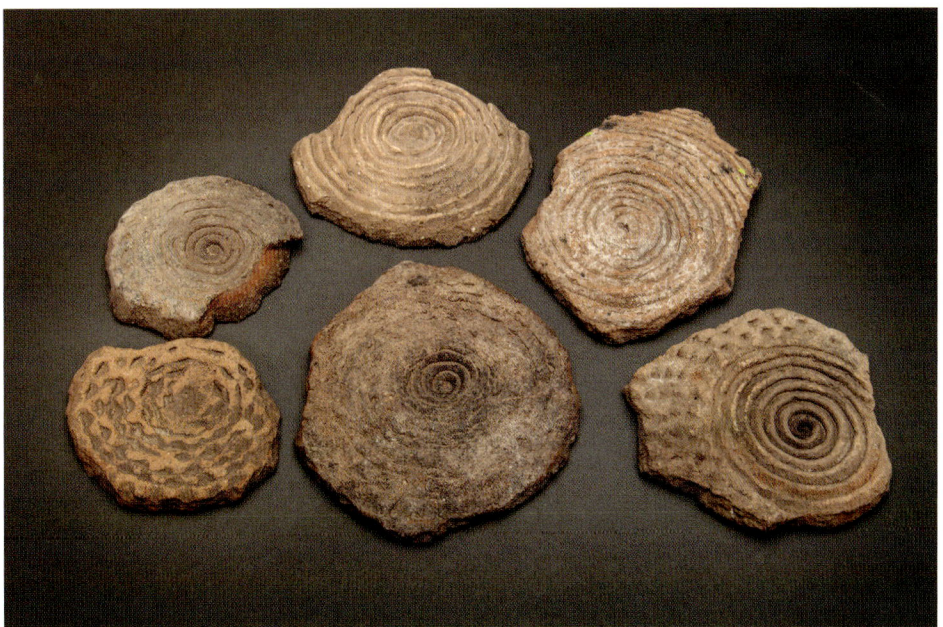

Figure 4.10. Corrugated ceramic vessel starts.

These sherds illustrate the variety of coiling starts for corrugated jars derived from prior experience weaving coiled basketry.

Figure 4.14. Kiva mural with interlocked dual spiral isomers painted in kaolin.

Photograph by Scott G. Ortman.

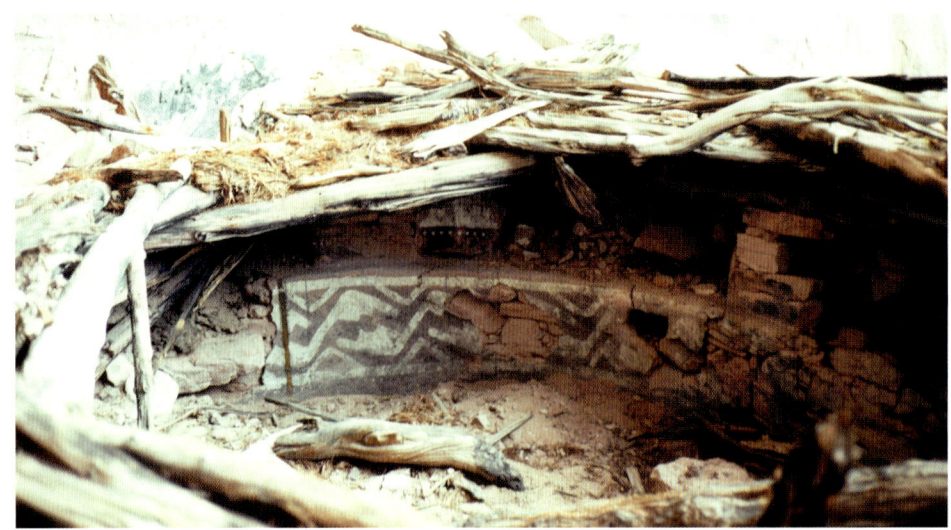

Another kiva from southern Utah (fig. 4.14) had an isomeric frieze painted on its interior wall. The design in this kiva bears a strong resemblance to the painting on the Mesa Verde Black-on-white mug also from Lowry Ruin (fig. 4.15) with its interlocked rectilinear spirals creating a diamondlike structure.

It is also important to note the woven character of the cribbed roof of the structure in figure 4.14 and figure 4.16, which seems to present the kiva as a microcosm of a world comprised of a vegetal sky basket and an earthen earth-bowl that meet at the horizon. This imagery seems to have been widespread, and the "weaving" of the roof beams to create an overturned, dome-shaped roof that mirrors the structure of a coiled basket is especially apparent in the photograph of an excavated kiva. These examples illustrate the metaphorical relationship between kiva architecture, basketry weaving technology, and isometric design strategies on contemporaneous painted pottery. These patterns further suggest that, at least in some areas, Pueblo people linked pottery design and weaving explicitly and consciously.

Kivas aren't the only locations where spiral isomers and ritual places merged with astronomical events. In their efforts to keep a calendar to guide the annual agricultural cycle, Ancestral Puebloans focused their keen observational skills on the daily motions of the sun, which rises and sets at different places on the horizon each day and follows different arcs as it travels to high noon and then back to sunset. The

Figure 4.15. Mesa Verde mug with interlocked dual spiral motifs similar to the kiva mural (see fig. 4.13).

The kiva mural uses chevrons to fill empty space around the spirals while the mug features stepped forms set within triangular spaces. Courtesy of the FM, neg. no. 85402.

painted designs. As painting skills and ceramic technology improved, ancestral artists began displaying the grid understructure for their designs and then inpainting the desired forms to create finished works. The best description for this style of design is a "woven painting." When the central element of a ceramic bowl is a circle, that sets up the structure for a tessellated design frieze around the rim of a bowl; but when the central motif is a square, the resulting four-part design radiates out from the center of the vessel and is divided into pie-shaped quadrants.

There is also a correspondence between these two types of layouts and the two primary basket-weaving methods, with banded friezes emerging naturally from coiling (figs. 4.7, 4.8), and centered, "draped" patterns emerging naturally from plaiting. Another important trend was the evolution of designs that drifted further and further from depictions of actual woven designs while maintaining the creative use of isomeric design principles.

Often the painting of spiral images bears a striking relationship to the process of coiling a woven basket and molding ceramic forms by coiling cylindrical ribbons of clay (fig. 4.9 *top*). The bottom image on the left displays the beginning of the coiling process. The artist smoothed the coils inside the vessel to lock them together structurally, but left the coils exposed on the exterior. A Mangas Black-on-white bowl decorated with a painted-and-unpainted spiral design (fig. 4.9 *bottom*) demonstrates a formal relationship to the initial coiling of a Pueblo jar.

A grouping of corrugated vessel starts (fig. 4.10) reveals slight differences in the starting of these ceramic objects but also affirms a strong relationship to basketry starts.

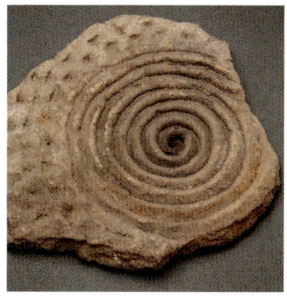

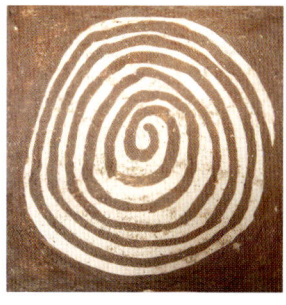

Figure 4.9. Coiling as cultural metaphor.

Both examples expand in a clockwise direction. The beginning coils of a corrugated jar (top) and a painted-and-unpainted isomer spiral on a Mangas Black-on-white bowl (bottom).

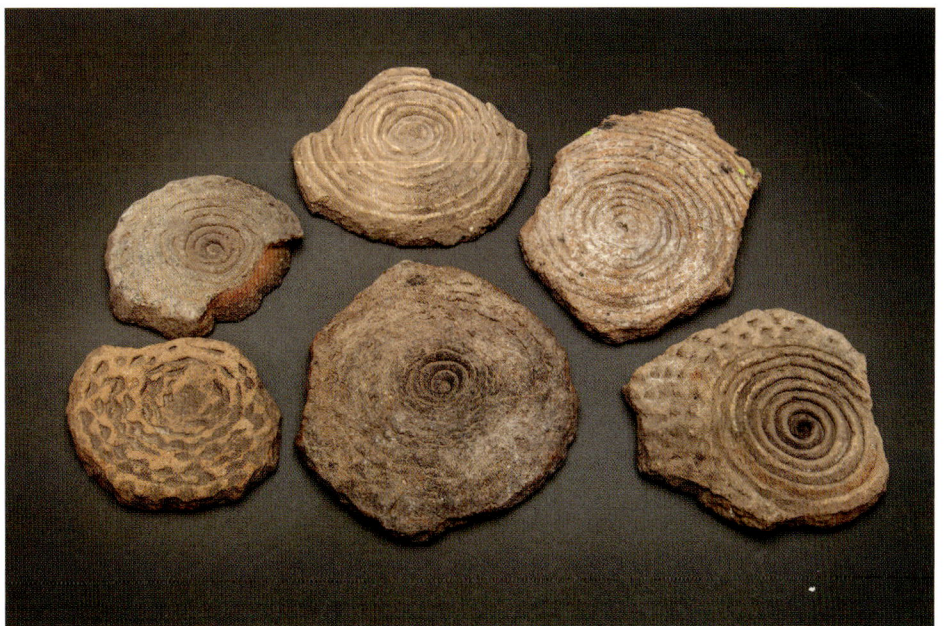

Figure 4.10. Corrugated ceramic vessel starts.

These sherds illustrate the variety of coiling starts for corrugated jars derived from prior experience weaving coiled basketry.

Figure 4.11. Woven paintings alluding to the coiling and the structure of basketry designs.

Tusayan/Betatakin Black-on-white bowl, 950–1150 CE, 3 ⅜ × 7 ½ in. dia., MIAC/LOA 43326/11 (left). *Tusayan/Betatakin Black-on-white bowl, 1200–1300 CE, 5 ½ × 10 ⅝ in. dia., MIAC/LOA 46588* (right).

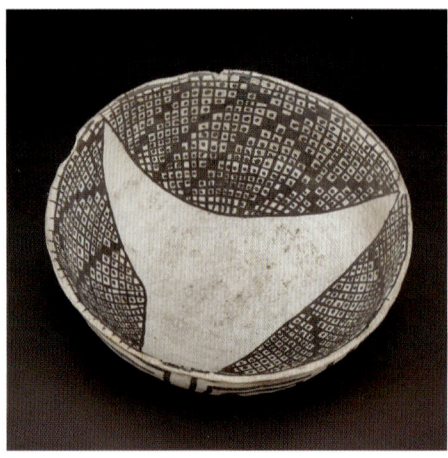 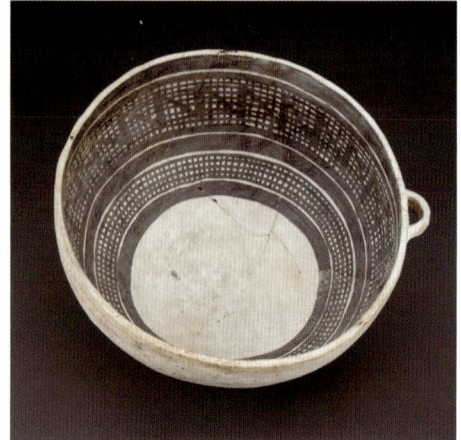

Artists devised other means of alluding to basketry form and structure using paint, creating woven paintings. The painting of checkerboard organizational structures imitates the surface of woven baskets in which the bundles or rods form the warp and sewn bindings act as the wefts. Using colored and plain bindings to create a design in a basket accentuated the gridded appearance of basketry surfaces.

A Betatakin Black-on-white bowl exemplifies the process of painting in a manner that mimicked basketry surface texture and design structure (fig. 4.11, *left*). The artist first outlined the central triangle to be left unpainted and then drew a series of concentric lines of latitude paralleling the rim of the bowl. Adding longitudinal lines radiating out from the center of the bowl finished the gridded structure. Inpainted cells in the grid created spiraling designs that produced figure-and-ground relationships. The painted squares pop forward against the plain grid, acting as negative ground. Optical reversals occur between the triangular center and the tessellated field.

A similar process produced the basketlike design friezes on a Tusayan Black-on-white bowl (fig. 4.11, *right*). The solid elements painted into the friezes created pairs of stepped designs, with the painted squares functioning like negative spaces behind the stepped elements. The artists painted the grids as squarely as possible; however, when an observer looks at these curved vessels from any angle the grid distorts visually and can appear haphazardly organized.

An important question raised by the parallels between weaving imagery and pottery designs discussed in this chapter is the degree to which Ancestral Pueblo people were conscious of the relationship. It is likely that at least in some areas potters drew upon weaving imagery in imagining pottery designs out of an implicit nonverbal awareness of the connections between these industries. But in at least a few areas it appears that people thought about, and talked about, these connections.

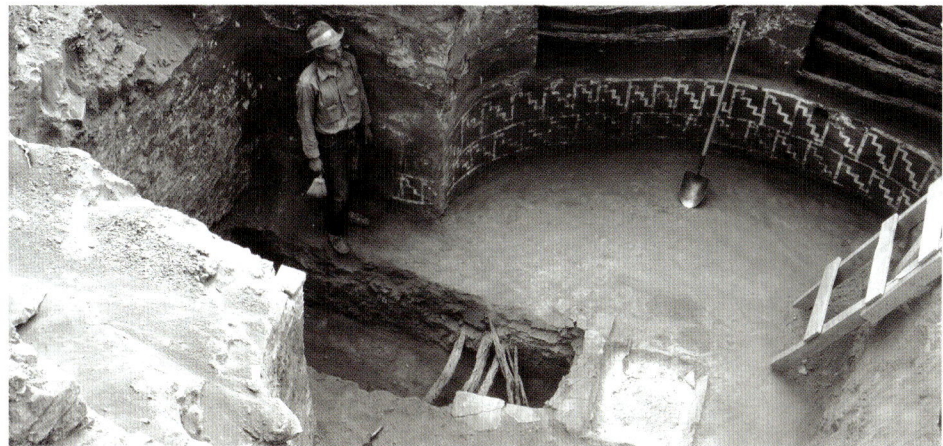

Figure 4.12. Excavation photograph of a kiva at Lowry Ruin, Colorado, with stepped elements separated by liminal spaces between elements.

This painted mural creates a strong figure-and-ground ambiguity. Courtesy of the FM, neg. no. 75659f.

The clearest evidence that supports this view comes from kiva architecture and mural paintings that express the same container imagery that appears on pots and baskets. Pueblo kivas are ceremonial chambers with central hearths that are accessed via ladders through a roof hatch. Today, these structures are viewed as microcosms of the spirit world from which Pueblo ancestors emerged into the physical world at the beginning of time. The archaeological record indicates that these structures evolved from Basketmaker Period pit houses; and by the Great Pueblo Period, if not sooner, they had acquired symbolic meanings similar to those of present-day kivas.

The plastered walls of Ancestral Pueblo kivas were sometimes decorated, and in the northern reaches of the San Juan drainage in particular a common form of this decoration involved the painting of isomeric pottery designs, which derived from weaving, around the wall of the structure. For example, a tessellated stepped design (fig. 4.12) adorns the well-known painted kiva at Lowry Ruin in southern Colorado. An interesting aspect of this painting is the use of white kaolin as the pigment; it bears a strong resemblance to the exterior painting of a Snowflake Black-on-white jar (fig. 4.13).

Figure 4.13. The stepped motifs painted on this jar are reminiscent of the kiva motifs at Lowry Ruin.

Snowflake Black-on-white jar, 8 ¼ × 11 ⅛ in. dia., MNA NA 9006.R.41.

Figure 4.14. Kiva mural with interlocked dual spiral isomers painted in kaolin.

Photograph by Scott G. Ortman.

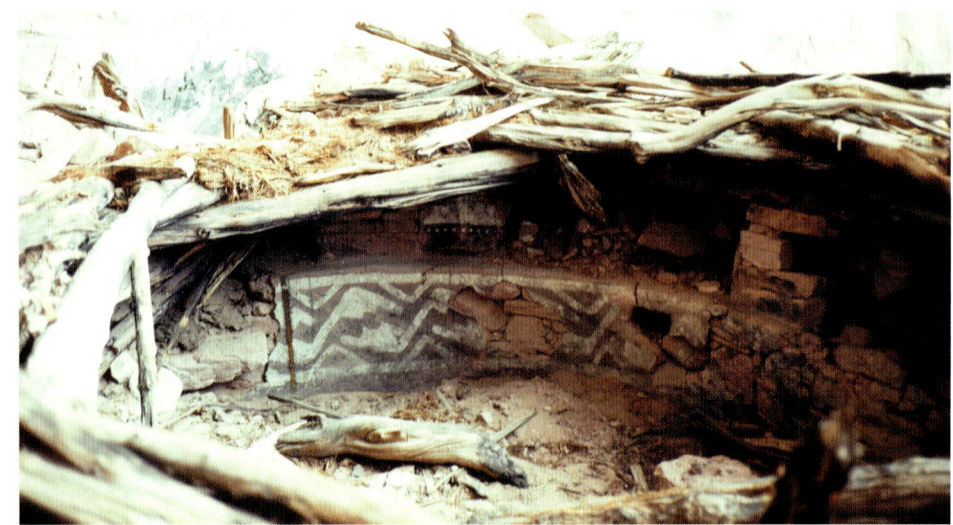

Another kiva from southern Utah (fig. 4.14) had an isomeric frieze painted on its interior wall. The design in this kiva bears a strong resemblance to the painting on the Mesa Verde Black-on-white mug also from Lowry Ruin (fig. 4.15) with its interlocked rectilinear spirals creating a diamondlike structure.

It is also important to note the woven character of the cribbed roof of the structure in figure 4.14 and figure 4.16, which seems to present the kiva as a microcosm of a world comprised of a vegetal sky basket and an earthen earth-bowl that meet at the horizon. This imagery seems to have been widespread, and the "weaving" of the roof beams to create an overturned, dome-shaped roof that mirrors the structure of a coiled basket is especially apparent in the photograph of an excavated kiva. These examples illustrate the metaphorical relationship between kiva architecture, basketry weaving technology, and isometric design strategies on contemporaneous painted pottery. These patterns further suggest that, at least in some areas, Pueblo people linked pottery design and weaving explicitly and consciously.

Figure 4.15. Mesa Verde mug with interlocked dual spiral motifs similar to the kiva mural (see fig. 4.13).

The kiva mural uses chevrons to fill empty space around the spirals while the mug features stepped forms set within triangular spaces. Courtesy of the FM, neg. no. 85402.

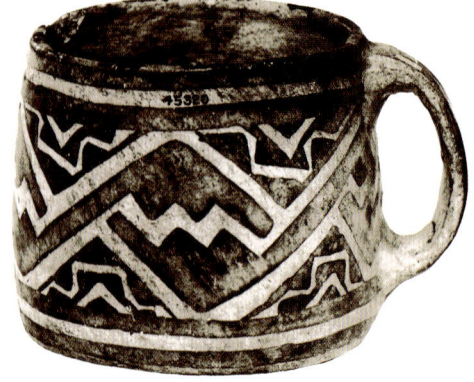

Kivas aren't the only locations where spiral isomers and ritual places merged with astronomical events. In their efforts to keep a calendar to guide the annual agricultural cycle, Ancestral Puebloans focused their keen observational skills on the daily motions of the sun, which rises and sets at different places on the horizon each day and follows different arcs as it travels to high noon and then back to sunset. The motions of the sun follow a yearly procession creating winter when the sun is low on the southern horizon and summer when it rises and sets at the northern range of its annual cycle. Similarly, the moon does not always rise and set at the same position of the horizon and it doesn't appear at the same height, or azimuth, but travels higher and lower in a slow eighteen-year cycle. Ancestral Pueblo sky watchers noted the changing positions of the sun and moon on the horizon and used the observational cycles that emerged to schedule rituals, plant crops, and otherwise coordinate their lifeways with nature to develop a successful agricultural economy despite the often unpredictable weather.

Pueblo sun watchers certainly noticed that rock formations and overhanging ledges cast cool shadows providing relief from the harsh summer sun and heat. The shadows in these spaces move in the opposite direction of the sun. The sun rises in the east and casts shadows to the west, but by late afternoon a reversal occurs as the setting sun casts shadows to the east. Depending on the formation of the rocks, overhangs and large boulders may allow rays of light to slip between rocks as the sun moves through its regular cycle. The resulting shafts of light within the shadows could change positions during the day and through the seasons.

Occasionally observers noticed that the curious motions of these changing light and shadow sensations corresponded with astronomical events, such as the sunrises and sunsets associated with the solstices and equinoxes. They marked these places for viewing celestial events with petroglyphs in the form of spirals and nested circles. In the previous chapter we presented formal relationships that connect the painting of curvilinear spirals, spiral forms beginning and ending with stepped elements, and geometric spirals. Tessellated stepped motifs and dual spirals on ceramics (see figs. 4.14, 4.16) relate to photographs documenting the painting of these isomeric elements as mural friezes in kivas (see fig. 4.13

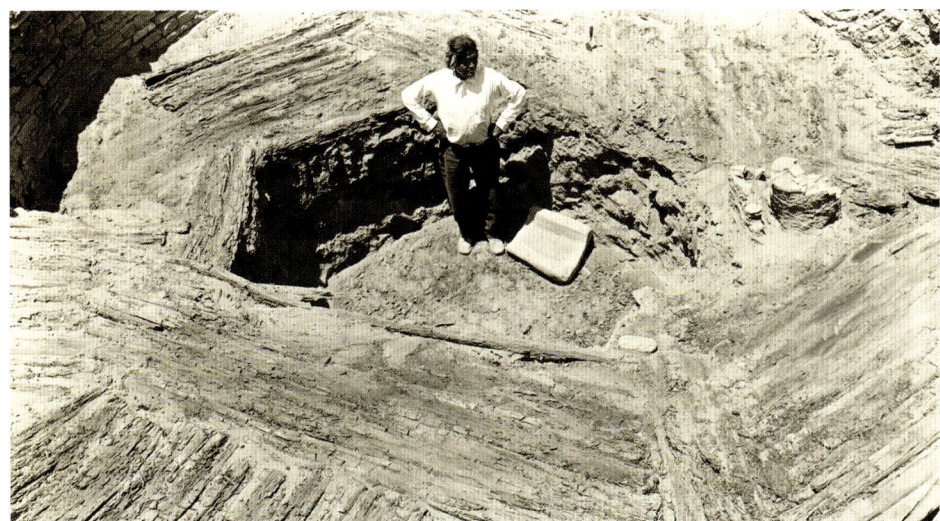

Figure 4.16. Excavation view of collapsed, cribbed kiva roof at Pueblo Bonito (Kiva I).

National Anthropology Archives, Smithsonian Institution, unidentified photographer (O. C. Havens?), neg. no. 22673 A.

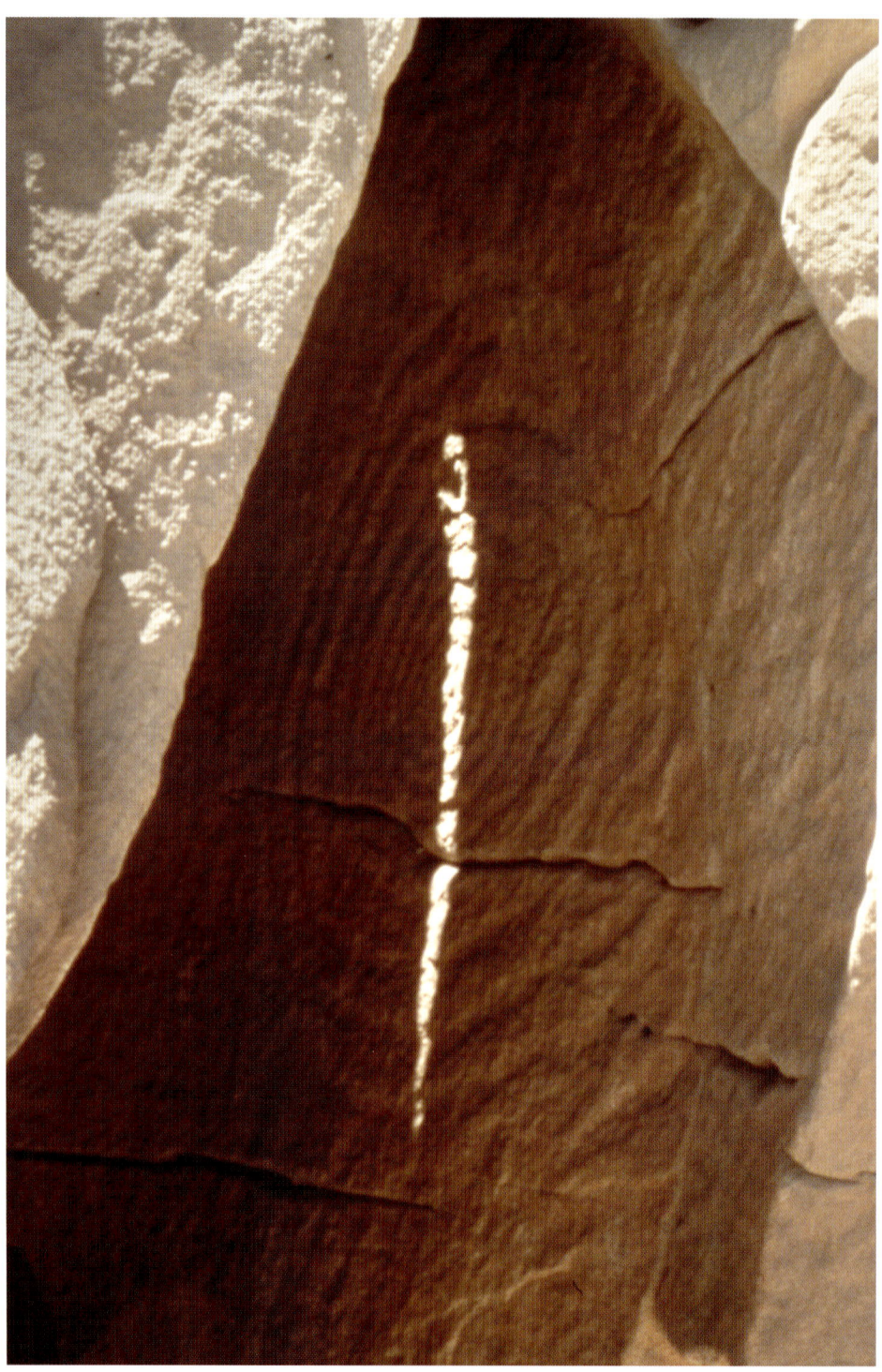

Figure 4.17. The Sun Dagger in Chaco Canyon, New Mexico.

Photograph by Karl Kernberger, © The Solstice Project.

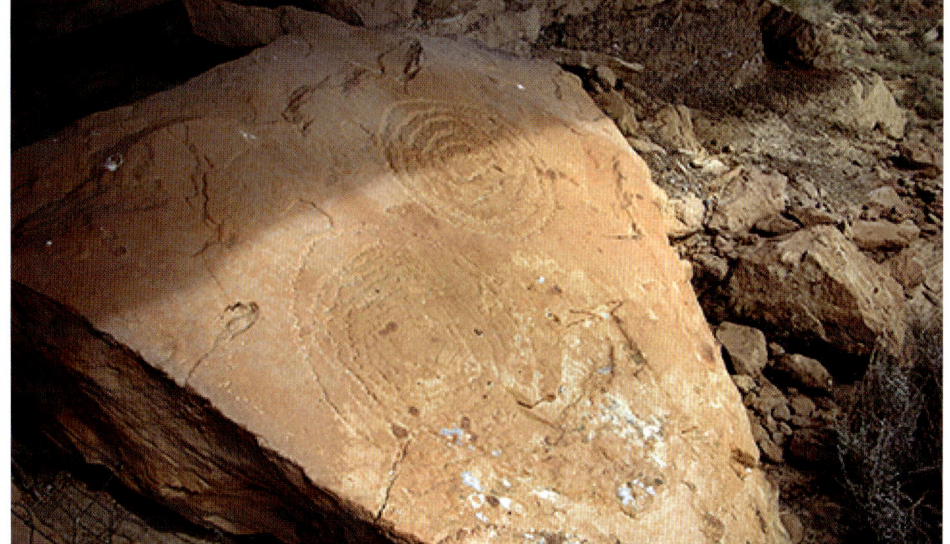

Figure 4.18. Equinox marker in Chaco Canyon, New Mexico.

Photograph by Joseph Traugott.

and 4.16 this volume, Ortman 2012:fig. 10.3). Such contexts for spiral and stepped elements suggest strong associations between these designs on pottery, astronomical observations, Pueblo rituals, and celebratory feasting.

The best known of these petroglyph markers is the Sun Dagger (fig. 4.17) near the top of Fajada Butte in Chaco Canyon National Historical Park (Sofaer 2008). Three naturally occurring rock slabs resting vertically on their edges cast unusual light and shadow images on the adjacent canyon wall. Multiple shafts of light move at different times of the day at specific times of year, slipping through the slabs when the sun lines up with the thin channels between them. Two spiral petroglyphs were carved on the canyon wall to align with sunshine streaming though the three rocks at different times of the year.

The larger petroglyph on the right of the Sun Dagger was pecked so that a triangular wedge of sunlight focused on the center of the spiral at midday on the June (summer) solstice. On the December (winter) solstice, two spears of light appear, touching the left and right edges of this spiral petroglyph. But on the equinoxes in March and September, a shaft of light aligns with the center of the small spiral petroglyph positioned just to the left of the larger marker. The site identifies the minor lunar standstill with a shadow covering the top of the large petroglyph, and the major standstill with a shadow just touching the western edge of the petroglyph. These details indicate that the Star Axis petroglyphs were pecked over at least an eighteen-year lunar cycle so that the shafts of light perfectly match the light and shadow phenomena.

Anna Sofaer identifies two additional solar sites near Sun Dagger on Fajada Butte with five more petroglyphs (including two spirals) that also interact with naturally occurring shadows and moving rays of light. Sadly, Sun Dagger no longer functions because the

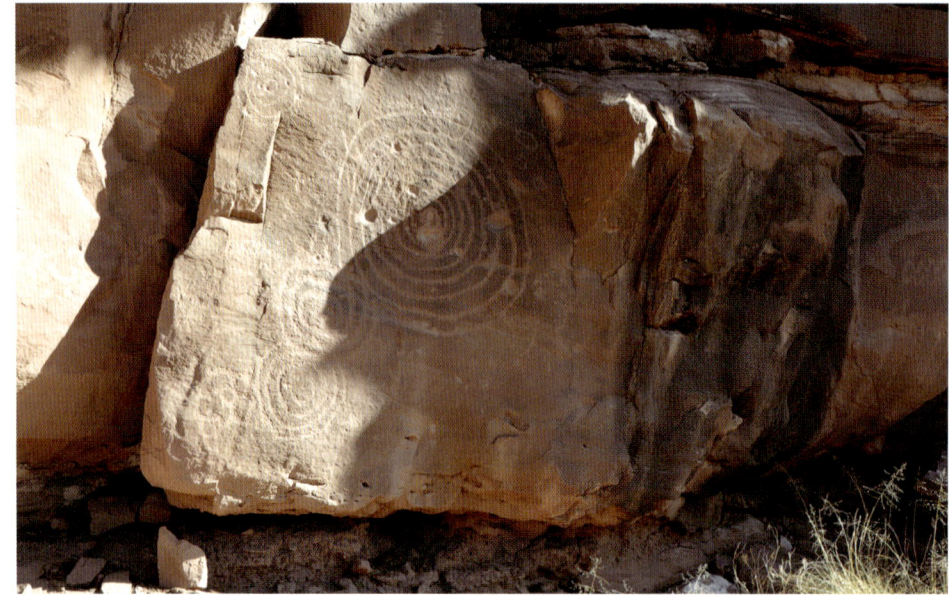

Figure 4.19. Winter solstice marker near San Ysidro, New Mexico.

Photograph by Dr. Ronald Costell.

three boulders became destabilized by visitors and have shifted, destroying this remarkable interactive site.

A flat boulder located under an overhanging ledge on the edge of a wash at Chaco also contains a pair of petroglyphs that serve as astronomical markers. The images pecked into the worn surface of the rock are either concentric circles or spirals. At high noon on vernal and autumnal equinoxes, the overhanging ledge casts a shadow that bisects the eastern petroglyph (fig. 4.18). However, on the summer solstice the shadow completely covers this large rock, and during the winter solstices the shadow misses the boulder. The western petroglyph appears to mark the major lunar standstill when the moon reaches the northernmost position in its cyclical precession. At this time the full moon should illuminate the bottom of the western petroglyph, beginning at the center of the marker.

Both the sites near Sun Dagger and the equinox marker also have partial rooms installed in nearby overhangs, suggesting that these were important spaces where observers could stay while conducting solar observations. These structures affirm the permanence of these places and suggest that they were more than casual markers. The careful construction of these spaces with their associated astronomical phenomena and Pueblo icons implies ritual power over an extended period of time.

A similar event occurs near San Ysidro, New Mexico, where a protruding pointed rock casts shadows on a rock wall just to the north. Petroglyphs pecked on the wall mark the winter solstice at high noon. Before noon the shadow moves down on the wall until it finally intersects with the central marker on the wall. Ron Costell's photograph of a cast shadow (fig. 4.19) captures the event, but not the dramatic, hour-long motion of the shadow.

Large boulders near Holly House at Hovenweep National Monument also create light and shadow singularities between the rocks and the panel behind them. Ancestral Puebloans transformed this performance space for solstice markers. Rays of light streaking horizontally across the canyon wall around the summer solstice created the context for the carving of three large petroglyphs. As the solstice progresses, the horizontal light rays cross the panel and intersect the centers of the three petroglyphs. Ortman also photographed this event and his image is similar to J. McKim Manville's photograph of the same site in his book *Prehistoric Astronomy in the Southwest*. In the image before the light show begins, two spirals on the left side of the panel are barely visible, but the concentric circles are clearly visible on the right. In the second photograph, the light is just beginning to cut through the two spirals and is also intersecting with the concentric circles. The light forms continue their inward path until they meet in the center of the panel, visually obscuring the three petroglyphs with blinding light in the dark theater.

Sunwatchers at Hovenweep Castle created their own light-and-shadow spectacle by cutting small holes in the walls of the buildings. The light entering through the piercings in these rooms aligns with the D-shaped tower to allow shafts of light to mark the solstices and the equinoxes. As these events approach, diffused light through the portholes announces their coming (Malville and Putnam 1989:41). Similar observation spaces are known at Chaco Canyon, and guides always point to a hole in a wall at Pueblo Bonito that aligns with a solstice sunrise. The importance of lines of sight to sunrise and sunset events is reaffirmed by the alignment of many exterior walls of the great houses and outliers in the Chaco regional system to correspond with sight lines to sunrise and sunset events, affirming their importance in organizing the Pueblo-made world with the natural order of the environment. The combination of Pueblo-made images and light and shadow phenomena underscore the metaphorical relationships between spiral motifs and natural occurrences.

In this chapter, we have begun to build an understanding of the significance of isomeric design by noting perceptual qualities of woven objects and historical and experiential reasons for the symbolic association of pottery and weaving in Ancestral Pueblo culture. We have also drawn connections between isomeric designs painted on vessels and murals painted in kivas, as well as with spiral petroglyphs serving as markers where astronomical and calendrical observations were made. In the following chapter, we work in the opposite direction, from concepts in contemporary Pueblo worldviews, to bridge the gap between ancient experience and meaning.

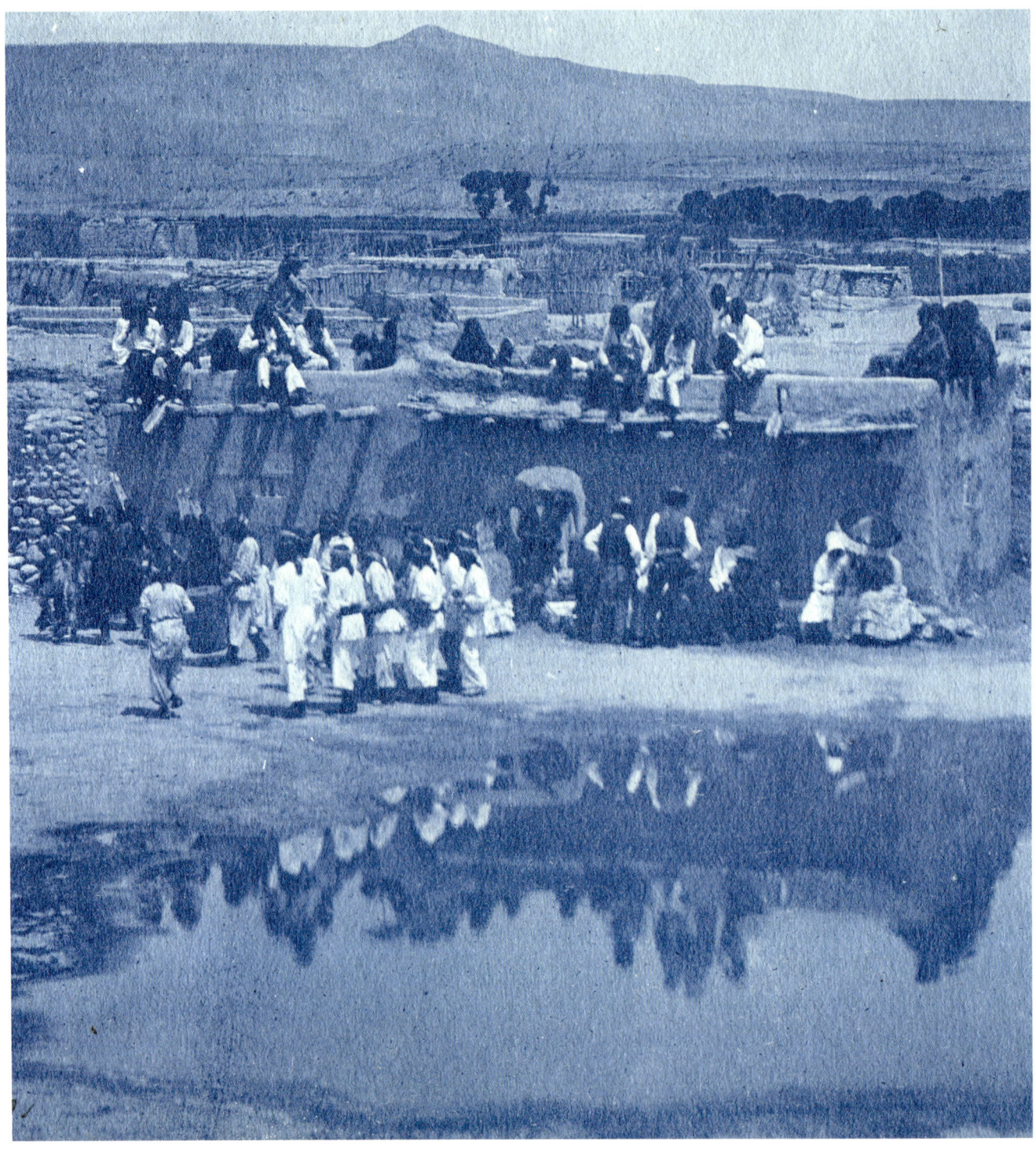

5 ISOMERIC DESIGNS AND PUEBLO PHILOSOPHY

In the previous chapter, we looked at historical, functional, and technological relationships between pottery and various other media. Woven clothing, baskets, and pottery vessels were all essential technologies that made the Ancestral Pueblo way of life possible, so it seems only natural that potters would have called attention to the unity of these various industries. In this chapter we connect pottery and weaving with Pueblo philosophy and social history to explore deeper layers of meaning of isomeric design in Ancestral Pueblo culture.

Philosophical concepts in contemporary Pueblo culture provide hints of the deeper significance of isomeric designs. Writings by Pueblo scholars, such as the late Rina Swentzell (1990), explain that Pueblo people conceive of reality as involving a spiritual world that is complementary and consubstantial with the physical world. In some communities this idea is expressed via the concept of *water-wind-breath*. Breath is the movement of air in and out of an animate being; wind demonstrates the animacy of the larger world; and water in its various forms is the ultimate source of animacy.

In this way of thinking, water is especially important because, in addition to being the source of life, a still body of water creates a window to the spirit world, which is viewed as a mirror image of the physical world. Consider what happens when one looks at the surface of a body of water on a calm day (fig. 5.1). What one will see is the surrounding landscape reflected in the water. However, this reflection does not match the world above exactly. Rather, it is a *mirror image* in which spatial relationships appear reversed, or opposite, to the way they are in the physical world.

This phenomenon of mirror-image reflection is apparent in a wider range of bodily experiences. If you look at your shadow on the wall of a canyon, for example, you will see a mirror image of yourself looking back at you. Your right hand in this world is the left hand of your shadow on the rocks. And, of course, you will see the same phenomenon even more clearly if you look at your reflection in a lake—if you raise your right hand in greeting, you will see your reflection in the water waving its left hand back at you. And if you walk across wet sand, the print of your left foot will be of a right foot, from the perspective of the sand looking back at you.

Mirror-image reflection is apparent even in the sky. In the northern hemisphere, the sun rises each morning in the east, then travels upward and southward until noon before turning downward and northward until it sets in the west each evening. During the night, the sun continues moving beneath the surface of the earth in the north, only to reappear on the eastern horizon the next morning. However, when one is inside a building with a skylight, such as a kiva, the beam of light cast by the sun inside the building moves opposite to the way it does in the world outside. In the morning, the sunbeam passing through

Figure 5.1. Example of reversed reflections in a pool of water.

Charles F. Lummis, Dance, Pueblo of Cochiti, NM; cyanotype, 1888, 5 × 7 in. Center for Southwest Research, University of New Mexico, 990-009-0036.

the roof hatch projects an image of the sun on the west wall of the kiva (see Martin and Plog 1973:133). Then as the day progresses, the image moves downward and northward until noon, at which time it reverses and moves upward and southward until the evening, when the image sets along the east wall. In short, the sunbeams inside the kiva move in a mirror image of the sun in the sky. The same thing also happens with the sunbeams that penetrate the surface of a lake, and this phenomenon likely lies behind Pueblo conceptions of the kiva as a microcosm of the spirit world from which people emerged in the beginning.

A Tewa story illustrates the way contemporary Pueblo people conceive of kivas and lakes as portals to the spirit world. In this story, Cactus Flower Girl runs away from home with Spider Grandmother after being scolded for misbehavior. According to the version recorded by Elsie Clews Parsons in the 1920s, "Soon they reached the edge of a lake. In the middle of the lake were two poles coming out of the water. As they watched, the poles grew higher and higher, soon there was a big ladder coming out of the water. This was a kiva, and out of it was a good-looking woman" (Parsons 1994[1926]:199). The story explicitly equates the surface of a lake with a portal to the spirit world. The Tewa term for the roof hole of a kiva, *p'o:kwikʰoyi*, or "Lake roof hole," further demonstrates that this story presents a widely understood and longstanding conception in Pueblo culture. The kiva represents the spirit world beneath the reflective surface of a lake.

Pueblo people use the phenomenon of mirror-image reflection to conceptualize the relationship between the spirit world and the physical world. In this construal of reality, the spirit world is a mirror image of the physical world, and one can contact this world at any number of places where water stands still—whether this is in the form of clouds and snow on mountains and hills, pools of water at mountain lakes, marshes or springs, moist caves, or even subterranean kivas. As water circulates through the physical world, so does animacy flow through both worlds.

This idea is expressed today in a variety of ritual practices. For example, when Pueblo men prepare for ceremonies they often cover their hands with wet white clay so that they can "lay the fog," making contact with the spirit world through their actions. The idea seems to be that the point of contact between the physical world and the spirit world is a wet surface, of a lake or of wet hands.

Archaeological evidence further suggests that these understandings have significant time depth. For example, they are reflected in the variety of ways the tau shape is employed in Ancestral Pueblo design. This shape is found on the handles of mugs used for drinking liquids (fig. 5.2) and on the backs of effigy vessels depicting waterfowl which can travel between the sky, the surface of a lake, and the world beneath (fig. 5.3). Tau-shaped doors are also common in Ancestral Pueblo architecture, primarily at thresholds between the inner world of the house and the outer world beyond (fig. 5.4). Such transition points are thus marked with a symbol of clouds or fog. Finally, a kiva from southeastern Utah explicitly

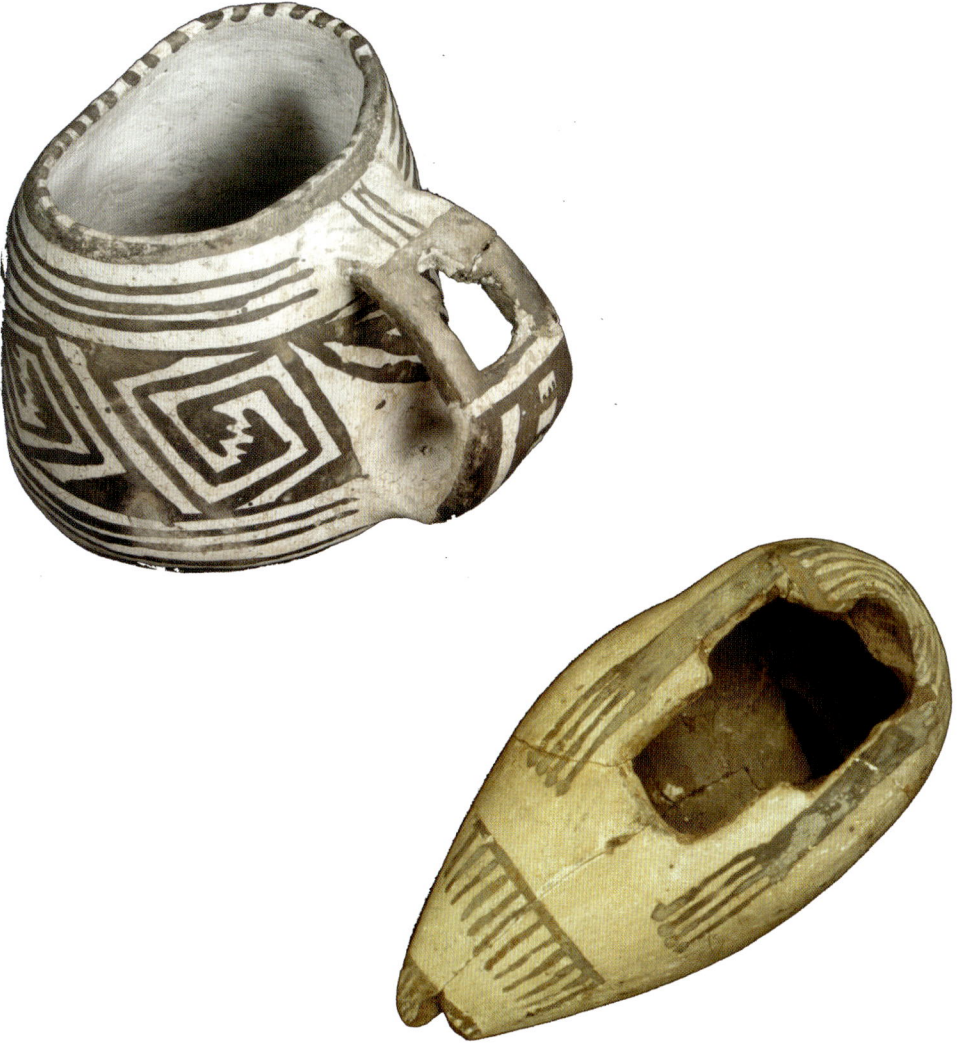

Figure 5.2. Mesa Verde Black-on-white mug with tau-shaped handle.
3 ⅜ × 4 ¼ in. dia., UCB 09332.

Figure 5.3. Effigy vessel with tau-shaped opening depicting a waterfowl, which can travel in the sky, on the water, and beneath the water.
18 cm, courtesy of the Clarence T. Hurst Museum Collection, Western State Colorado University.

connects the tau shape with the transition between the physical world and the spirit world (fig. 5.5). Owing to the low roof of the alcove in this location, the builders created a side entrance to the kiva through a dark recess at the back of the cave. This threshold, through which people passed from the outside world to the spirit world, was a tau-shaped opening. These various bits of evidence support the notion that contemporary conceptions of the spirit world as a mirror image of the physical world have been a part of Pueblo philosophy since at least the Great Pueblo Period.

We believe the logic of mirror-image reflection is also embedded in isomeric design. Indeed, isomers are themselves an additional form of mirror imaging. As we have shown

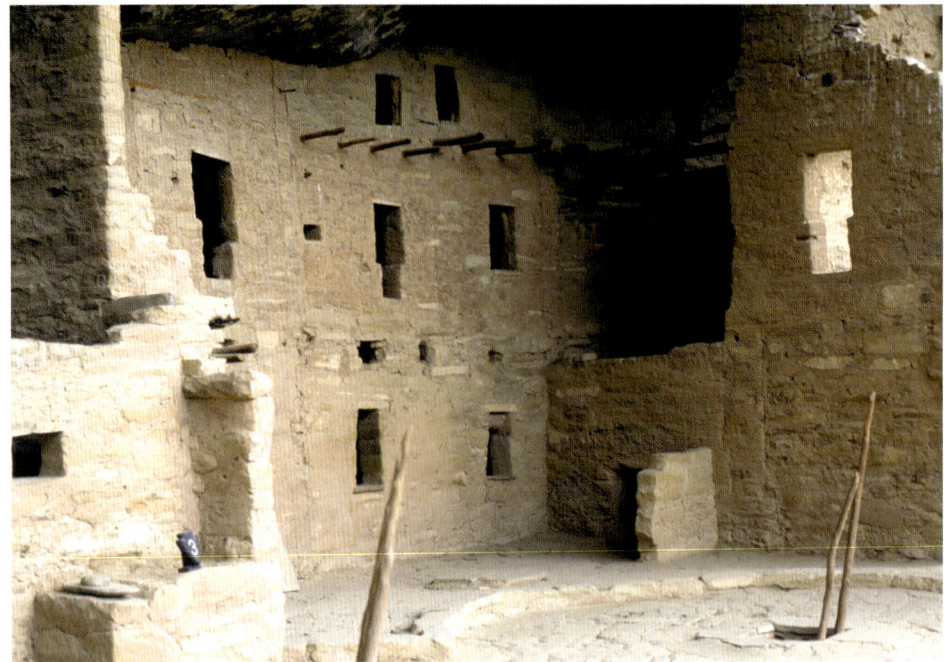

Figure 5.4. Tau-shaped doors are common in Ancestral Pueblo architecture, primarily at thresholds between the inner world of the house and the outer world beyond.

Photograph by Scott G. Ortman.

throughout this book, isomeric designs are designs in which the negative, unpainted space has a shape complementary to the positive, painted space. The inspiration for these optical illusions probably originated in weaving, but it is important to note that these designs often create mirror images as well.

In the case of liminal-space isomers, the liminal space can be viewed as the "moist" point of contact between isomeric designs in bifold rotation that reflect the complementary, mirror-image reality of the physical and spiritual worlds. This relationship is especially apparent when one of the painted elements is solid and the other hatched, as on the Puerco Black-on-red bowl (see fig. 2.15) discussed previously.

In the case of painted-and-unpainted isomers, the process of creating the painted design also creates a mirror-image, unpainted design that interdigitates with the painted elements and thus reflects the consubstantiality of the physical and spiritual worlds.

Finally, incomplete-element and tessellated isomers both involve interacting isomeric elements that are connected by liminal unpainted spaces. Importantly, it is the unpainted liminal spaces, and not the painted figures, that do the work of "weaving" the isomers together. Although we are not sure if these relationships between painted design and concepts emanating from mirror images were ever discussed explicitly, we feel the popularity of isomeric designs must have derived, at least in part, from the way they alluded to and reinforced the simultaneity and consubstantiality of the physical and spiritual worlds and their watery points of near contact as implied by the experiential properties of reflection.

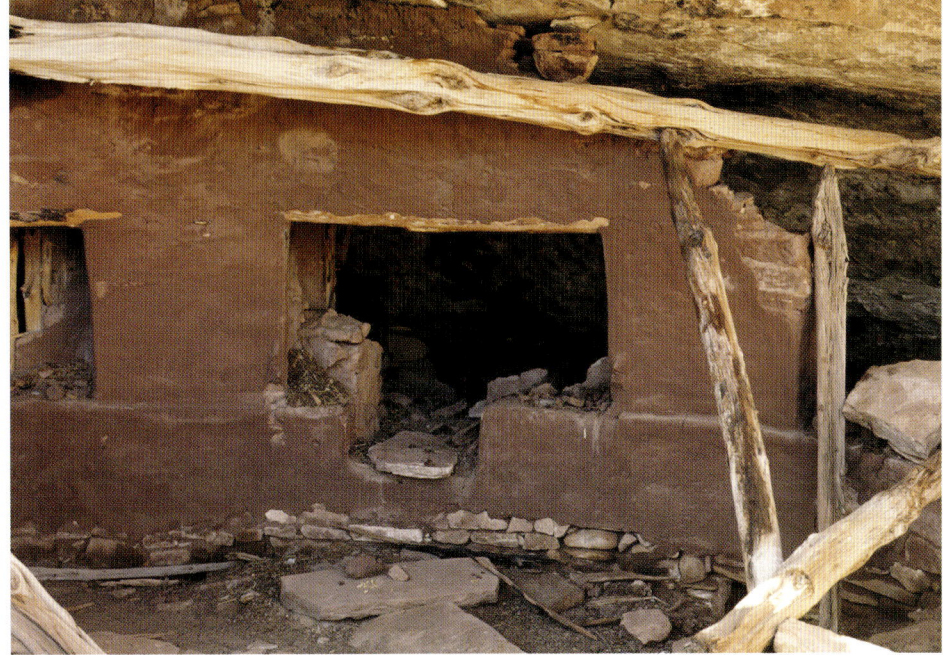

Figure 5.5. A tau-shaped door from a kiva in southeastern Utah explicitly connects the physical world and the spirit world.

Photograph by Scott G. Ortman.

Even if isomeric designs do reflect the spiritual realities we have discussed above, this does not, by itself, explain why such designs became so popular during the Great Pueblo Period. Part of the answer surely lies in the coincidental timing of the innovations that created isomeric patterns in weaving, as discussed in the previous chapter. But we think there is also a deeper reason that is related to the emergence of large-scale social organization during the Great Pueblo Period. Once again, the best place to begin in building this argument is with contemporary Pueblo ideas.

Today, Pueblo people view the various forms of water as sentient beings that impinge on human affairs. For example, clouds have the capacity to bring life through the transport of water from the mountains down to fields, streams, and villages, and clouds are normally accompanied by wind, indicating that they are alive. Clouds exist and can be seen and felt, but not grasped, even when they pass by as fog. And clouds vary in the ways they move and the kind of rain they bring, and thus have personalities.

The ancestors of Ancestral Pueblo people were hunters and gatherers. Hunting and gathering people depend on plants that have adapted to specific environments through natural selection over long periods of time. As a result, their food resources are not very sensitive to the whims of the weather, and the forces that produce weather are thus not of critical importance. Pueblo food crops, on the other hand, derive from wild plants that originated in tropical regions of Mexico. As a result, for an agricultural people living in a semiarid plateau, weather can make the difference between abundance and starvation, and in this setting one would expect an intense interest in understanding what causes weather and in influencing it, if possible.

In this context, Pueblo people came to understand weather as a phenomenon that emanates from ancestral spirit-beings who have become clouds. These beings, often referred to as *katsinas* or *kachinas*, watch over the people and signal their approval of the community's behavior by bringing moisture and their disapproval by withholding it. What the ancestral rain beings desire most in people's behavior is the proper performance of public rituals, prayers, and songs, and adherence by individuals to the communal values of the Pueblo. As Sekaquaptewa, Hill, and Washburn (2015:12) explain, "The katsinas promise in their songs that, in return for the people's sincere prayers and moral living, they will come as clouds, thunder, lightning and rain. By this means, the planted fields of the people will bloom, the yellow jackets and butterflies will flutter about pollinating the flowers, and the people will sing and dance with happiness at these signs of the promise of new life."

Importantly, Pueblo people understand that the ancestral rain beings can see the true, internal mental states of community members regardless of their outward behavior. So, if the community is being monitored by these beings the people cannot receive their approval by just "going through the motions." Rather, each person's heart and mind must generate respectful and helpful thoughts for one's surroundings and for other people. In this way, the spiritual world of thought, in each person and in larger natural forces, influences the state of the physical world.

It is important to emphasize the real-world, practical benefits this philosophy generates in a community that depends upon cooperation among its members to maintain itself, whether through sharing with those in need, participating in community work projects, or the fair exchange of goods and services. The philosophical and ceremonial life of Pueblo people is designed to bring the desired state of the spirit world into being, and in so doing they also encourage the mirror image of this desired state to occur in the human community. In this way, Pueblo conceptions of the spirit world have practical benefits for real Pueblo communities which help them to survive and thrive.

We suspect that the emergence of isomeric designs in Ancestral Pueblo pottery reflects the initial crystallization of these philosophical ideas which made it possible for large groups of people, many of whom were not relatives, to live and work together. Experimental research by psychologist Ara Norenzayan (2013) shows that people generally behave more cooperatively when they are being watched by others, or feel that they are being watched, even if by purely spiritual beings.

So it would seem that the emergence of isomeric designs, which emphasize the coexistence of the seen and unseen world, each the complementary mirror image of the other, was part of this process of recognizing the forces that produce a properly functioning universe and creating a society that took these forces into account in its activities. In our view, isomeric designs, which were first noticed in specific weaving techniques, became a powerful expression of, and aid to memory for, the accumulating philosophical and practical knowledge that made Ancestral Pueblo society possible.

If this is the case, why did Pueblo potters stop painting isomeric designs after 1300 CE, despite the continued relevance of the knowledge they seem to materialize? We suspect the answer lies in the transformation in Pueblo life that occurred in the thirteenth century CE. In this book we have emphasized positive aspects of social and technological developments during the Great Pueblo Period, but it is important to acknowledge that there were also darker aspects of these developments. Archaeological studies show, for example, that substantial material inequalities emerged during this period. Very few people lived in the great houses in Chaco Canyon, but those who did ate better food and could command resources and labor from much farther afield than the average person. Stories maintained in Pueblo and Navajo communities also allude to excessive gambling and slavery in Chaco Canyon. These bits of evidence suggest that material inequality was a growing problem in Ancestral Pueblo society. Given this, the pattern of change in material culture associated with the thirteenth century migrations and reorganizations of Pueblo society suggests one of its underlying goals was to resolve some of these problems.

The archaeological record shows that, as Pueblo people left their ancestral homes for the Rio Grande and Little Colorado drainages, many things that had previously been hidden were revealed to public view. Community ceremonies that had occurred inside great kivas for many centuries came to be performed in plazas where all, including the clouds, could see the assembled community. Also, the smaller kivas in which private rituals occurred were moved from the interiors of great houses to the centers of plazas, where the comings and goings of the participants were also visible to the entire community and its spiritual counterparts.

Finally, mural painting and rock art shifted to explicit anthropomorphic representation of sentient natural forces, especially cloud beings (katsinas). And in many communities it became possible for these natural forces to inhabit community members directly through donning of the appropriate katsina mask. The pattern of change in these activities suggests that prior to 1300 CE the ancestral spirit beings, and the activities that people undertook to influence them, had been largely hidden in Ancestral Pueblo society; and that one of the changes people desired at this time was for these beings, and the activities through which people develop relationships with them, to be more visible and open. To the extent that isomeric designs were associated with the old society, and the old way of thinking, they would have been discouraged. In this way, a paradigmatic expression of these core ideas could have faded from use, even as many of the ideas themselves continued to influence Pueblo culture in other ways down to the present.

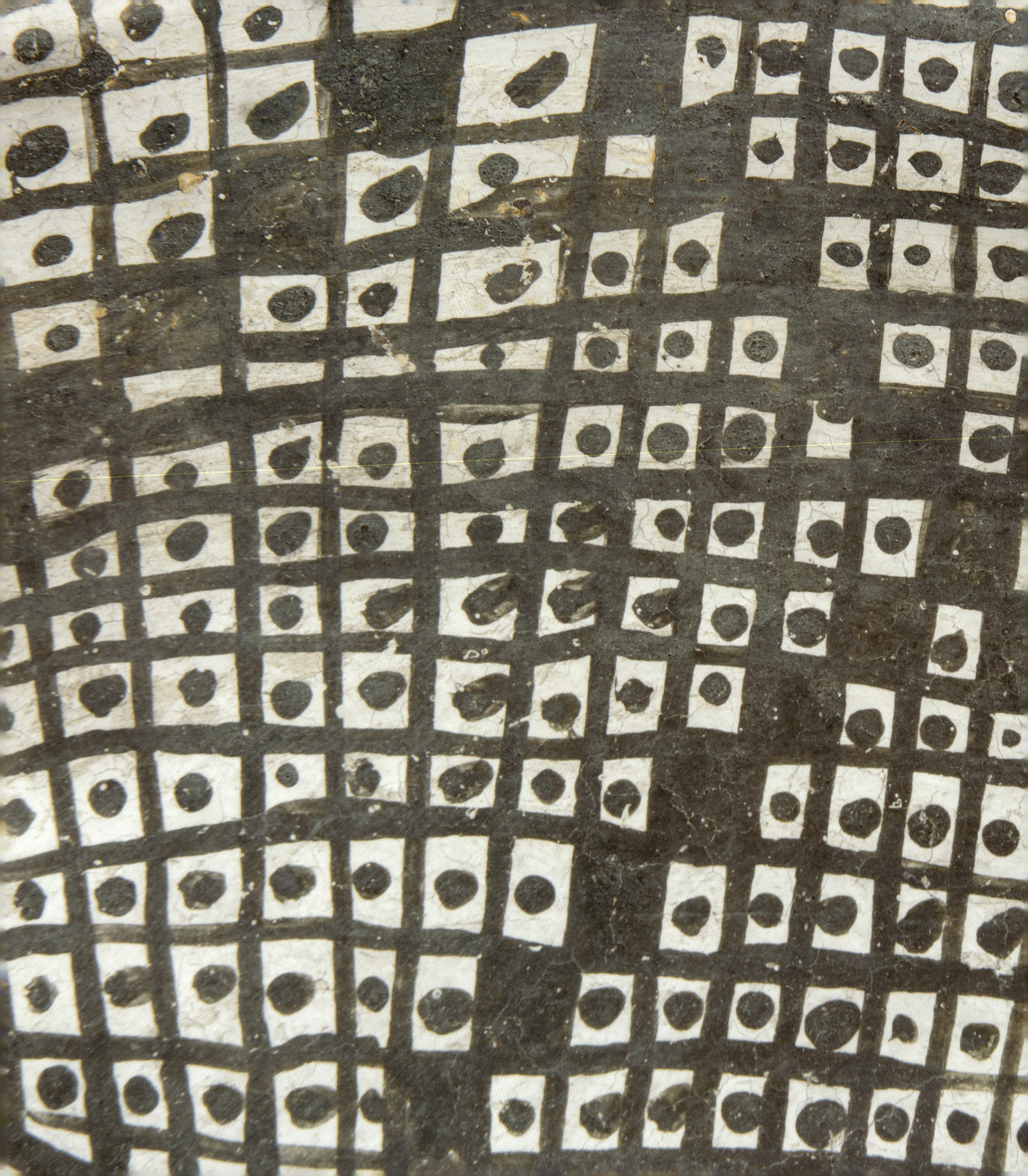

6 ISOMERS, ART, AND SOCIETY

In this book we have made an argument that Ancestral Pueblo people developed their distinctive and timeless pottery style by paying attention to a variety of experiential phenomena, including properties of visual perception, their reflection in weaving processes, the beneficial applications of these processes to pottery, and the connection of all this to water, wind, and breath. In this final chapter, we return to the more technical aspects of isomeric design and its implications for the role of art and artists in Ancestral Pueblo society. We also allude to some of the issues raised by this analysis that we hope will be addressed in future investigations.

The concept of dualities is the basis for our comprehension of isomeric designs and their optical reversibility in the Great Pueblo Period. These designs can produce perceptual dualities—reversible figure-and-ground relationships that can be interpreted as either black shapes in front of white backgrounds or white figures in front of black backgrounds. When artists painted shapes that created unpainted areas of similar size and shape, they created consubstantial mirror images. Tessellated elements produced chains of interlocked motifs or fields of repeated forms such as a checkerboard design. In other situations painters created dualities by separating a pair of isomeric elements with another shape, and the separation became the subject. And finally, viewers can perceptually produce dualities in their minds when they comprehend abbreviated elements as versions of well-known motifs.

The perceptual reversals associated with isomeric designs are accentuated by other optical tricks. Border-contrast phenomena intensify the boundaries between elements; the law of simplicity allows observers to perceive the essences of known forms; size relationships alter spatial perceptions; and afterimages transform lingering images into ghostlike reversals. What modern viewers may dismiss as unimportant negative spaces take on new meaning as intended figures that reflect the harmony of consubstantial and interdependent realities in the Pueblo world.

We have shown formal relationships among isomeric motifs, including curvilinear spirals, rectilinear spirals, interlocked dual spirals, motifs ending in pronged elements, and pairs of stepped elements. The use of stepped isomeric motifs on kiva murals and spirals as locations for observing astronomical phenomena alludes to a relationship with Ancestral Pueblo ritual. But these designs also extend to metaphors of basketry and its physical and cultural functions, and to isomers marking the fusion of ritual knowledge and light phenomena in the landscape. All of this suggests Ancestral Pueblo people developed an idea of the human community as a mirror of a harmonious, cyclical, and animate natural world.

Curiously, the four design strategies identified in this study do not seem to have succeeded one another in a linear progression. All began about the same time, during the first century of the Great Pueblo Period, and more precise dating of the origin of these design strategies is probably impossible. The rise of dual-element designs corresponds with the changes that occurred during the Great Pueblo Period in food acquisition and preparation, architecture, residency patterns, social relationships, and ritual practices related to kivas. The development of painted isomeric designs can be associated with a number of paired traits well established during this period, including divisions based on gender, economic activity, relationships between dwellers in unit pueblos and great houses, and stratification by status among individuals.

It makes sense to think of the dualism in Pueblo pottery designs as a visual manifestation of lifeways begun during the Great Pueblo Period, and as a complex metaphor for weaving and woven objects of the past. These isomeric designs imply dual economic roles between women and men within these communities, as well as differences in ritual knowledge between individuals entrusted with secret knowledge and those without such knowledge. We conclude that the production of isomeric designs on pottery, and their ability to be perceived as ambiguous figure and ground relationships, served as metaphors of social relationships and as metonyms of society and reality itself during the Great Pueblo Period.

The most sophisticated isomeric designs were created by painters who lived in core areas of regional systems: Chaco/Mesa Verde, Mimbres, and Hohokam. These designs required the highest degree of skill in molding vessels symmetrically and then organizing the designs on a three-dimensional surface. The designs demanded exceptional skill in visualizing how to lay out these designs on curved surfaces. That formal skill supports arguments about the division of labor in these regional systems. It seems probable that the artists who created isomeric designs were valued for their skill at creating pottery featuring designs of iconological significance, and they may have had specialized to some extent in making pottery. The production of isomeric designs went far beyond what was minimally necessary to produce functional vessels with relevant designs. From an aesthetic point of view, these skills transcend what a family would need to produce for their own needs. So it is clear that painted pottery was deeply enmeshed in the social life of Ancestral Pueblo communities.

To further delineate the importance of isomeric designs and the artists who created them, future scholars may be able to identify the works of individual artists in collections from intensively excavated settlements where many usable vessels were left behind. For example, Ortman has noticed that several of the vessels left on the floors of houses at Sand Canyon Pueblo, a thirteenth-century village in southwestern Colorado, appear to have been painted by the same hand. The next step is to trace the distribution of such vessels to determine just how broadly the works of individual artists were used in ancient communities.

Our dissection of the four isomeric design strategies and the techniques used to produce them lead us to conclude that most previous assessments of Ancestral Pueblo pottery painting have underestimated the perceptual and technical skills needed to produce these works. As a result, studies of these designs have been limited to formalist analysis. The resulting interpretations have not connected these designs with other social developments associated with the rise and disintegration of regional systems in the US Southwest. In our view, there is a clear connection between the emergence of new scales of social, economic, and political integration and the technical mastery with which ancestral potters created vessels that intrigue and inspire across vast chasms of time, culture, and technology.

We would be remiss if we did not mention a few points that we have not discussed but which deserve more attention in future work. Perhaps the most important are the relative and perhaps changing roles of women and men in the history of Pueblo pottery. The classic studies of Pueblo pottery, such as Ruth Bunzel's *The Pueblo Potter* (1972[1929]), give the impression that in the past almost all pottery was made by women, as is common across cultures. Yet over the years archaeologists have uncovered vessels with unusual shapes and/or designs that could easily have been associated with men's activities. And in more recent times, men participated in forms of craft production, including weaving of cotton cloth on upright looms, which are performed by women in many other societies. Given that some forms of weaving were viewed as men's work in Pueblo society, it could also be that men painted more Ancestral Pueblo pottery vessels than one might at first assume. There is nothing physical that would have kept women from painting designs that reference male-associated aspects of the world or men from painting designs that reference female-associated aspects. Thus it would seem important for archaeologists to put more effort into engendering Ancestral Pueblo pottery production by looking for specific evidence regarding the sex of the producers of specific vessel forms or design styles.

This being said, we find no reason to doubt that most of the vessels we have discussed in this book were made by women, and this leads to an important point. Our interpretation of isomeric design connects the spatial illusions that emerge from light-and-dark patterns, border-contrast phenomena, and figure-and-ground relationships to some of the central concepts and concerns of Pueblo philosophy. An additional important element of this philosophy is gender complementarity, where men and women are viewed as embodying distinct but complementary realms that come together in the process of "seeking life." Thus women are to corn as men are to water, the house is the realm of women and the kiva the realm of men, summer activities are feminine and winter activities masculine, and leaders are enjoined to "be a woman, be a man." One might extend this line of reasoning to suggest that in the Ancestral Pueblo world the maintenance of ritual and thus spiritual knowledge lay in the male realm and was localized in the kiva. Our analysis shows that this was not the case. The rich but perhaps implicit spiritual realities expressed in isomeric design reinforced relationships between earth and sky, the physical and spiritual worlds, the female and male worlds, and fundamental forces in nature and society. And in a society that did not use writing to maintain its accumulated knowledge, expressive material culture must have been an important mnemonic device, something psychologist Merlin Donald (1991) has labeled "external symbolic storage." The key point then is that our analysis suggests Ancestral Pueblo potters, and primarily women, were central players in the creation and maintenance of a conceptual system that governed life for everyone.

A second point that we have not addressed, but deserves more attention, is interpretation of specific designs by Pueblo people. Many people who purchase contemporary Pueblo pottery at a feast day or at Indian Market in Santa Fe have experienced artists who explain the iconographic content of the designs on specific pieces. Terraces reflect mountains and clouds, spirals the wind, zigzags lightning or flowing water, and so forth. Contemporary potters are clearly cognizant of these ideas and associations as they compose designs. This sensibility could have emerged through the market for Native arts in recent times. The more often an artist is asked, "What does the design mean?" by a potential buyer, the more motivation there is to think about designs in iconographic terms so as to please the client. Nevertheless, it seems unlikely that Ancestral Pueblo designs were devoid of iconographic content. There are direct representational images of animals, animal tracks, and other objects on some vessels; and on others there are embellishments on geometric motifs that suggest the painter had something specific in mind. We have not focused on the explicit representational or symbolic content of Ancestral Pueblo design in this book, but we suspect investigation of relationships between isomers and iconography would be fruitful.

Finally, we want to call attention to the fact that the spatial illusions we have discussed are grounded in aspects of visual perception, but the fact that these processes are automatic does not determine the cultural significance attached to these phenomena. We have inferred that these phenomena were viewed as significant, at least implicitly, based on evidence for their intentional incorporation into isomeric design, the extension of such designs beyond pottery and weaving, and their resonances with concepts expressed by contemporary Pueblo writers and thinkers. But it remains an open question just how widespread these understandings were. The most innovative artists in any society exert their influence by finding new and creative ways of expressing resonant ideas, but many other artists simply follow suit with varying degrees of awareness of what the original artist intended to convey. Given this, the fact that isomeric design is common in Ancestral Pueblo art need not imply that the ideas we think they expressed were understood the same way or to the same extent across the population. We think it is important to keep in mind that the art and architecture of past societies probably did not express the same ideas or associations to everyone. Isomeric design was likely no exception.

Scholars who work in the US Southwest are fortunate on two accounts. First, the region boasts one of the most complete, compelling, and well-studied archaeological records of any non-Western society. Second, Pueblo society continues today and is a vibrant part of the cultural tapestry of the region. This fortunate confluence has made it possible for interested people to delve much more deeply into the practical, historical, and philosophical dimensions of material culture than is possible in most other contexts. Such depths are likely present in the artistic traditions of every people, but our ability to see them is perhaps clearer in the US Southwest than it is anywhere else.

This study demonstrates the potential of isomeric designs for understanding the philosophical bases of Ancestral Pueblo societies and the importance they placed on visual culture. It also illustrates the rich, multilayered, and multidimensional ways in which art encodes knowledge and facilitates its maintenance in oral societies. Indeed, in oral cultures the encoding of ideas in material form, through visual culture, is an important way that people retain their accumulated knowledge and transmit it to others in the community and to future generations. In creating isomeric designs, Ancestral Pueblo potters simultaneously expressed the functional relationships among various technologies they depended on, the philosophical concepts that structured their societies and worldviews, and the capacity of individuals to produce objects exhibiting technical and aesthetic mastery of the medium. We hope this book will help others to better appreciate this unique artistic tradition and its continuing importance for Native people of the US Southwest today.

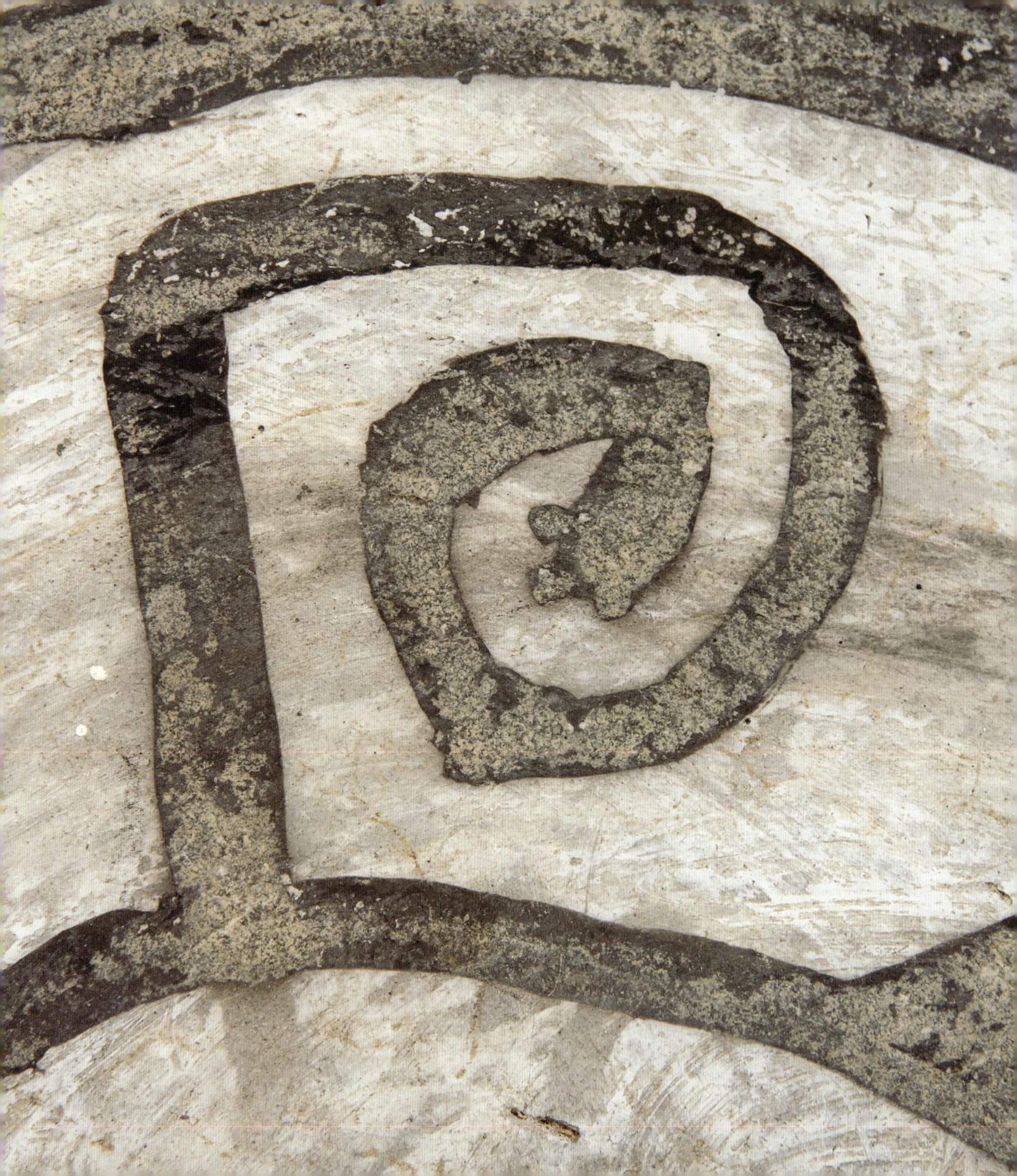

A PORTFOLIO OF ISOMERIC DESIGNS

The following plates reproduce vessels from the Great Pueblo Period with isomeric designs that have the ability to create optical transformations or figure-ground reversals. We organized these works chronologically to emphasize some of the subtle changes through time in design strategies, layouts, elements, and motifs. Most of these examples incorporate more than one of the design strategies discussed in chapter 2. The captions identify the relevant design strategies associated with each vessel, as well as the related optical phenomena produced by each design. Virtually all of these examples highlight the visual importance of the unpainted areas to the perception of these optical phenomena.

    We have attempted to organize the vessels chronologically, but doing so is not so simple. Chronologies usually are not detailed enough to indicate if a vessel was produced during the early, middle, or late period of each pottery type. Chronologies are also complicated because artists often produced many pottery types for several centuries and over vast geographical areas in the US Southwest. In addition, these objects came from several museum collections and were often typed and dated well in the past by unknown researchers. Nonetheless, some examples may be slightly out of chronological order despite our best efforts.

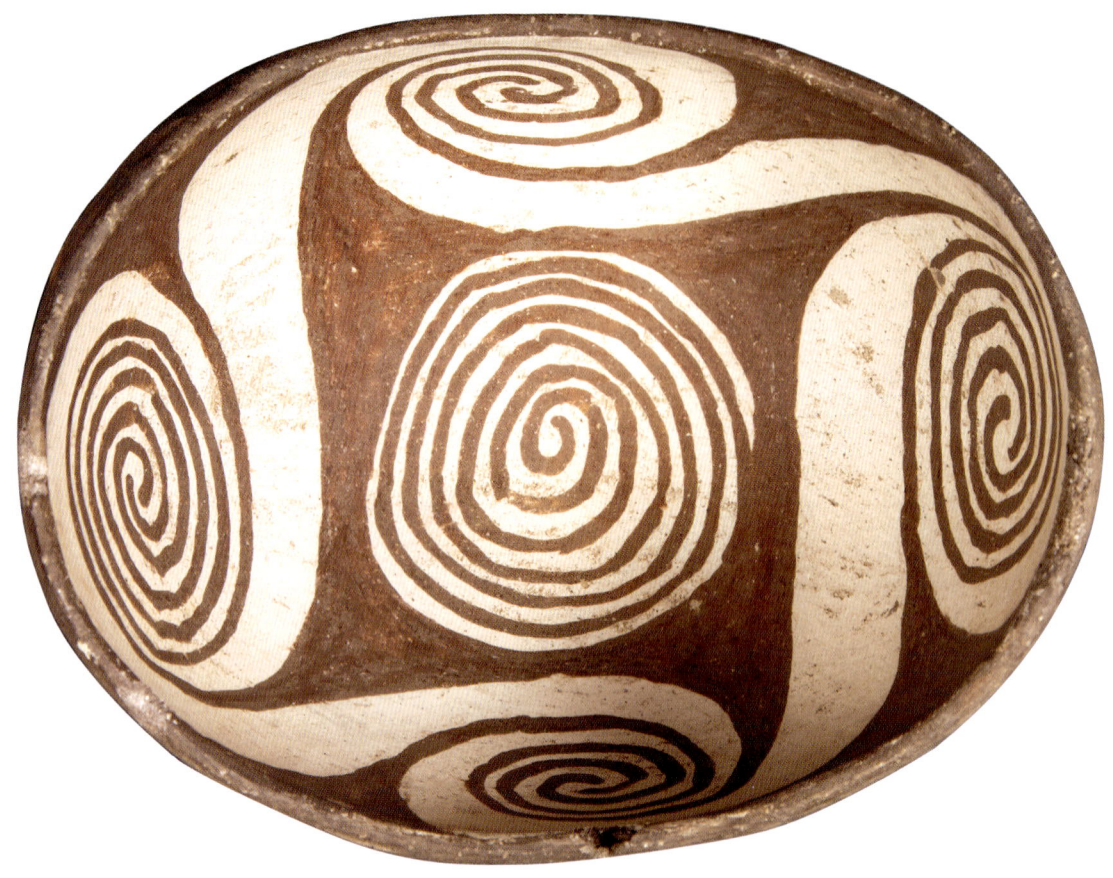

PLATE 1. MANGAS BLACK-ON-WHITE BOWL
750–1000 CE, 3 ¼ × 6 IN. DIA., MNA A7849

Artists in the Mimbres region of New Mexico often painted variations of this five-spiral composition on bowls and jars. The balance between light and dark areas produces ambiguous figure-ground relationships.

Design strategies: liminal-space isomers, tessellated isomers
Optical phenomena: figure–ground spatial reversals, border-contrast phenomena

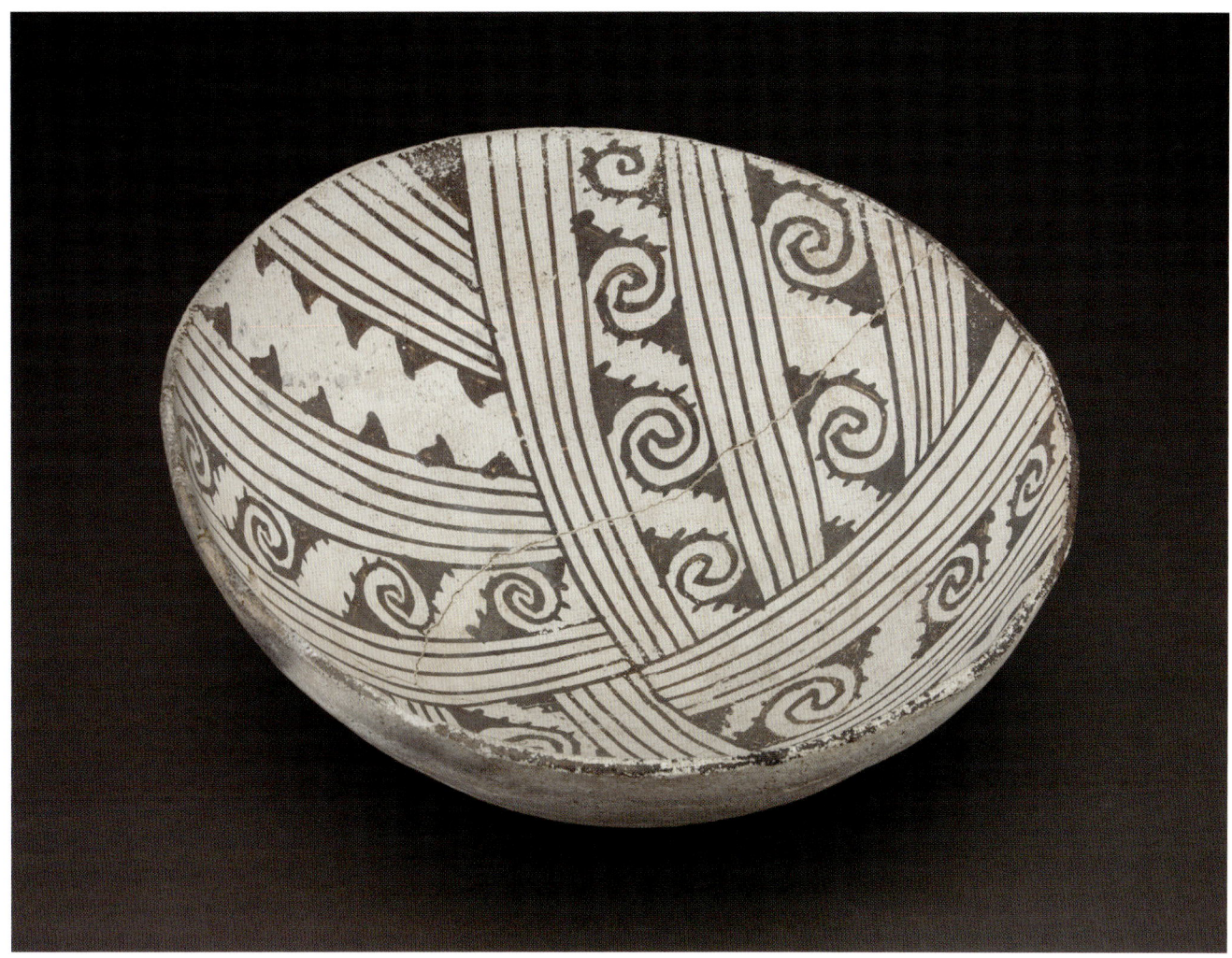

PLATE 2. KIATUTHLANA/RED MESA BLACK-ON-WHITE BOWL
850–950 CE, 3 ¼ × 7 ¾ IN. DIA., MIAC/LOA 8224.8224

This design alludes to the design and structure of plaited basketry. The spirals are painted as both complete and incomplete spiral motifs. At first the panel with triangular forms may appear as mistakes, but these panels seem intentional because they are repeated.

Design strategies: liminal-space isomers, incomplete-element isomers, tessellated isomers, and painted-and-unpainted isomers
Optical phenomena: figure–ground spatial reversals, border-contrast phenomena, law of simplicity

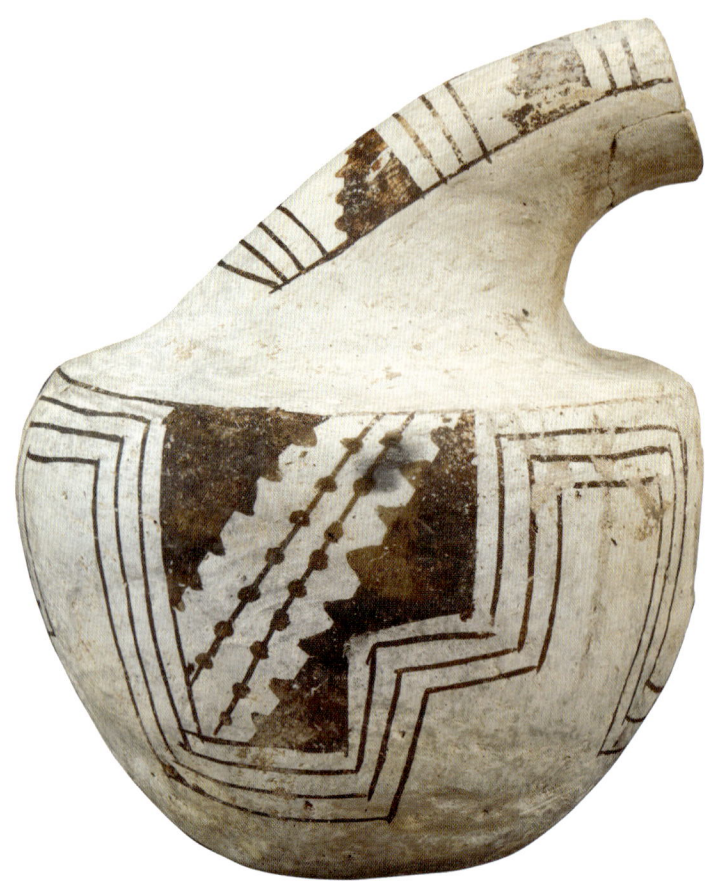

PLATE 3. KIATUTHLANA BLACK-ON-WHITE GOURD-SHAPED JAR
850–950 CE, 6 ¾ × 5 ¾ IN. DIA., MIAC/LOA 8280

This jar presents painted stepped elements separated by liminal spaces painted as three parallel lines. Within the pairs of stepped forms, one is painted and the other is an implied, unpainted, reciprocal part of the body of the vessel.

Design strategies: liminal-space isomers, painted-and-unpainted isomers
Optical phenomena: figure–ground spatial reversals, border-contrast phenomena, law of simplicity

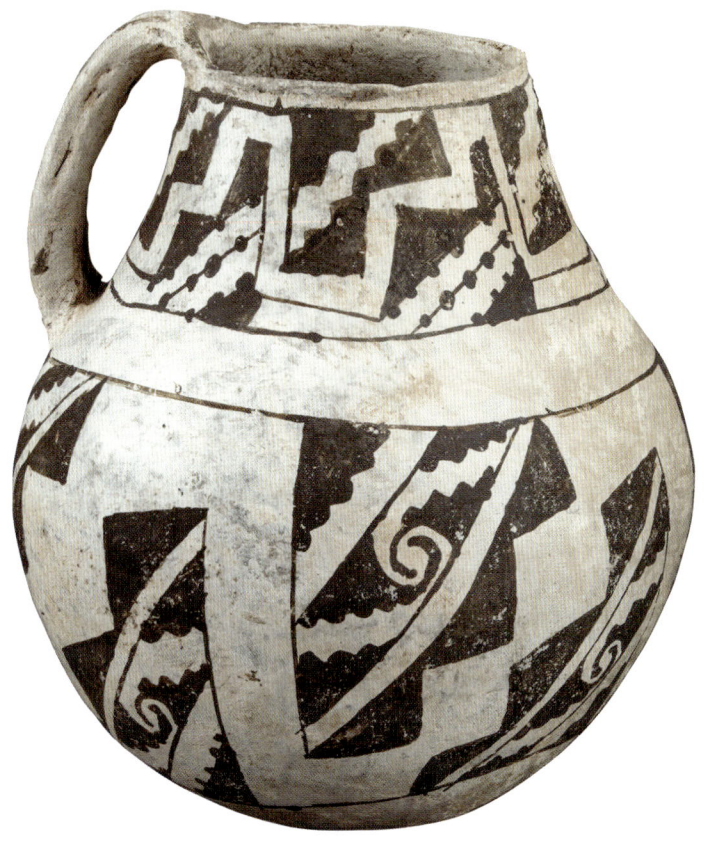

PLATE 4. RED MESA BLACK-ON-WHITE PITCHER
875–1050 CE, 6 ½ × 6 IN. DIA., MIAC/LOA 8277/11

The stepped motifs painted on the body of this pitcher are separated by unpainted liminal spaces. Internally each stepped motif features an interlocked spiral composed of incomplete shapes. The diagonal divisions of the stepped forms create several layers of ambiguous figure-and-ground relationships. The busy painted stepped forms cause the unpainted liminal spaces to pop forward spatially.

Design strategies: liminal-space isomers, tessellated isomers, and incomplete-element isomers
Optical phenomena: figure–ground spatial reversals, border-contrast phenomena, law of simplicity

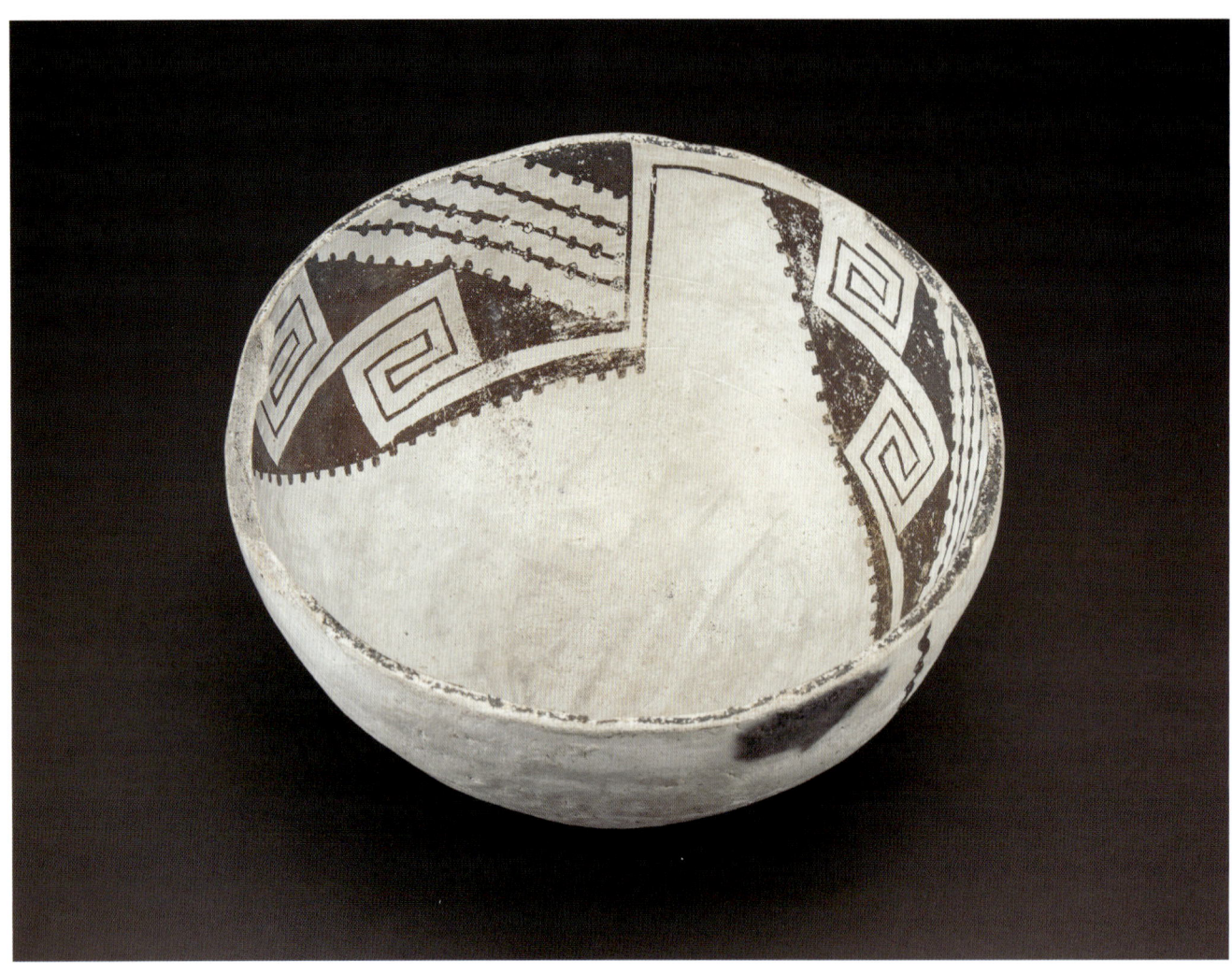

PLATE 5. RED MESA BLACK-ON-WHITE BOWL
875–1050 CE, 2¹⁵⁄₁₆ × 5¹³⁄₁₆ IN. DIA., MIAC/LOA 8222/11

Linear painting outlines three pairs of interlocked spirals presented as rectilinear forms within triangular friezes. Z-shaped lines at the center of these spirals complete the outlines of interlocking forms. The ticked forms are reminiscent of the textures and designs associated with woven baskets. Optically the outlined dual spirals appear as both foreground and background with the triangular painted shapes.

Design strategies: liminal-space isomers, painted-and-unpainted isomers
Optical phenomena: figure–ground spatial reversals, border-contrast phenomena, law of simplicity

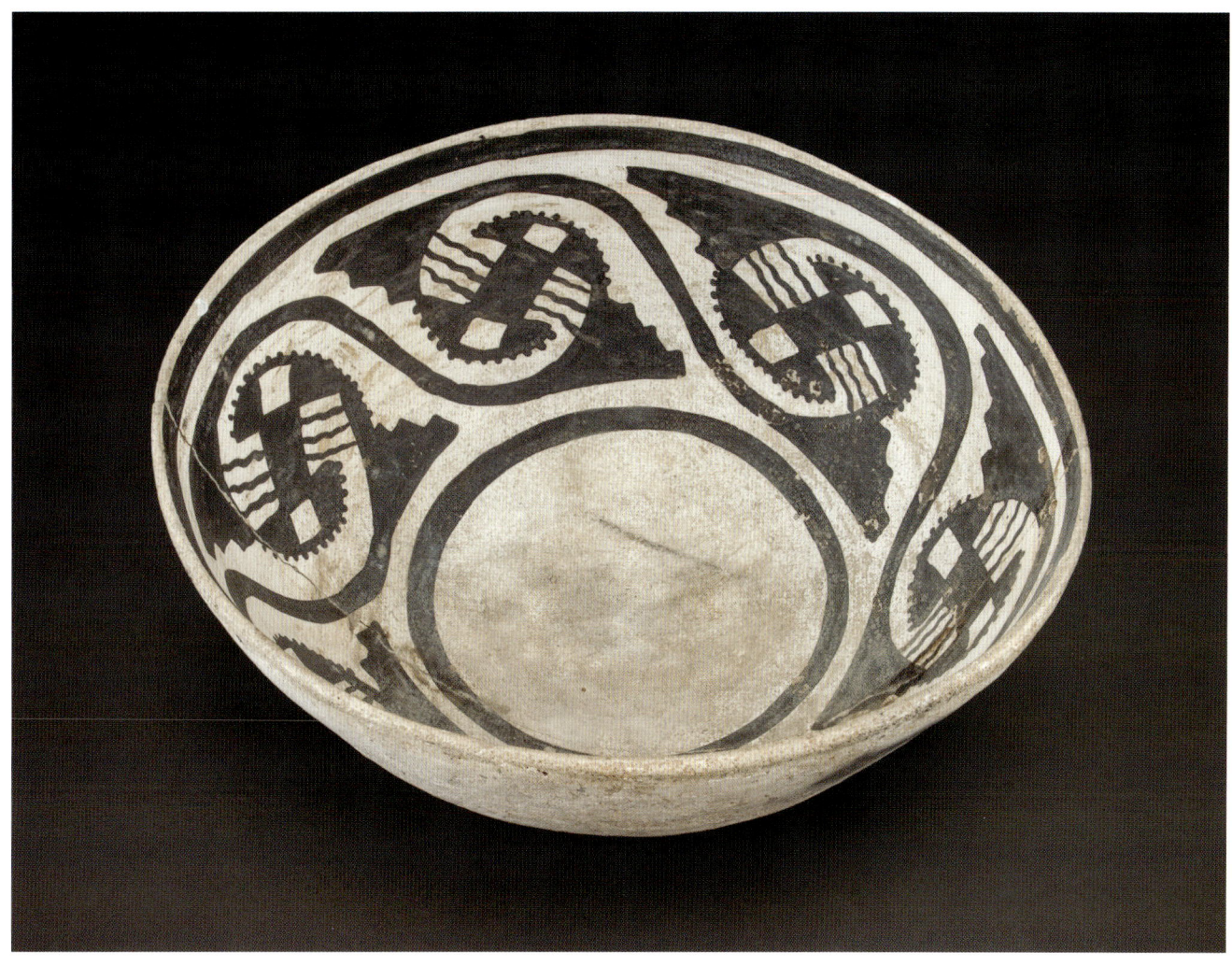

PLATE 6. BLACK MESA BLACK-ON-WHITE BOWL
1100–1170 CE, 4 15/16 × 10 IN. DIA., MIAC/LOA 8833/11

The interlocking spiral motifs painted in the design frieze of this bowl present a variation of spiral motifs connected to stepped elements. Ticked forms and squiggly lines produce flickering, border-contrast phenomena that accent the black-and-white patterning. Areas of the design do reverse optically, but the busy design seems to limit spatial perceptions.

Design strategies: liminal-space isomers, incomplete-element isomers, tessellated isomers
Optical phenomena: figure–ground spatial reversals, border-contrast phenomena, law of simplicity

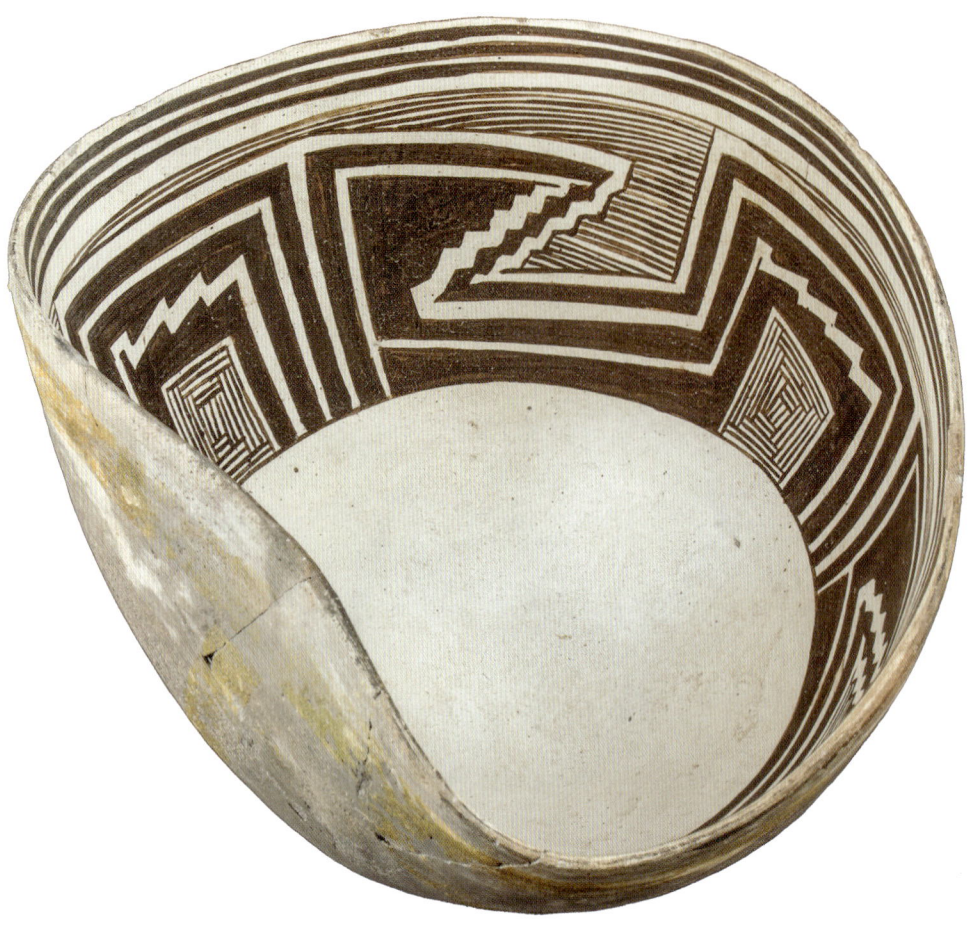

PLATE 7. MIMBRES BLACK-ON-WHITE BOWL
880–1010 CE, 12 × 8 ⅞ IN. DIA., MIAC/LOA 48178/11

On this bowl, the zigzag edges of the liminal spaces separate interlocked stepped motifs and function optically as a series of figure-ground reversals. Border-contrast phenomena associated with the zigzag edges intensify the spatial relationships created by painted forms and bright white slip. Perhaps an accident during molding caused the irregular shape, but the artist successfully painted the design in spite of the deformed shape.

Design strategies: painted-and-unpainted isomers, liminal-space isomers
Optical phenomena: figure–ground spatial reversals, border-contrast phenomena, law of simplicity

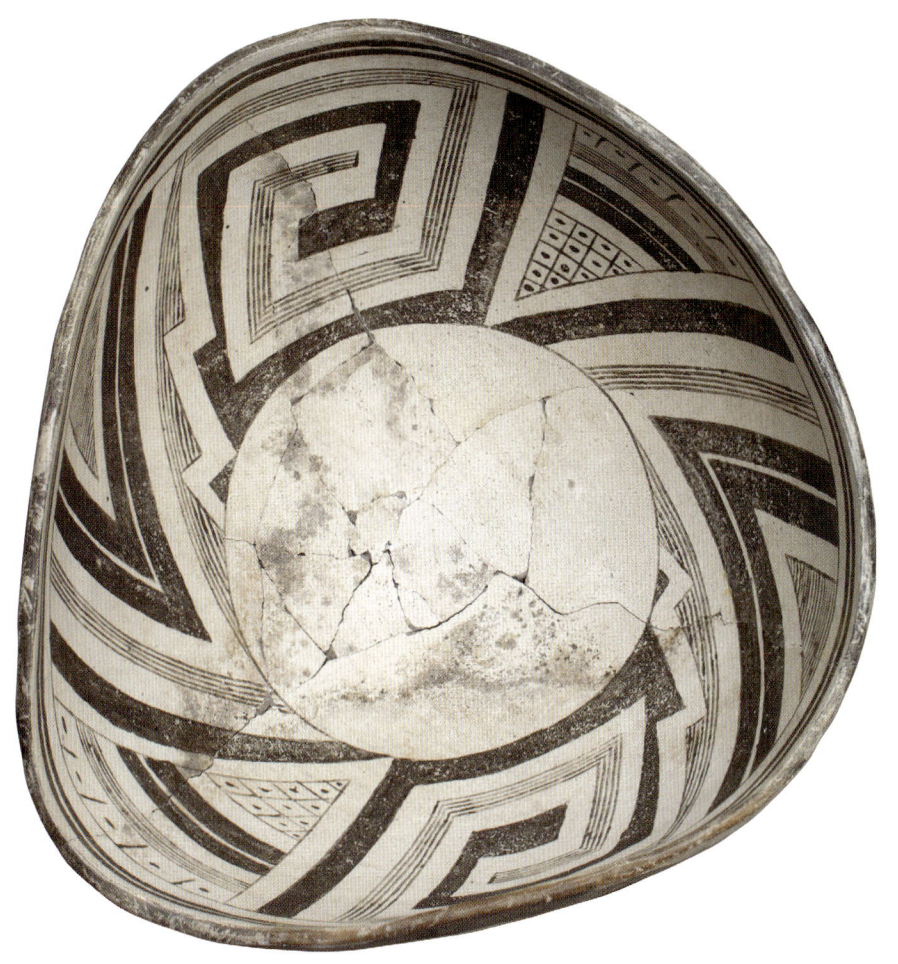

PLATE 8. MIMBRES BLACK-ON-WHITE BOWL

880–1010 CE, 5 9/16 × 10 3/8 IN. DIA., courtesy of the School for Advanced Research, SAR.1965-27, photograph by Jennifer Day

The design frieze of this bowl presents two rectilinear spiral motifs painted as interlocked, solid, and hachured elements. The spirals are separated by chevrons containing tessellated square elements with a dot in the center.

Design strategies: liminal-space isomers, painted-and-unpainted isomers, tessellated isomers
Optical phenomena: figure–ground spatial reversals, border-contrast phenomena, law of simplicity

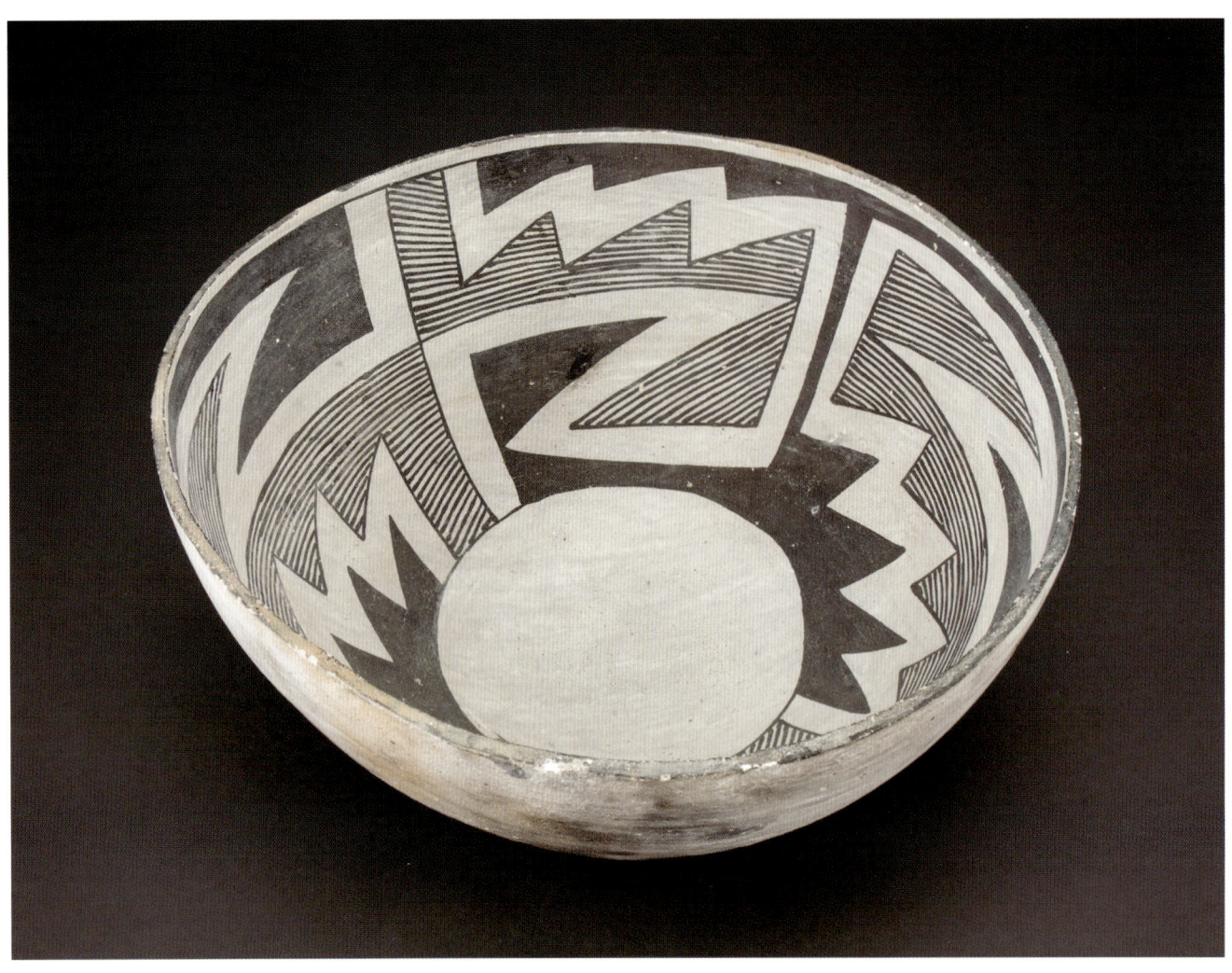

PLATE 9. SOCORRO BLACK-ON-WHITE BOWL
900–1350 CE, 8 ⅝ × 13 IN. DIA., MIAC/LOA 8179

Border-contrast phenomena abound in this design. The zigzag forms produce intensified perceptions between the unpainted, hachured, and solid forms. The energized design can be understood as white shapes floating in front of painted backgrounds, or as dynamic painted forms with unpainted backgrounds.

Design strategy: liminal-space isomers
Optical phenomena: figure–ground spatial reversals, border-contrast phenomena, law of simplicity

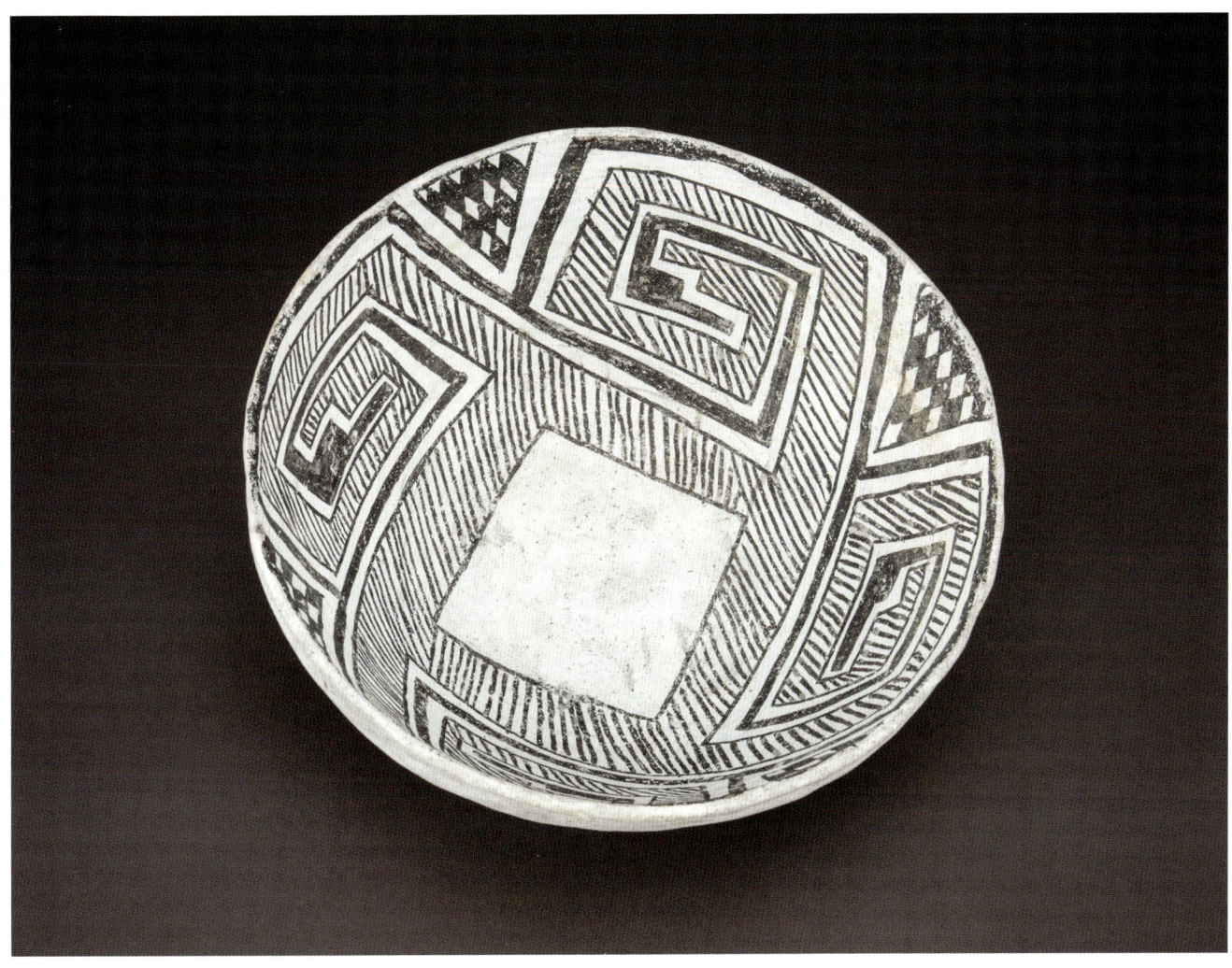

PLATE 10. GALLUP BLACK-ON-WHITE BOWL
950–1150 CE, 3 × 6 ⅛ IN. DIA., MIAC/LOA 18530/11

The dual spiral motifs on this bowl are painted as solid and hachured elements leaving pie-shaped remnants at the rim. Adding checkerboard triangles solved the problem graphically and is also a simple form of a tessellated isomer.

Design strategies: liminal-space isomers, tessellated isomers
Optical phenomena: figure–ground spatial reversals, border-contrast phenomena, law of simplicity

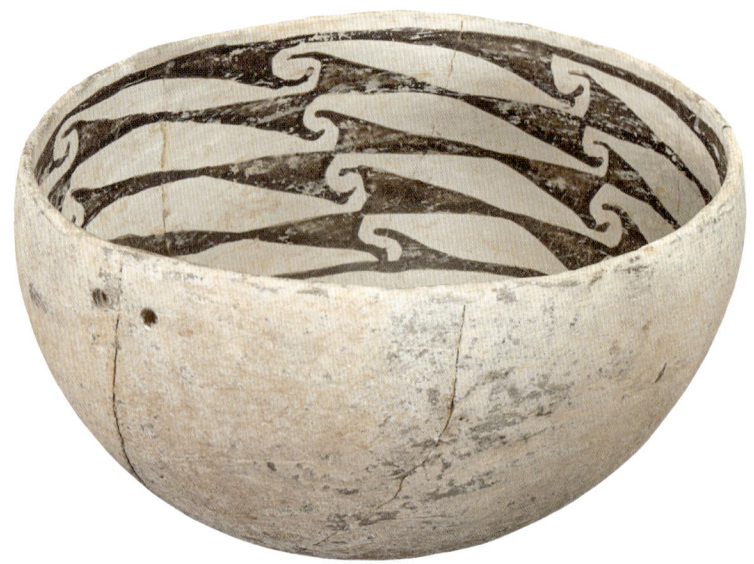

PLATE 11. NEWCOMB BLACK-ON-WHITE BOWL
975–1050 CE, 4 ½ × 8 IN. DIA., MMA 72.43.172

This design presents incomplete spiral elements above and below five concentric framing lines. The painted forms merge and appear simply as curved lines that camouflage the underlying structure. Perceptions of the design flip between partially-interlocking painted spirals and friezes of unpainted, S-shaped elements positioned in front of a dark ground.

Design strategies: incomplete-element isomers, liminal-space isomers, tessellated isomers
Optical phenomena: figure–ground spatial reversals, border-contrast phenomena, law of simplicity

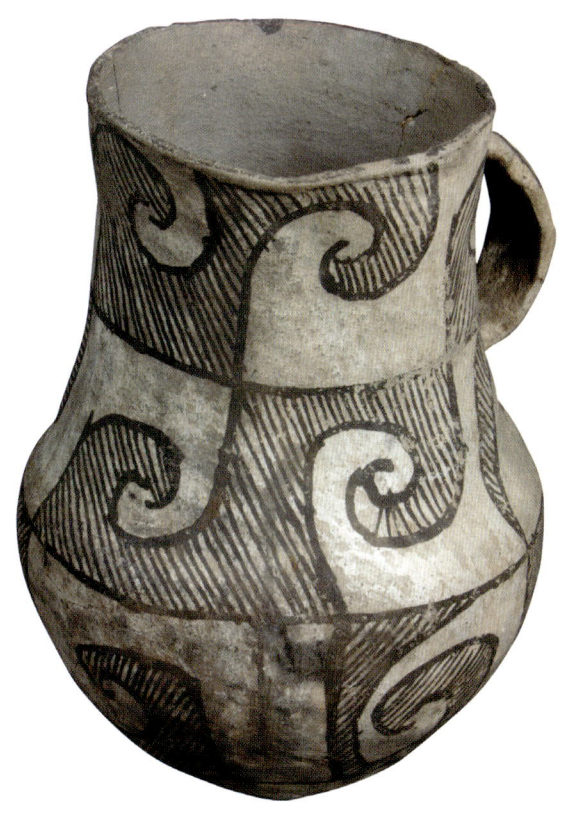

PLATE 12. GALLUP BLACK-ON-WHITE PITCHER
950–1150 CE, 7 ⅜ × 5 ½ IN. DIA., UCB 09501

The motifs on this jar alternate between hachured and unpainted shapes that create interlocked dual spirals. The hachured lines have an uneven quality, producing a border-contrast intensification of the design.

Design strategies: tessellated isomers, painted-and-unpainted isomers
Optical phenomena: figure–ground spatial reversals, border-contrast phenomena

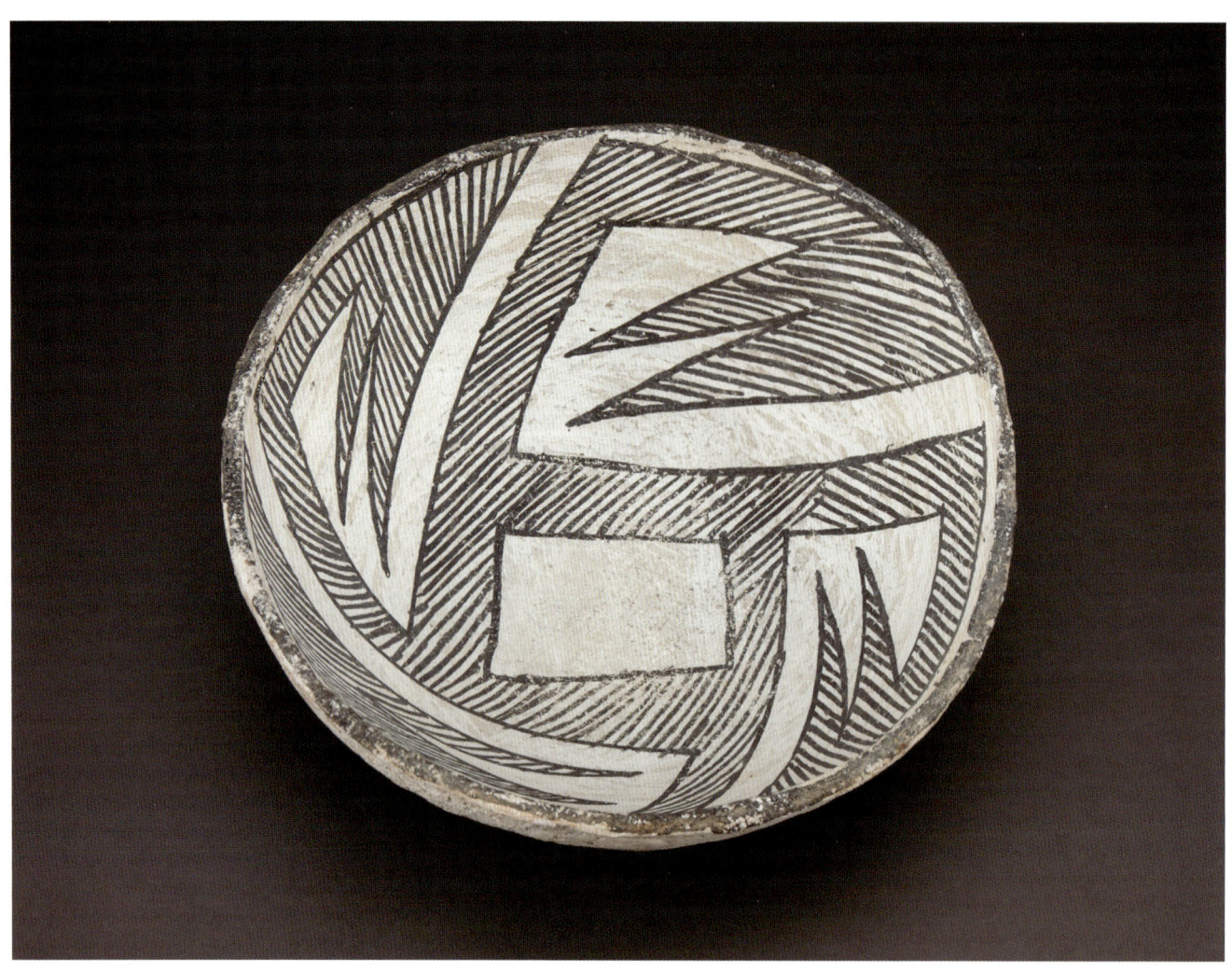

PLATE 13. GALLUP BLACK-ON-WHITE BOWL
950–1150 CE, 2 ½ × 6 IN. DIA., MIAC/LOA 43323/11

The pronged forms on this vessel appear as simplified versions of interlocked spirals with abstracted stepped forms. The balance between painted-and-unpainted shapes allows the composition to alternate between figure and ground perceptions.

Design strategies: painted-and-unpainted isomers, tessellated isomers
Optical phenomena: figure–ground spatial reversals, border-contrast phenomena, law of simplicity

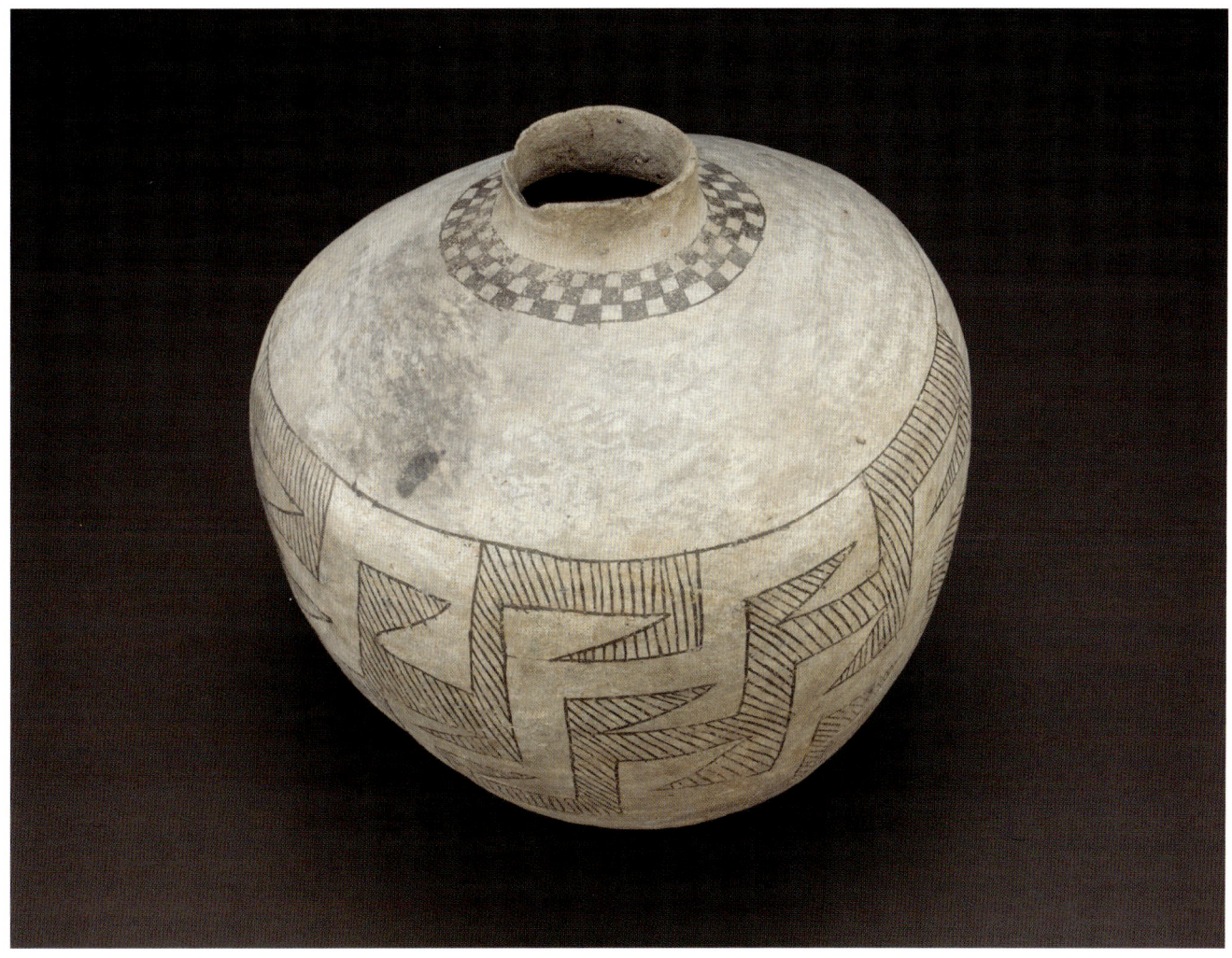

PLATE 14. GALLUP BLACK-ON-WHITE JAR
950–1150 CE, 11 ½ × 11 ¾ IN. DIA., MIAC/LOA 43334

The hachured forms on this tessellated design also produce similar shapes as painted-and-unpainted isomers. The complex design interlocks seamlessly without the need for additional liminal spaces. The checkerboard design encircling the neck of the jar is a simple form of tessellation that probably helped the artist set the spacing for the designs on the body of the jar.

Design strategies: tessellated isomers, painted-and-unpainted isomers
Optical phenomena: figure–ground spatial reversals, border-contrast phenomena, law of simplicity

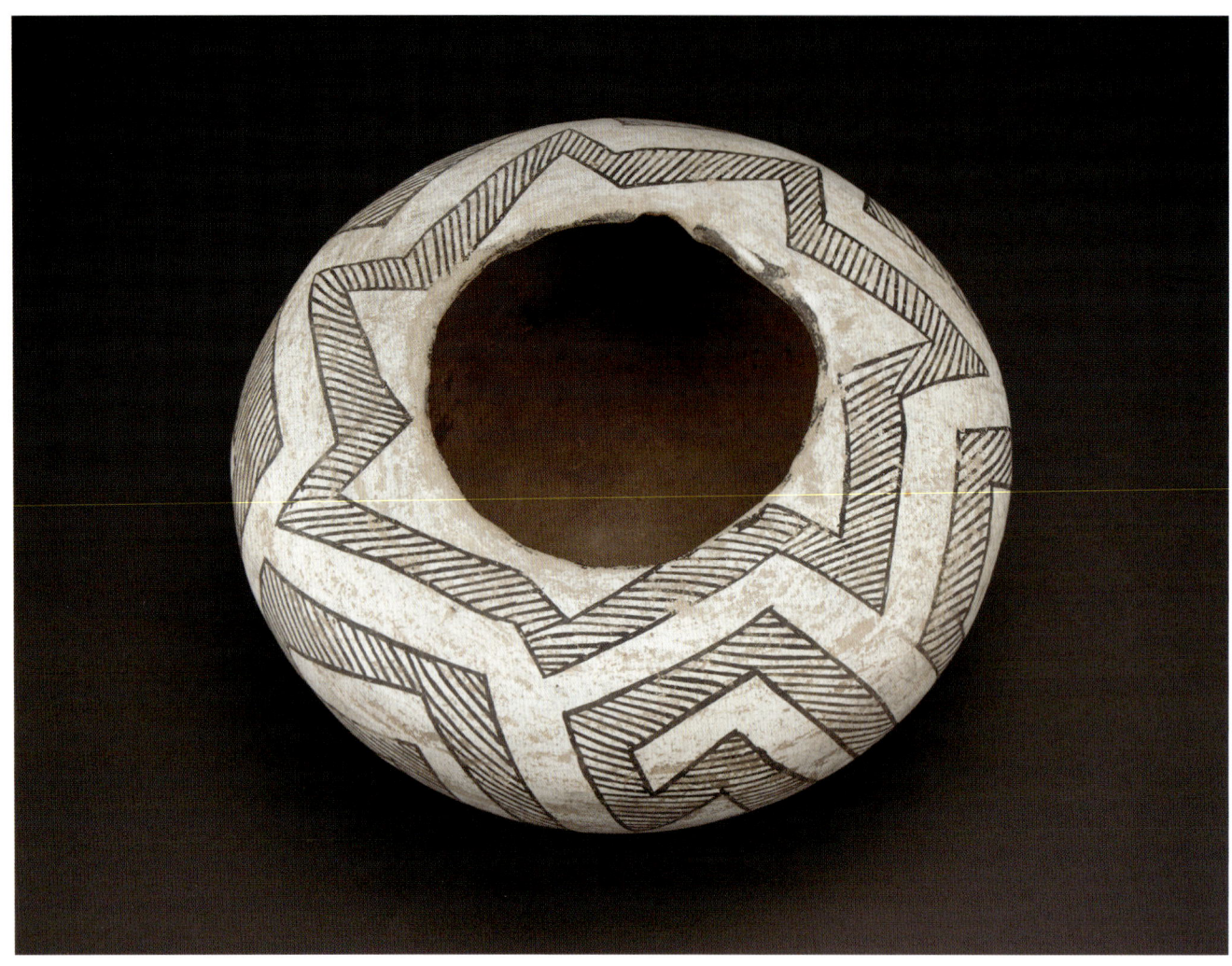

PLATE 15. GALLUP BLACK-ON-WHITE JAR

950–1150 CE, 5 ½ × 9 ¼ IN. DIA., Honorable Daniel H. McMillan Collection, MIAC/LOA 8842/11

The hachured forms painted on this seed jar separate pairs of L-shaped unpainted isomers. The artist carefully balanced the isomers and the liminal space so they are the same width, a difficult task on a spherical form. Part of the solution to this challenge involves the motif encircling the mouth of the vessel. This motif set the spacing for the design and the correct angles for the L-shaped isomers. The equal balance of hachured and unpainted areas allows the composition to be perceived as both a black-on-white and a white-on-black design.

Design strategies: liminal-space isomers, tesellated isomers
Optical phenomena: figure–ground spatial reversals, border-contrast phenomena, law of simplicity

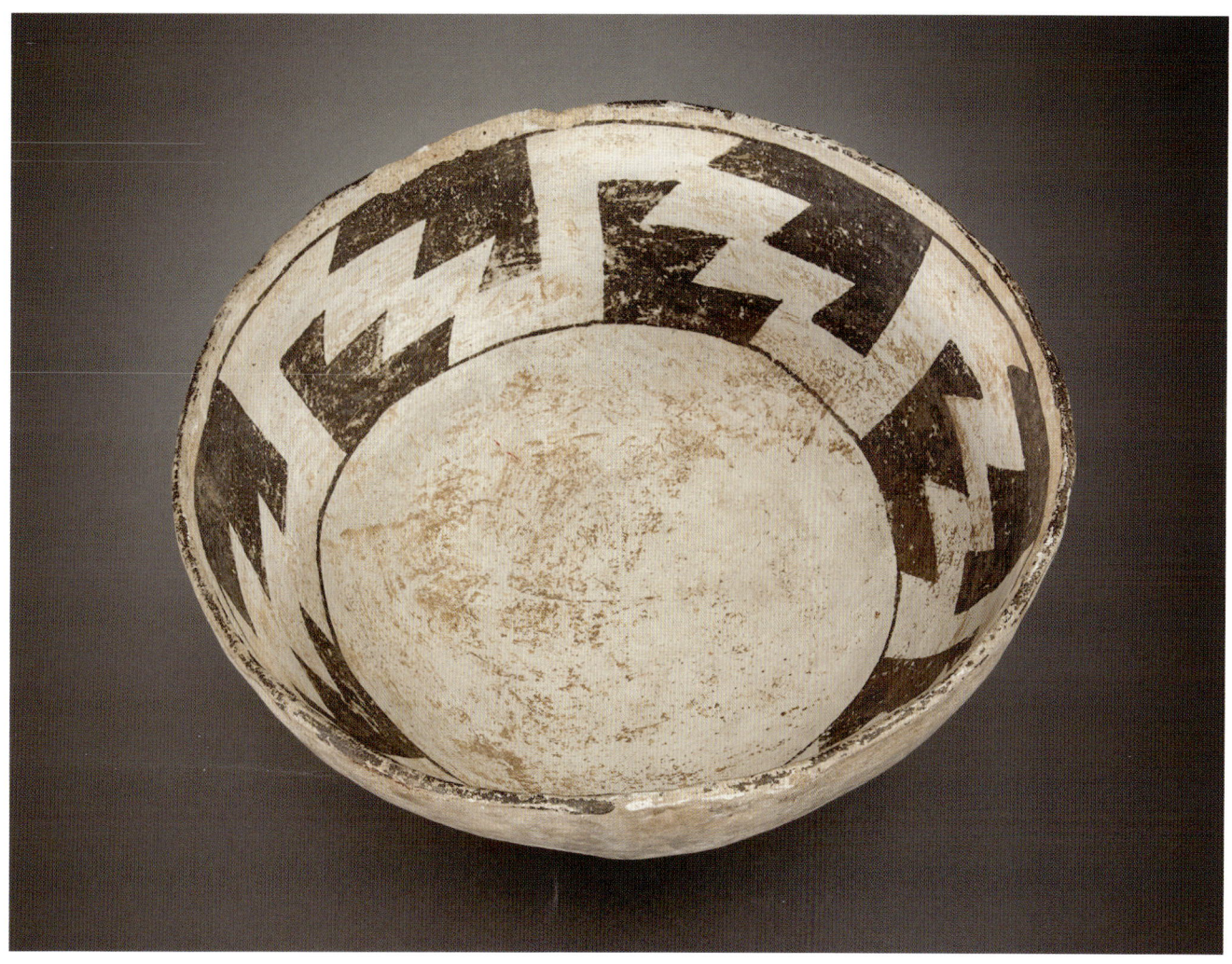

PLATE 16. ESCAVADA BLACK-ON-WHITE BOWL
950–1150 CE, 3 × 9¼ IN. DIA. MMA 76.68.51

This vessel presents a carefully balanced composition in which pairs of stepped isomers produce optical reversibility. The liminal-space reads as both a black-on-white and a white-on-black perception.

Design strategies: liminal-space isomers
Optical phenomena: figure–ground spatial reversals, border-contrast phenomena, law of simplicity

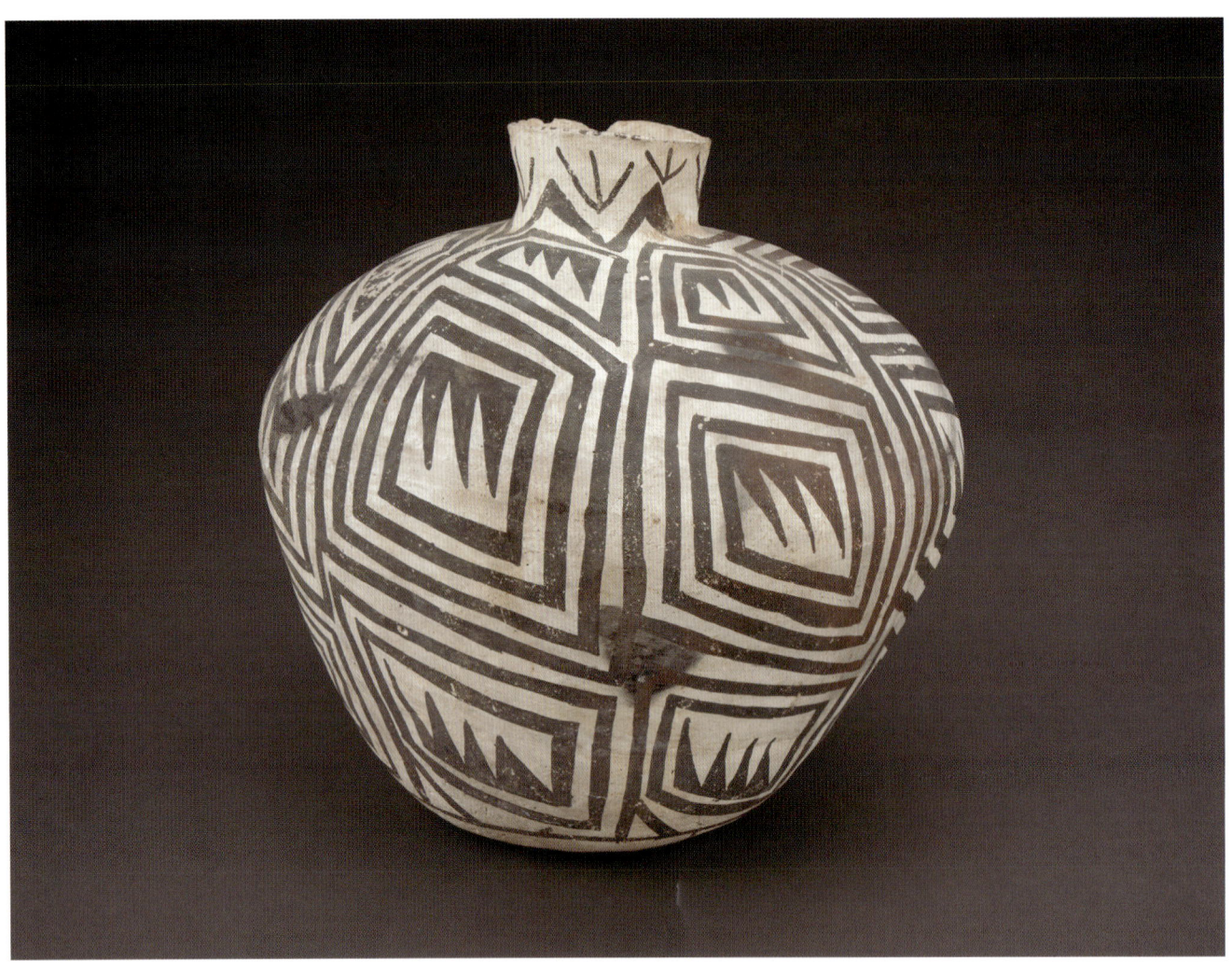

PLATE 17. ESCAVADA BLACK-ON-WHITE JAR
950–1150 CE, 11 ⅞ × 12 ¼ IN. DIA., MIAC/LOA 20175

The light and dark equilibrium on this vessel allows the painting to be understood as both a black-on-white and a white-on-black design. The simplification of stepped elements as pronged forms creates a more dynamic interaction between painted and unpainted elements than does rectilinear stepped shapes. Focusing on the border-contrast phenomena of the pronged forms intensifies the spatial ambiguity of this design.

Design strategies: painted-and-unpainted isomers, tessellated isomers
Optical phenomena: figure–ground spatial reversals, border-contrast phenomena, law of simplicity

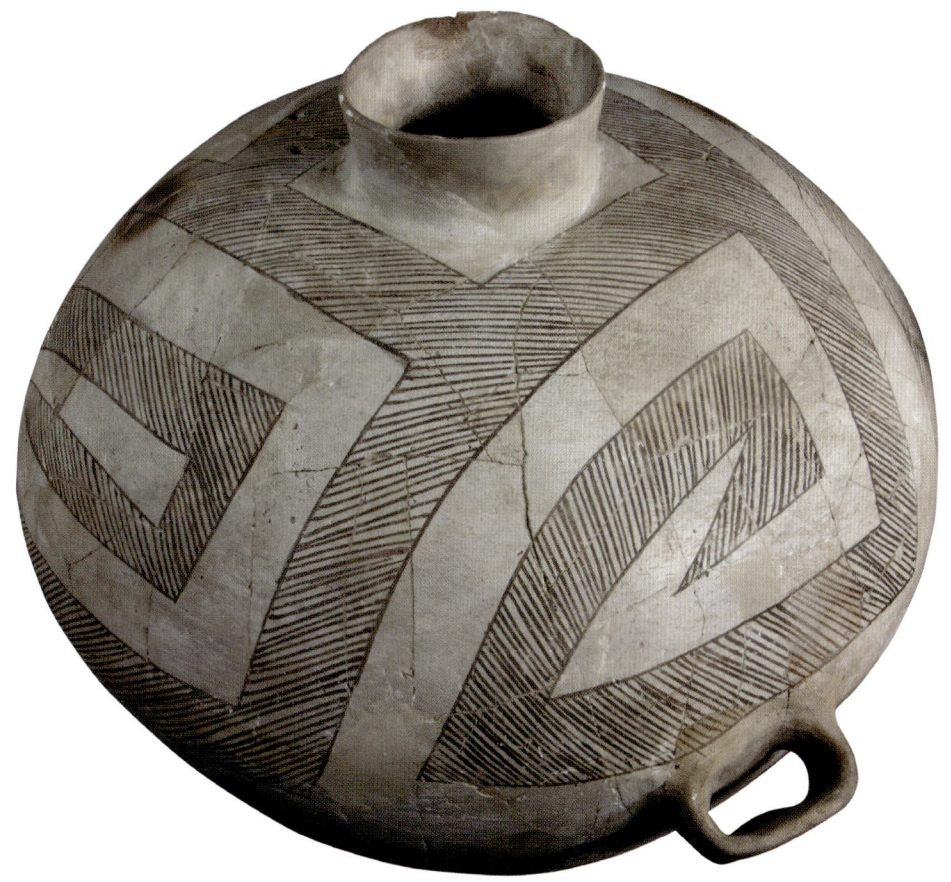

PLATE 18. GALLUP BLACK-ON-WHITE JAR
950–1150 CE, 14 ⅝ × 15 ⅝ IN. DIA., UCB 04032

The rectilinear design painted on this jar laps over the shoulder of the vessel. The uniform width of the hachured and unpainted forms is difficult to produce and allows for figure–ground reversals.

Design strategies: painted-and-unpainted isomers
Optical phenomena: figure–ground spatial reversals, border-contrast phenomena

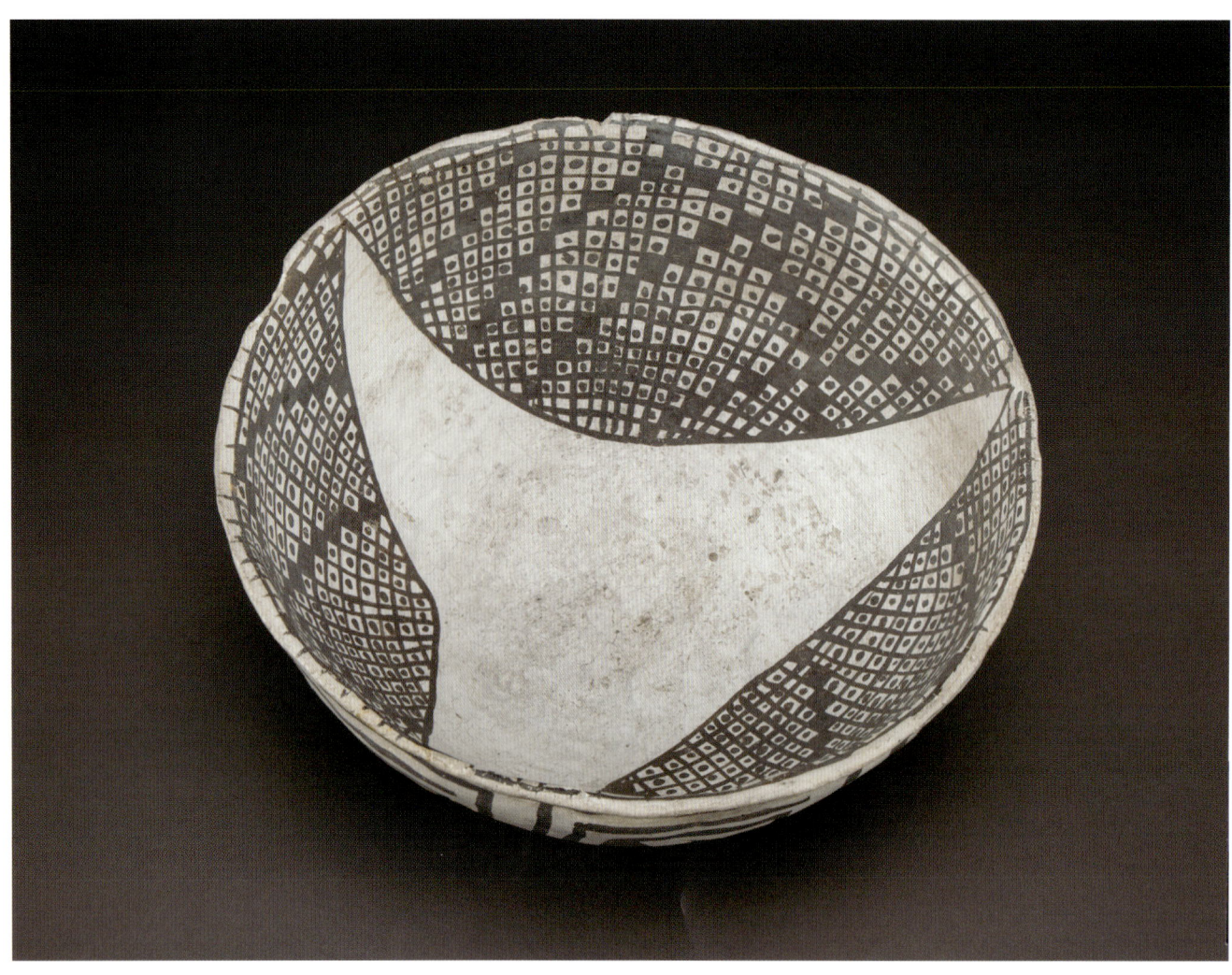

PLATE 19. TUSAYAN/BETATAKIN BLACK-ON-WHITE BOWL
980–1150 CE, 3 ⅜ × 7 ½ IN. DIA., MIAC/LOA 43326/11

This example of a woven painting demonstrates a conceptual relationship to the structure of coiled baskets and the process of weaving basket designs. The filled-in cells produce the curved, diagonal design. Optically the rather dark painting on this bowl forces the unpainted center to pop forward and appear as a triangular figure spatially in front of a dark background formed by the design frieze.

Design strategies: tessellated isomers, painted-and-unpainted isomers
Optical phenomena: figure–ground spatial reversals, border-contrast phenomena, law of simplicity

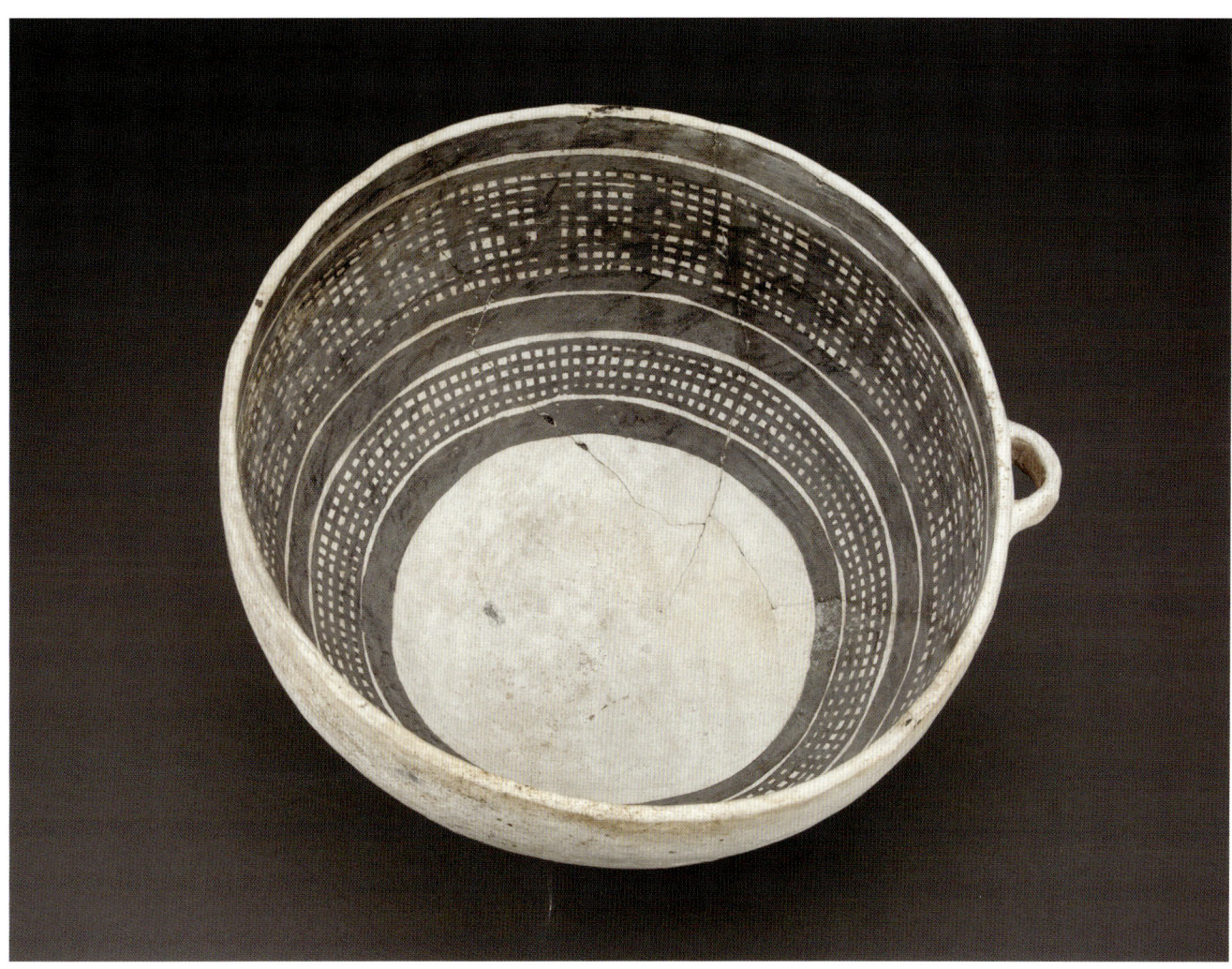

PLATE 20. TUSAYAN/BETATAKIN BLACK-ON-WHITE BOWL
1200–1300 CE, 5 1/16 × 10 5/8 IN. DIA., MIAC/LOA 46588

The painted weaving on this bowl mimics the warp and weft structure of a coiled basket. Within the tile-like structure of this painted basket design, some cells are filled in to funtion like liminal spaces. These painted friezes create a figure–ground relationship with the unpainted center, allowing this area of slip to be perceived as physically in front of the painted bands.

Design strategies: tessellated isomers, painted-and-unpainted isomers
Optical phenomena: figure–ground spatial reversals, border-contrast phenomena, law of simplicity, size-based optical reversals, size-based optical illusions

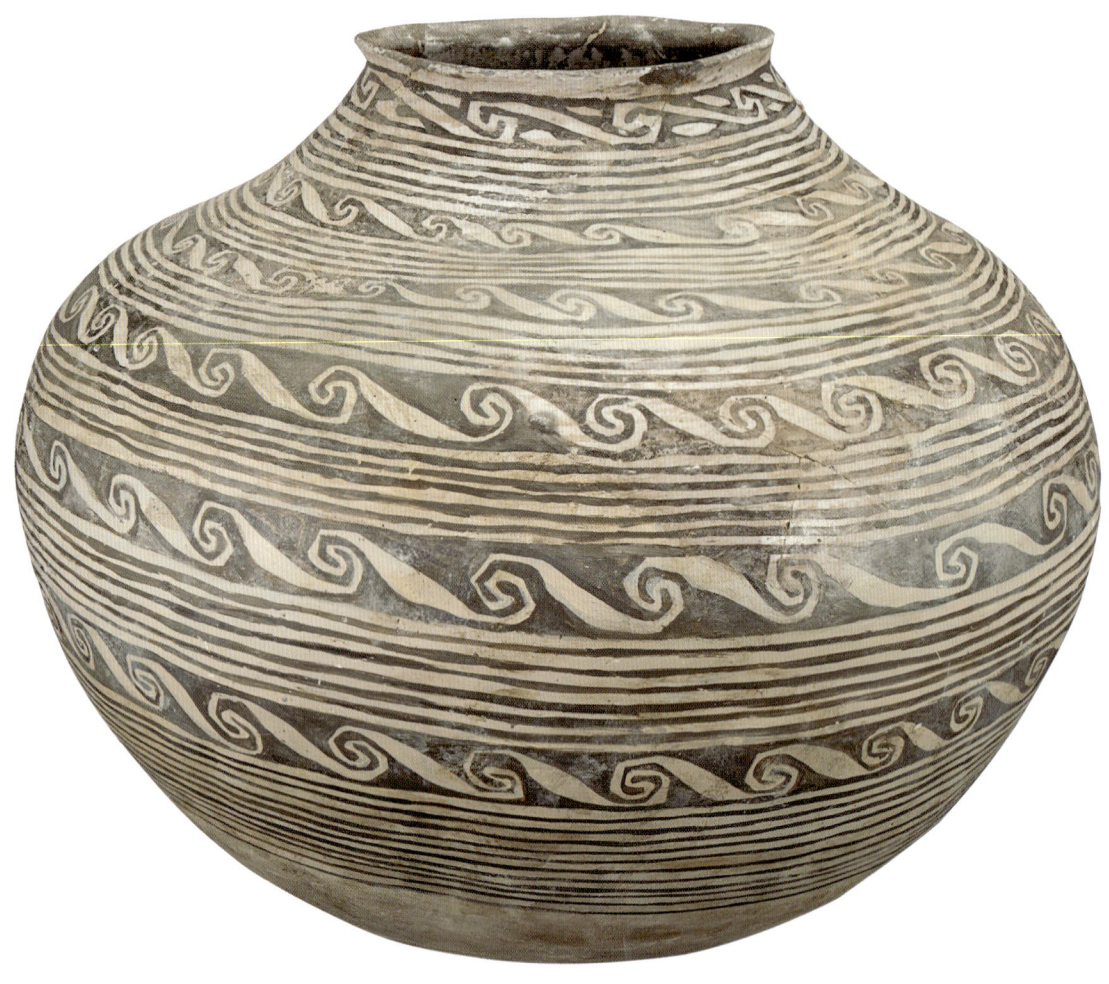

PLATE 21. WALNUT BLACK-ON-WHITE JAR
1000–1100 CE, 13 ½ × 17 IN. DIA., MMA 35.6.1

Curvilinear spirals dominate the composition painted on this jar. But a close look reveals that the spirals are not smooth curves, but mostly a series of short straight lines. The law of simplicity aids the perceptual transformation of straight lines into curved forms. Perceptually the design friezes can be understood as both incomplete painted spirals and unbroken, unpainted dual spirals.

Design strategies: incomplete-element isomers, liminal-space isomers, tessellated isomers, painted-and-unpainted isomers
Optical phenomena: figure–ground spatial reversals, border-contrast phenomena, law of simplicity

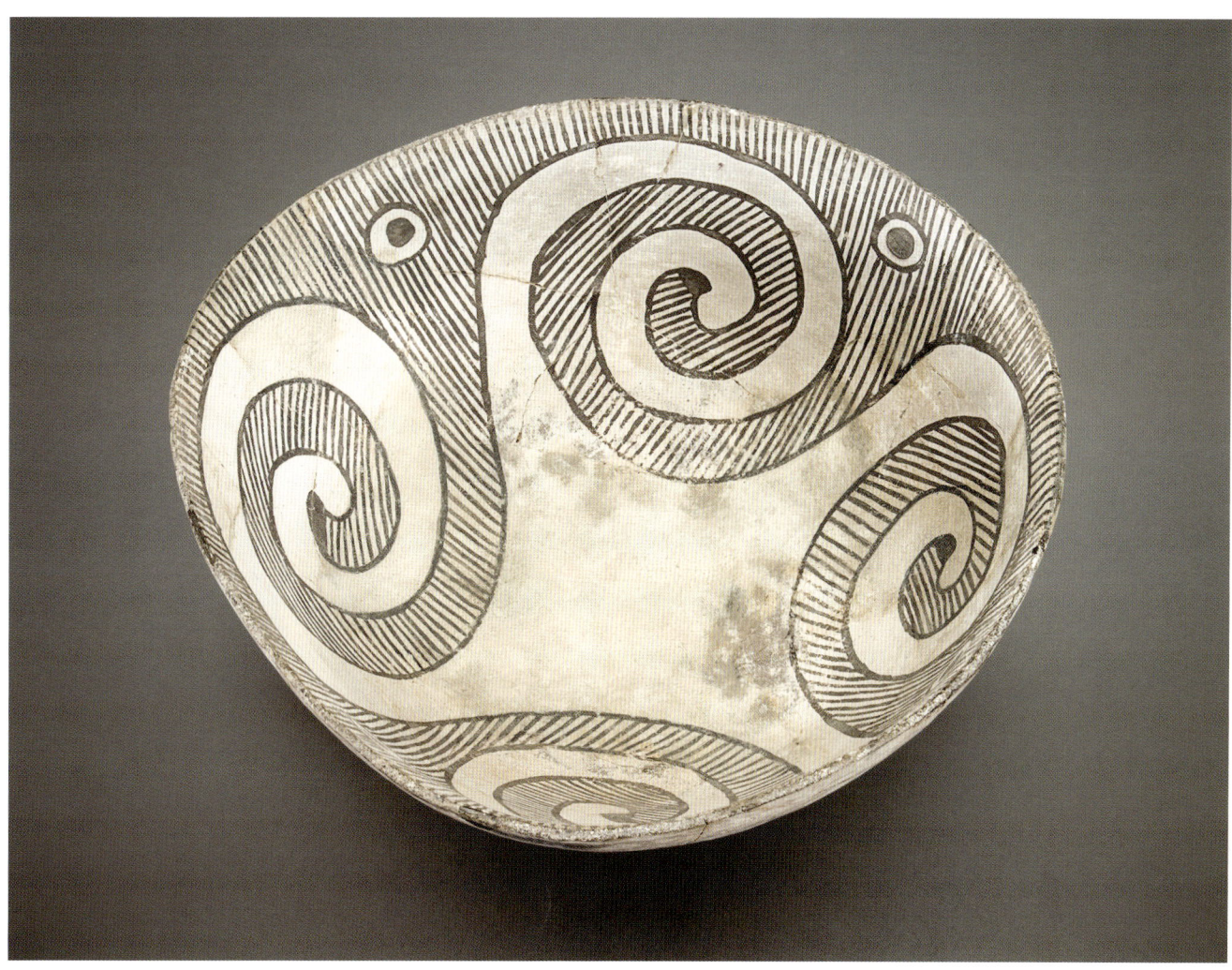

PLATE 22. CHUSKA BLACK-ON-WHITE BOWL
1000–1125 CE, 4 ⅞ × 11 IN. DIA., MMA 42.12.131

The spiral motifs on this bowl intertwine hachured and unpainted shapes. The unpainted elements expand from the center of the bowl and mesh with the painted spirals at the rim. The balance between hachured and unpainted elements creates a figure-and-ground uncertainty producing dual perceptions as spatial reversals.

Design strategies: painted-and-unpainted isomers, liminal-space isomers
Optical phenomena: figure–ground spatial reversals, border-contrast phenomena, law of simplicity

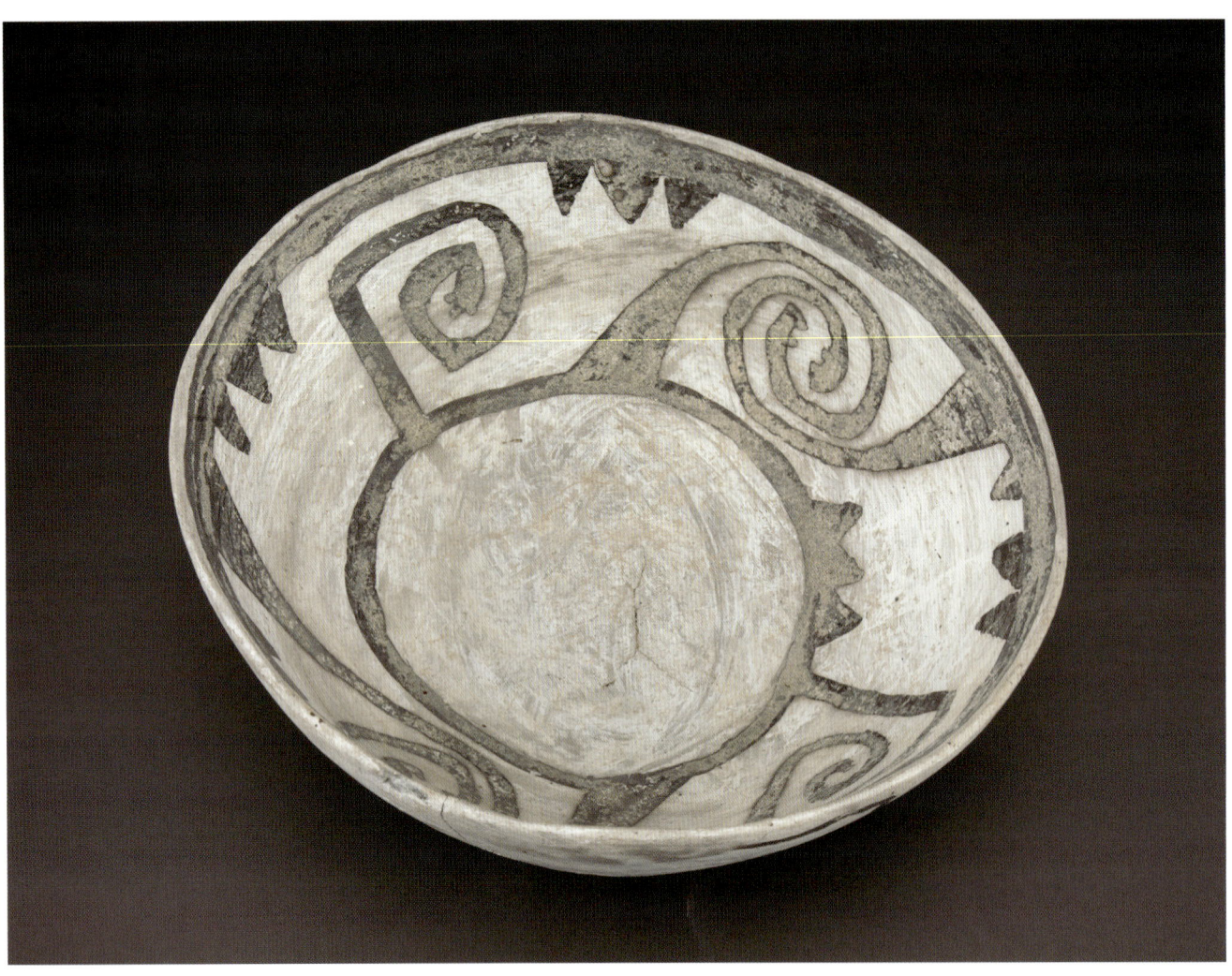

PLATE 23. BLACK MESA BLACK-ON-WHITE BOWL
1100–1200 CE, 5 ¾ × 9 ⅞ IN. DIA., MIAC/LOA 8832/11

The linear design on this bowl presents spiral motifs that alternate between individual spirals and interlocked spirals as a duality in the layout. The preponderance of unpainted slip makes it difficult for linear motifs to reverse perceptually.

Design strategies: painted-and-unpainted isomers, liminal-space isomers
Optical phenomena: figure–ground spatial reversals, border-contrast phenomena, optical reversals

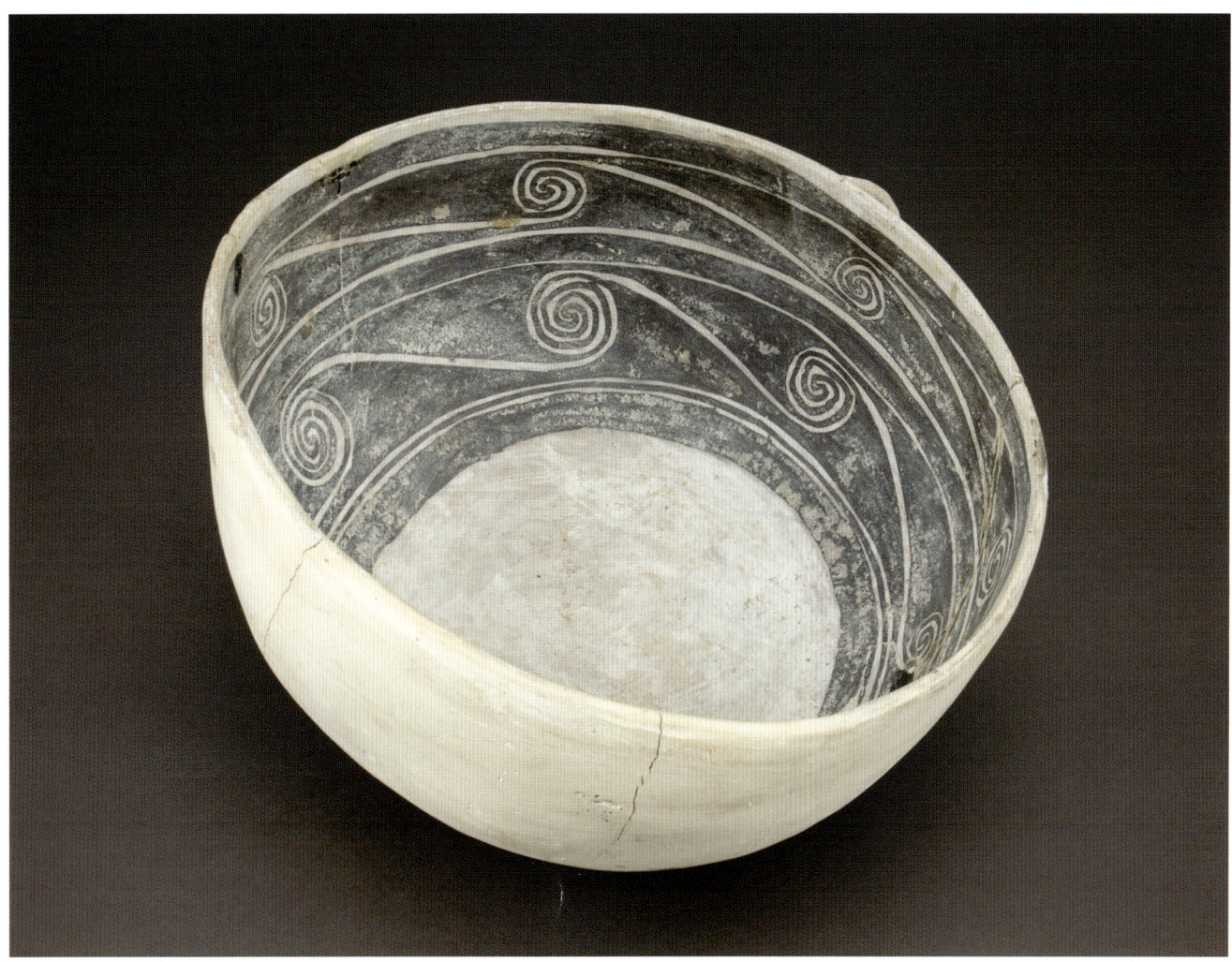

PLATE 24. TUSAYAN BLACK-ON-WHITE BOWL
1200–1300 CE, 4 ½ × 9 ¾ IN. DIA., MIAC/LOA 45527

The artist painted this bowl as a "negative" design by filling in all but the fine, unpainted lines of slip. Size differences between the painted and unpainted areas create a stable figure-and-ground relationship making it difficult to see the painted areas as the figure in the design.

Design strategies: liminal-space isomers, tessellated isomers
Optical phenomena: figure–ground spatial reversals, border-contrast phenomena, law of simplicity, size-based optical reversals

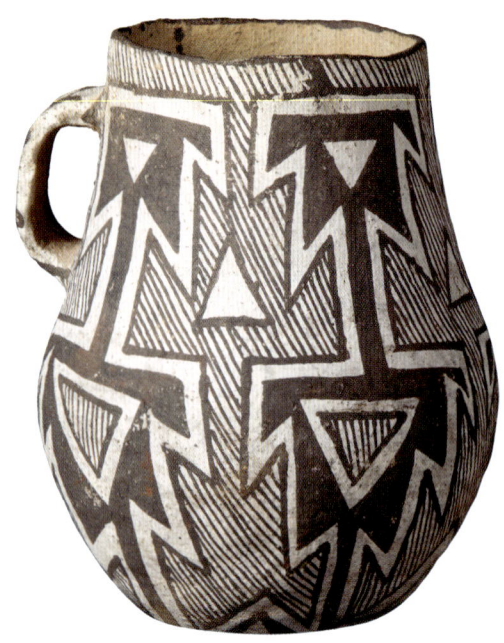

PLATE 25. MESA VERDE BLACK-ON-WHITE PITCHER
1000–1150 CE, 7 × 6 ¼ IN. DIA., MNA NA6004.6

The tessellated form on this pitcher repeats a single motif that is flipped so the motifs can interlock seamlessly. The edges of the motifs include pairs with lock and key elements permitting adjustments to the widths of the motifs to the circumference of the vessel.

Design strategies: tessellated isomers, painted-and-unpainted isomers
Optical phenomena: figure–ground spatial reversals, border-contrast phenomena, law of simplicity

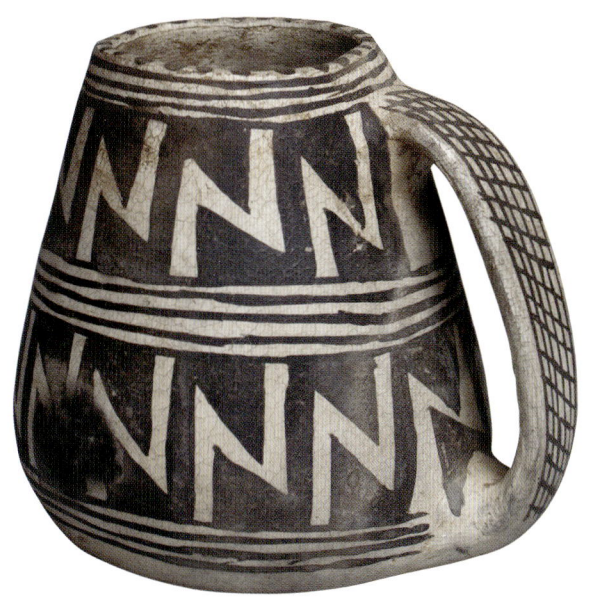

PLATE 26. MESA VERDE BLACK-ON-WHITE MUG
1200–1300 CE, 3 ⅞ × 4 ⅜ IN. DIA., courtesy of the School for Advanced Research, IAF.2387, photograph by Jennifer Day

This mug exhibits design friezes created by pairs of Z-shaped elements oriented vertically. The pairs of painted Zs define similar, unpainted elements. Optically this design creates a figure–ground reversal allowing the solid and unpainted areas to flip back and forth spatially, between background and foreground.

Design strategies: tessellated isomers, painted-and-unpainted isomers
Optical phenomena: figure–ground spatial reversals, border-contrast phenomena, law of simplicity, size-based optical reversals

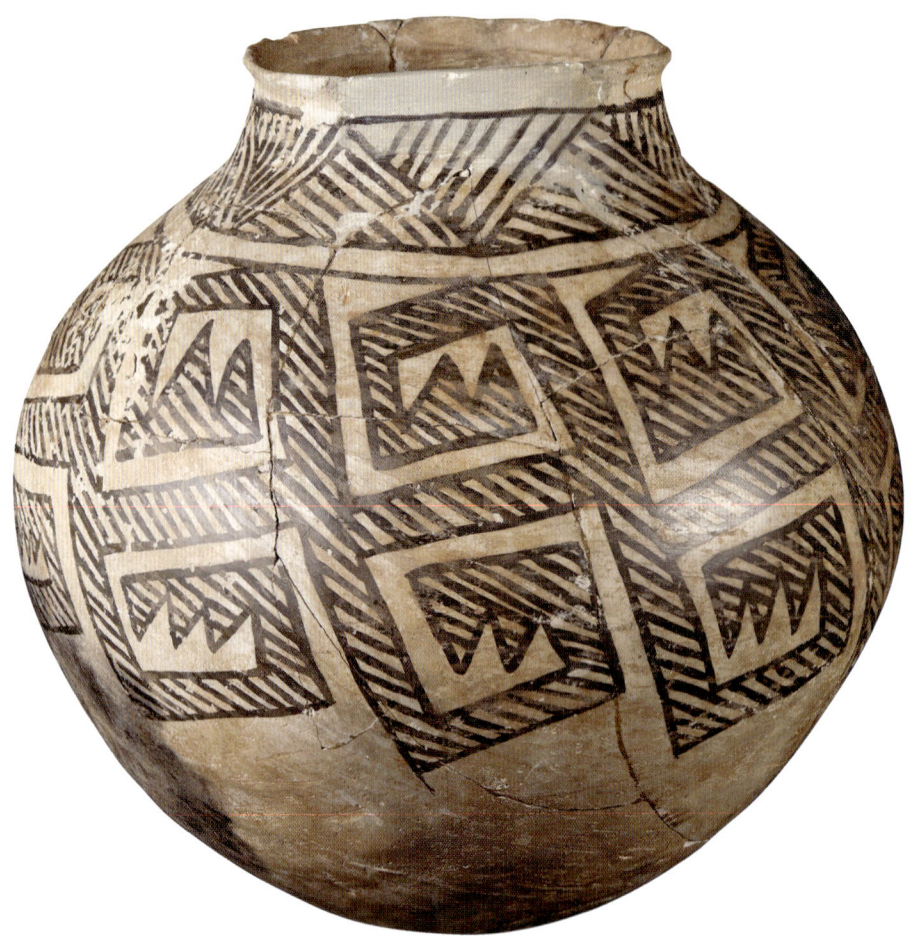

PLATE 27. DOGOSZHI BLACK-ON-WHITE JAR
1040–1220 CE, 12 ⅜ × 13 ⅜ IN. DIA., MNA OC281

The hachured shapes on this jar are slightly wider than the unpainted liminal spaces they create. This visual arrangement facilitates the ability of the unpainted shapes to appear as foregrounds against darker hachured shapes. Organizing design on a diagonal makes inaccuracies in spacing less noticeable. Curiously, the hachured triangles painted on the neck do not adhere to the apparent axiom that painted spaces should not touch.

Design strategies: painted-and-unpainted isomers, tessellated isomers
Optical phenomena: figure–ground spatial reversals, border-contrast phenomena, law of simplicity

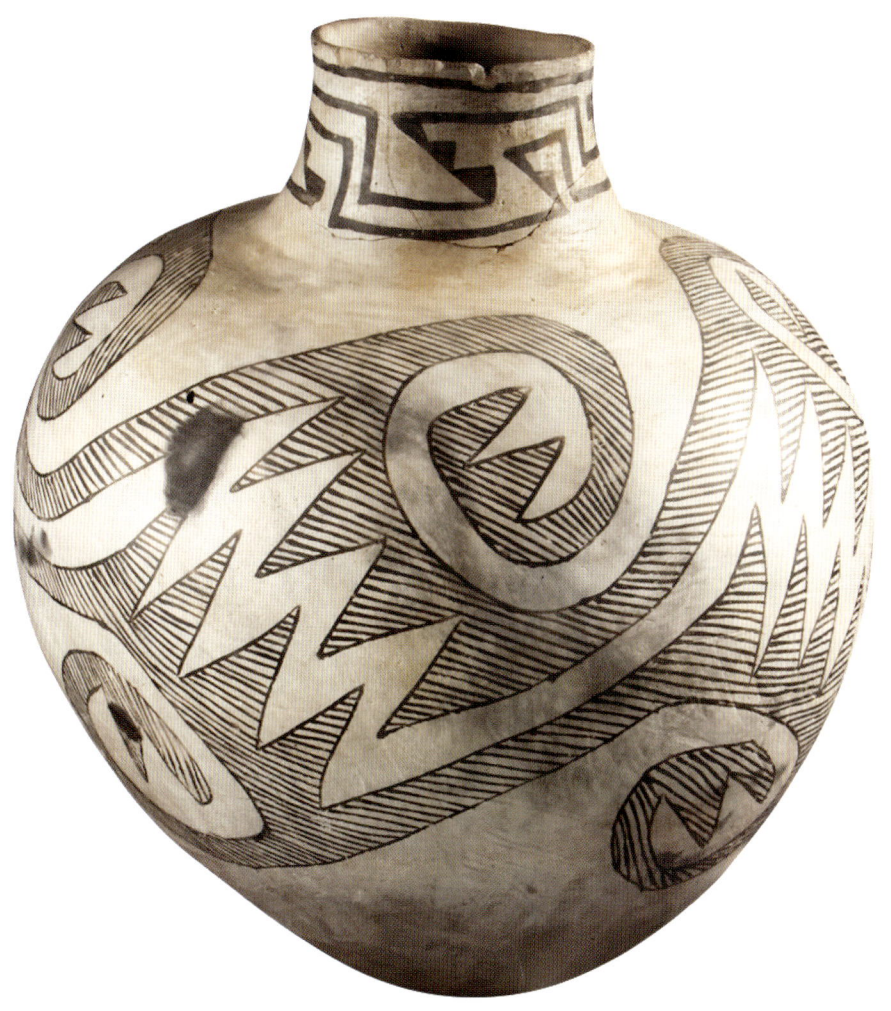

PLATE 28. DOGOSZHI BLACK-ON-WHITE JAR
1040–1220 CE, 17 ⅝ × 16 ½ IN. DIA., MNA A5095

The design frieze on this jar appears as if it were a single form divided in half with the two parts pulled apart, leaving a liminal space in between. Border-contrast phenomena associated with the pronged elements energize the zigzagging liminal space.

Design strategies: painted-and-unpainted isomers, liminal-space isomers
Optical phenomena: figure–ground spatial reversals, border-contrast phenomena, law of simplicity

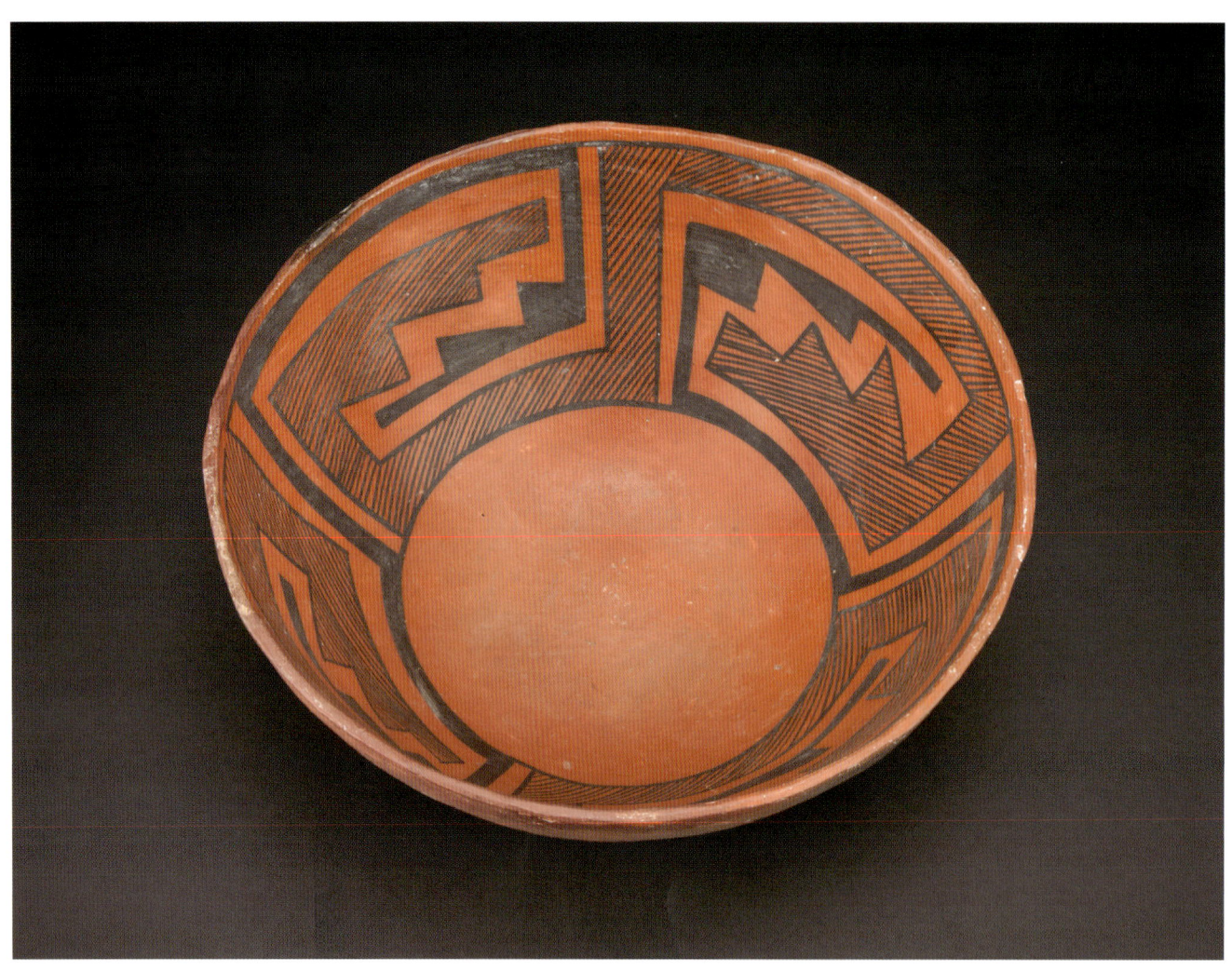

PLATE 29. PUERCO BLACK-ON-RED BOWL
1050–1175 CE, 4 1/8 × 9 1/4 IN. DIA., MIAC/LOA 43321

The dual spirals on this bowl are painted as solid and hachured shapes, separated by unpainted liminal spaces. This can be considered another version of a tessellated isomer design even though the solid and hachured forms are not repeated exactly. Figure-ground reversals occur as the unpainted, intensely red slip dominates visually and appears spatially in front of the solid and hachured painted elements.

Design strategies: liminal-space isomers, tessellated isomers, and painted-unpainted isomers
Optical phenomena: figure–ground spatial reversals, border-contrast phenomena, law of simplicity

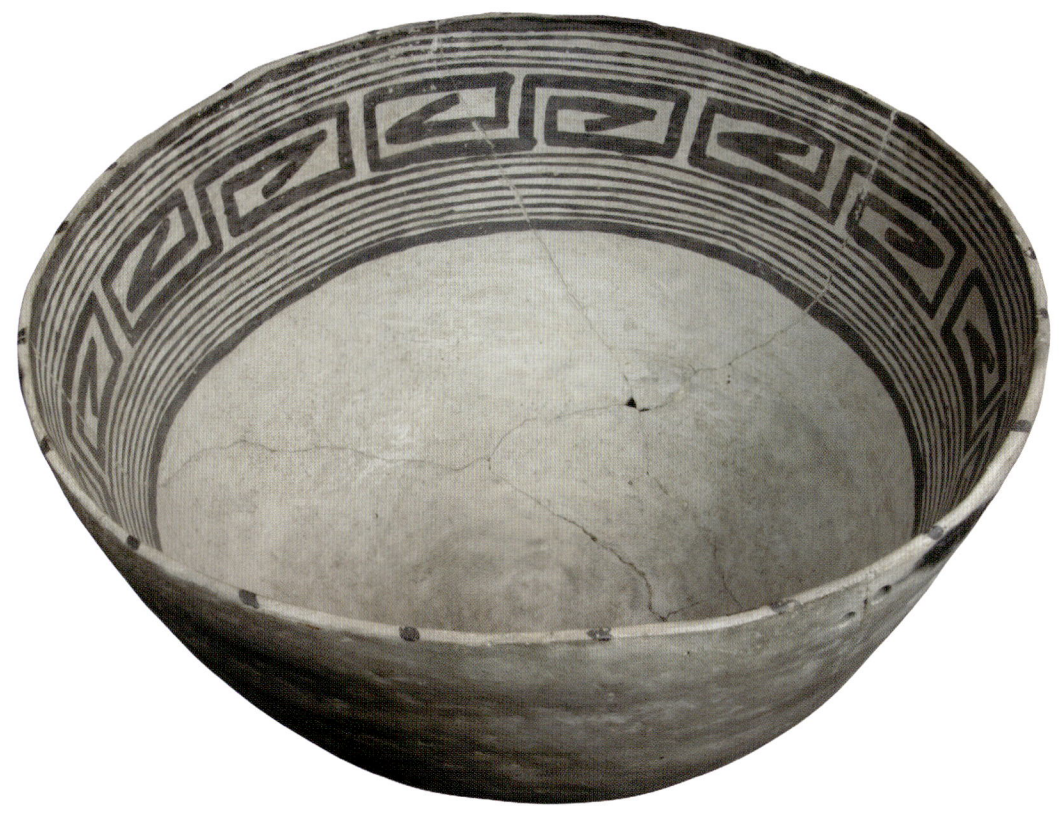

PLATE 30. MESA VERDE BLACK-ON-WHITE BOWL
1150–1280 CE 5 ⅞ × 12 ⅛ IN. DIA., UCB 09324

This design frieze on this bowl incorporates a band of eight dual-spiral motifs centered between bands of parallel lines. At first the unpainted liminal spaces of these motifs may appear as backgrounds to the painted motifs, but they easily reverse optically and appear in front of the painted elements. Each of the dual-spiral motifs ends with an angled form, a simplification of a pronged form derived from a stepped element.

Design strategies: tessellated isomers, painted-and-unpainted isomers, incomplete-element isomers

Optical phenomena: figure–ground spatial reversals, border-contrast phenomena, law of simplicity

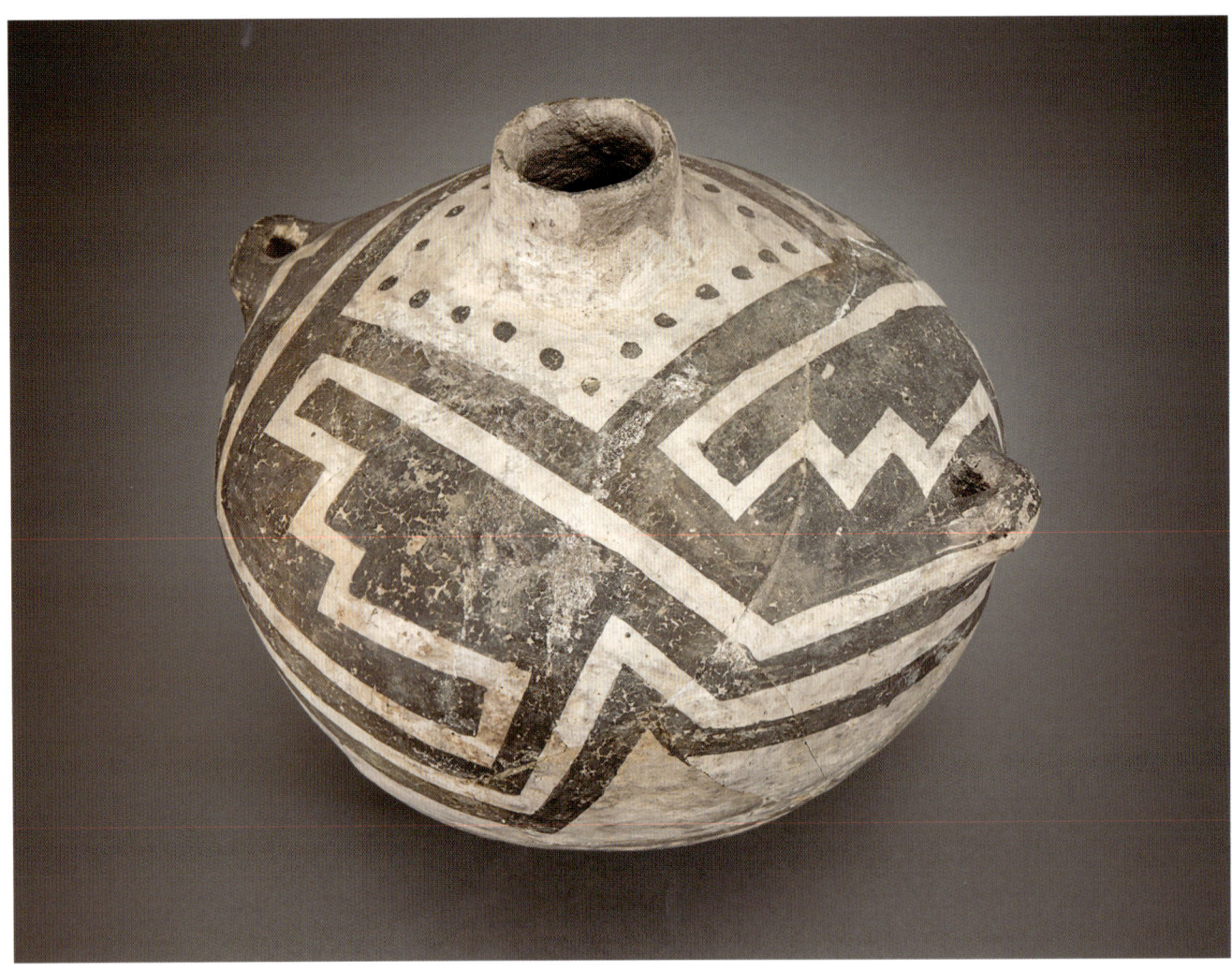

PLATE 31. LEUPP BLACK-ON-WHITE JAR
1100–1225 CE, 7 ¼ × 11 IN. DIA., MMA 73.43.160

Ancestral artists carefully adapted this popular composition to multiple forms, including bowls, jars, and dippers. As the design drapes over the top of the jar, the triangular, unpainted spaces adjust for the changing circumference of the vessel. Conceptually this design alternates visually between perceptions; one conception understands the painted elements as the intended subject while the other recognizes the meandering liminal spaces as the foreground.

Design strategies: liminal-space isomers
Optical phenomena: figure–ground spatial reversals, border-contrast phenomena

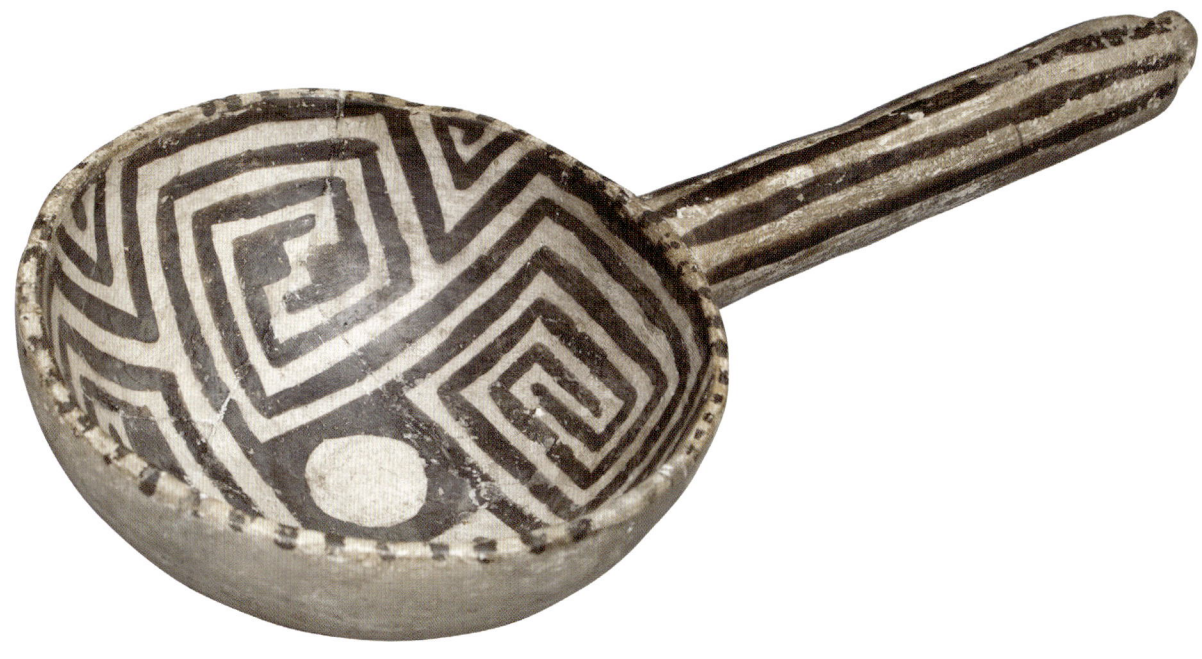

PLATE 32. McELMO BLACK-ON-WHITE DIPPER

1150–1300 CE, 2 ⅜ × 10 × 5 ¼ IN. DIA., courtesy of the School for Advanced Research, IAF.2400, photograph by Jennifer Day

The artist painted a balanced design of interlocked spirals ending with stepped elements radiating out from a square in the center of the dipper. The equilibrium between painted and unpainted areas allows the observer to understand this design as an example of figure–ground reversal. This design is virtually the same as the image adapted to the exterior of the Leupp Black-on-white jar (see plate 31).

Design strategies: liminal-space isomers, tessellated isomers
Optical phenomena: figure–ground spatial reversals, border-contrast phenomena, law of simplicity

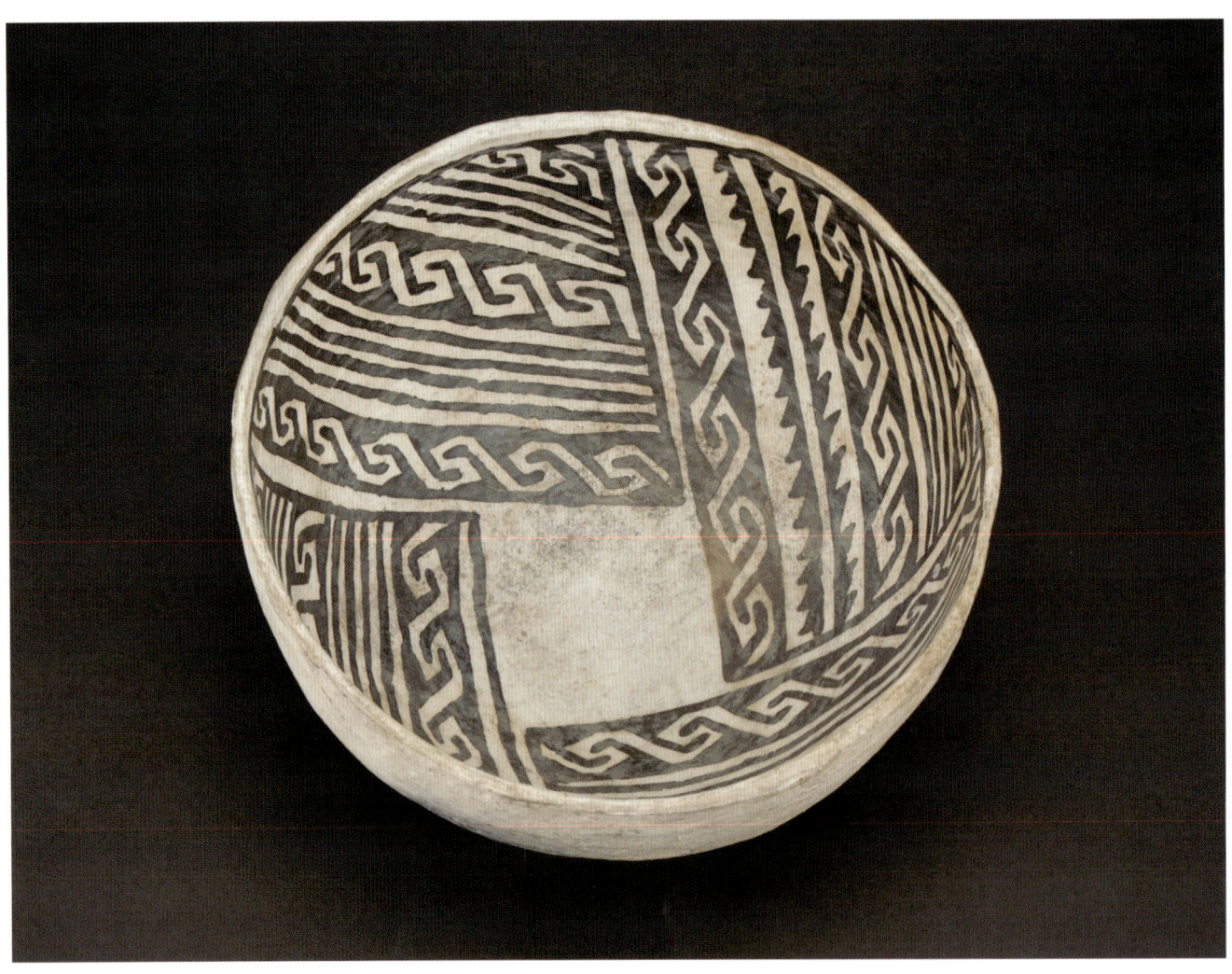

PLATE 33. FLAGSTAFF BLACK-ON-WHITE BOWL
1125–1200 CE, 3 ½ × 7 IN. DIA., MIAC 53295

On this bowl, pairs of triangular shapes ending with angular crooks form simplifications of incomplete spiral motifs. Perceptually these dual motifs appear as interlocked spirals, but they can also be perceived as abstract representations of twisted yucca cordage.

Design strategies: incomplete-element isomers, liminal-space isomers, painted-and-unpainted isomers, tessellated isomers
Optical phenomena: figure–ground spatial reversals, border-contrast phenomena, law of simplicity

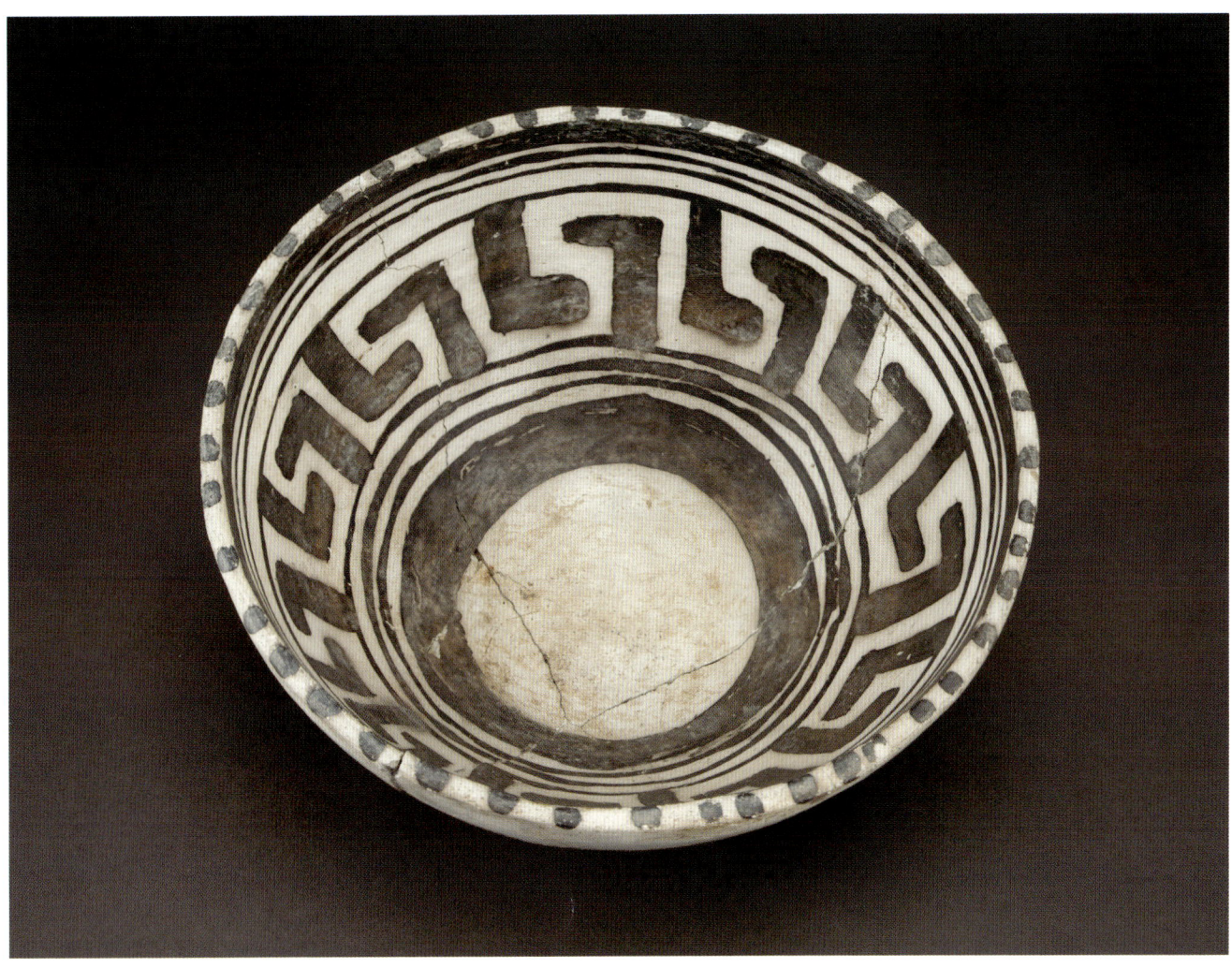

PLATE 34. MESA VERDE BLACK-ON-WHITE BOWL

1150–1280 CE, 2 ¾ × 6 IN. DIA., MIAC/LOA 43345/11

The L-shaped isomers on this bowl are separated by an unpainted liminal space. Optically the unpainted center of the vessel appears to pop forward spatially against the painted frieze. The L-shaped motifs may seem like simplifications of the stepped motifs painted in other liminal-space designs.

Design strategies: tessellated isomers, liminal-space isomers
Optical phenomena: figure–ground spatial reversals, border-contrast phenomena, law of simplicity

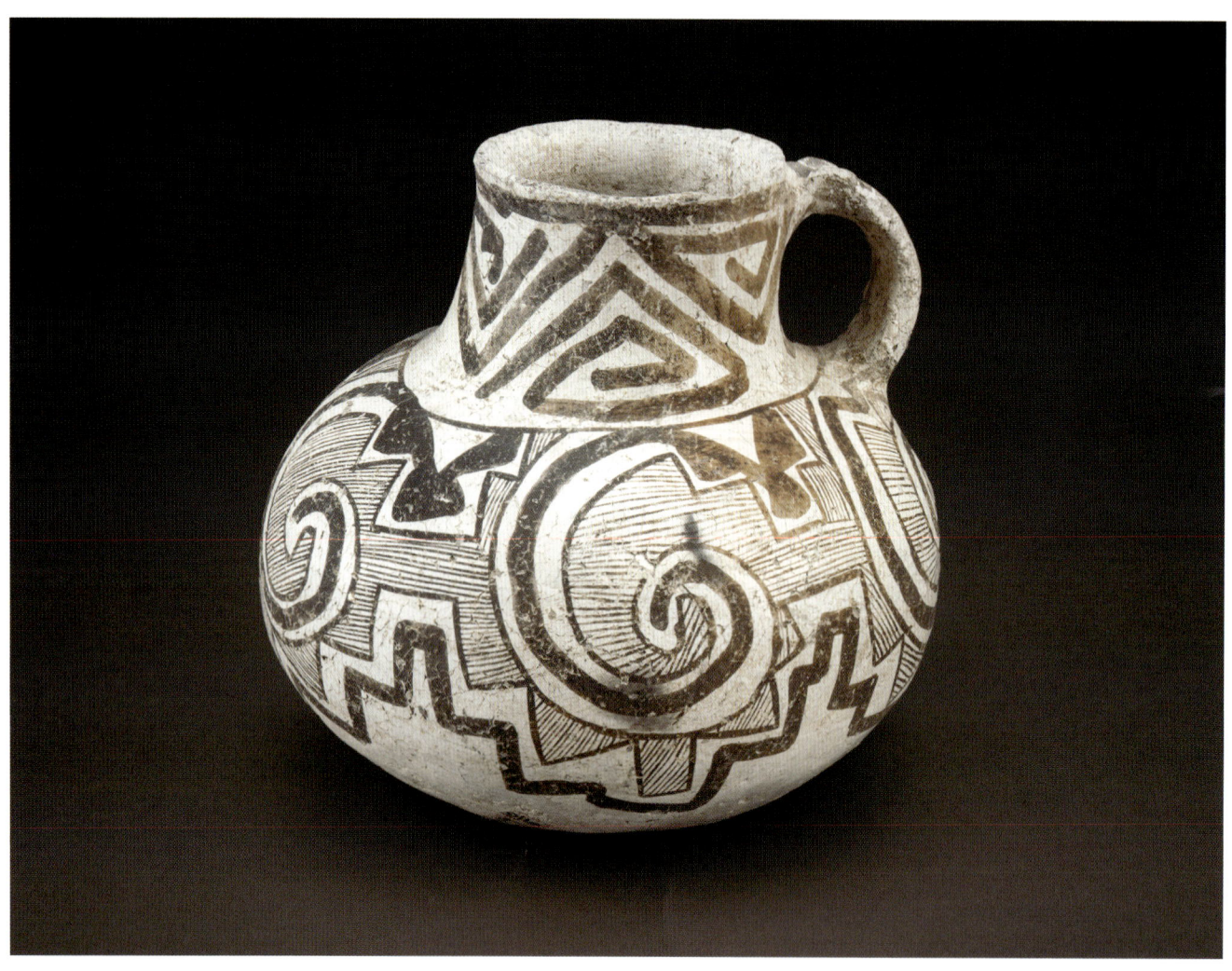

PLATE 35. TULAROSA BLACK-ON-WHITE PITCHER
1100–1250 CE, 6 ¾ × 7 IN. DIA., MIAC/LOA 19720

The motifs painted on this pitcher combine curvilinear spirals painted on the body with rectilinear spirals produced on the neck. It appears that an experienced potter produced the solid and hachured shapes on the body of the vessel, but an inexperienced painter added upper and lower framing elements that do not carefully follow the hachured shapes.

Design strategies: liminal-space isomers, tessellated isomers, painted-and-unpainted isomers
Optical phenomena: figure–ground spatial reversals, border-contrast phenomena, law of simplicity

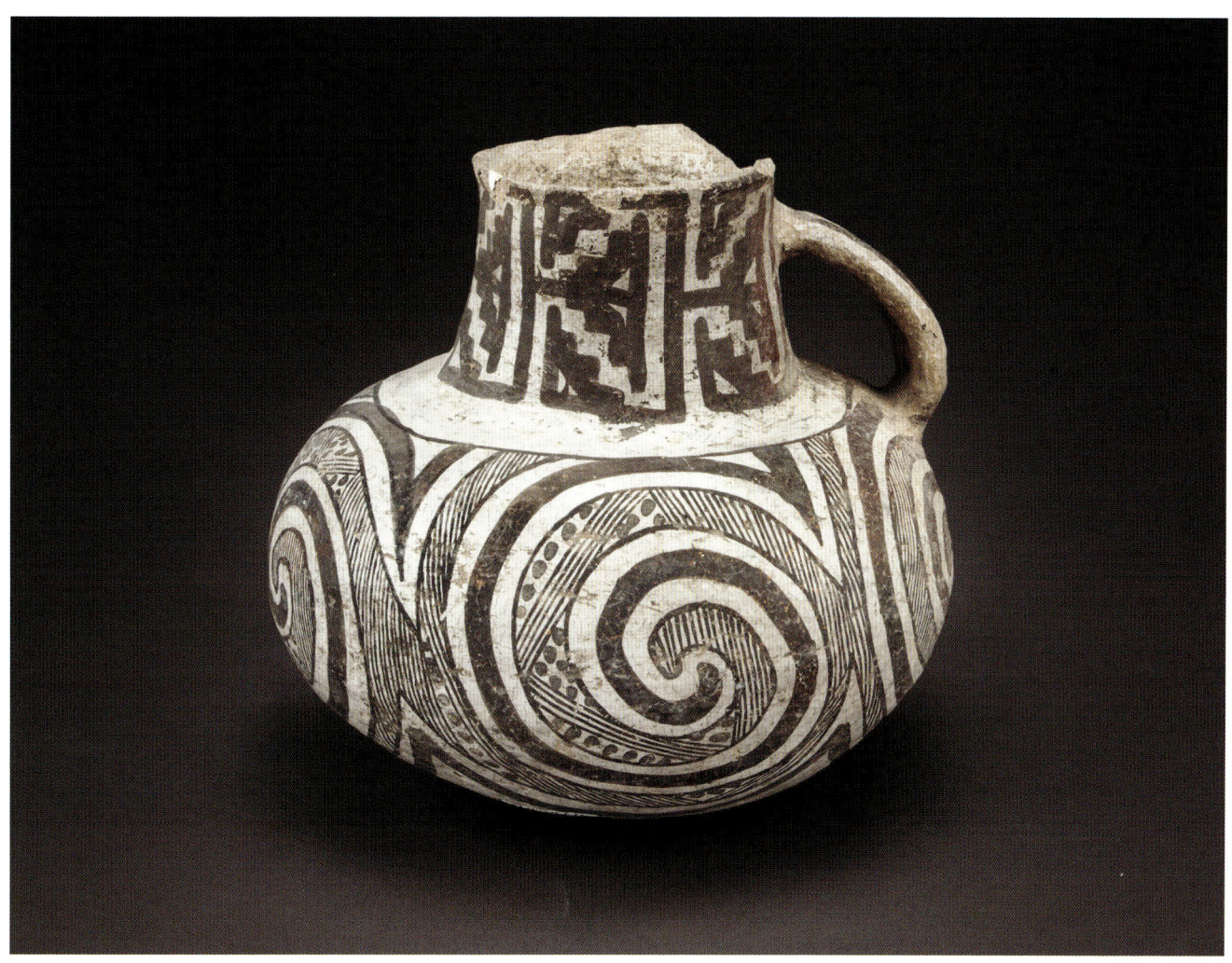

PLATE 36. TULAROSA BLACK-ON-WHITE PITCHER
1125–1250 CE, 6⅛ × 6⅞ IN. DIA., MIAC/LOA 11478

The frieze on the neck of this jar presents a tessellated motif that includes lock and key segments that mesh seamlessly. The design frieze on the body of the vessel presents solid and hachured spirals separated by unpainted liminal spaces. The preponderance of painted areas on the pitcher make the spirals difficult to interpret as reversible motifs, but the design is dominated by the combination of solid spirals outlined with unpainted slip.

Design strategies: tessellated isomers, liminal-space isomers
Optical phenomena: figure–ground spatial reversals, border-contrast phenomena, law of simplicity

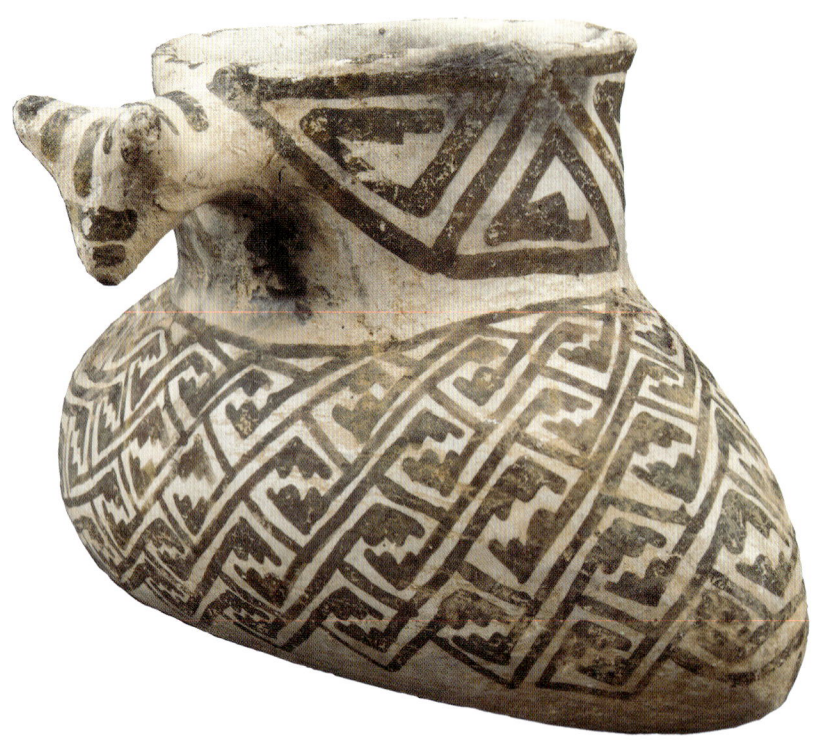

PLATE 37. TULAROSA BLACK-ON-WHITE JAR WITH EFFIGY HANDLE
1100–1250 CE, 4 3/16 × 6 5/8 IN. DIA., MIAC/LOA 19722/11

This pitcher, with a small handle in the form of an animal effigy, presents two friezes of abstracted spirals ending in stepped elements. The neck of the jar displays triangular spirals ending in stepped forms while the lower frieze presents interconnected pairs of stepped motifs that tessellate into long friezes. This endlessly repeated design can be understood as painted forms representing positive motifs, or the unpainted, liminal spaces can be interpreted as the positive image. Take your pick.

Design strategies: liminal-space isomers, tessellated isomers
Optical phenomena: figure–ground spatial reversals, border-contrast phenomena, law of simplicity

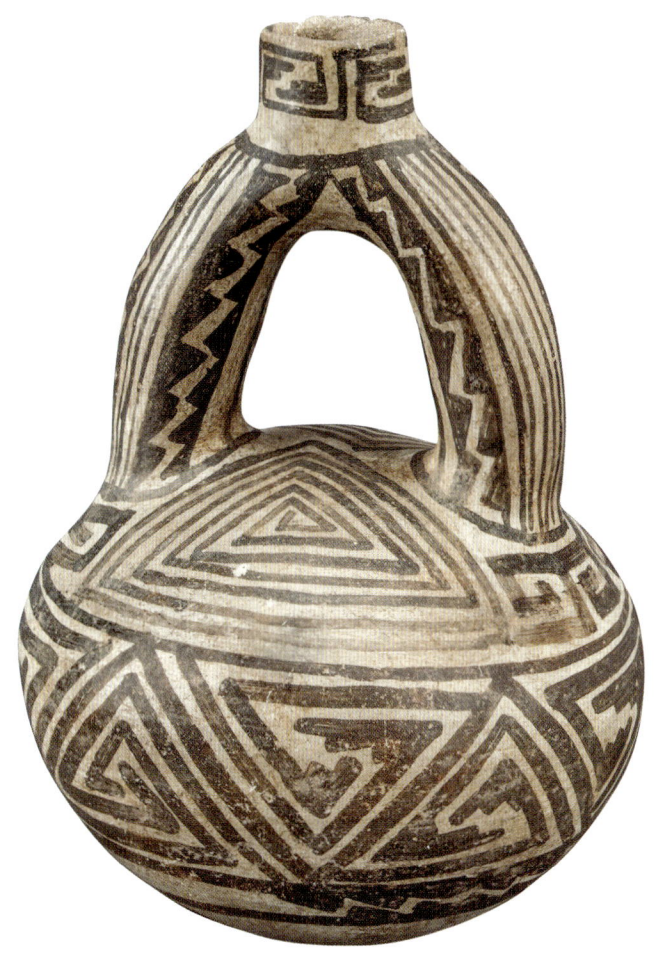

PLATE 38. KLAGETOH BLACK-ON-WHITE CANTEEN

1125–1300 CE, 6 ¾ × 6 ⅛ IN. DIA., John and Linda Comstock
and the Abigail Van Fleck Charitable Trust, MIAC/LOA 43341

The unpainted liminal spaces between repeated triangular forms on the double spouts of this canteen reverse to become a dominant image empowered by border-contrast phenomena. Similarly, the triangular spirals painted as a frieze on the body tessellate around the vessel and end with stepped elements at the center of these spirals. This concept worked well until the artist ran out of room and eliminated the stepped elements on the motifs to the left. This mistake reveals that the spirals were painted from the exterior to the interior of the motifs.

Design strategies: liminal-space isomers, tessellated isomers
Optical phenomena: figure–ground spatial reversals, border-contrast phenomena,
law of simplicity

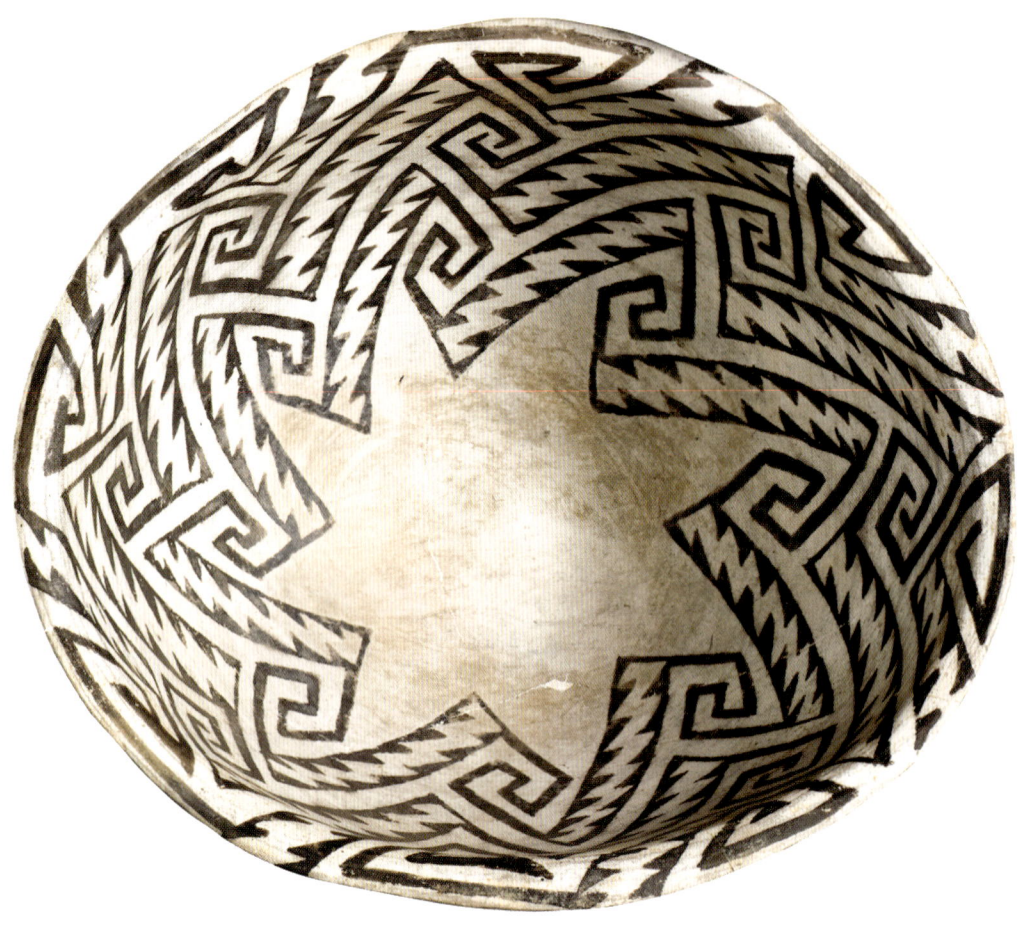

PLATE 39. FLAGSTAFF BLACK-ON-WHITE BOWL
1150–1200 CE, 5 ⅞ × 11 IN. DIA., MNA A10990

The painting on this bowl presents zigzag motifs ending with stepped elements incorporating Z-shaped elements. Multiple zigzag elements energize the design frieze with border-contrast phenomena. The painted frieze defines an eight-pointed star in the center of the bowl. The calmness of the central star foils the frenetic visual activity of the painted design frieze.

Design strategies: liminal-space isomers, incomplete-element isomers
Optical phenomena: figure–ground spatial reversals, border-contrast phenomena, law of simplicity

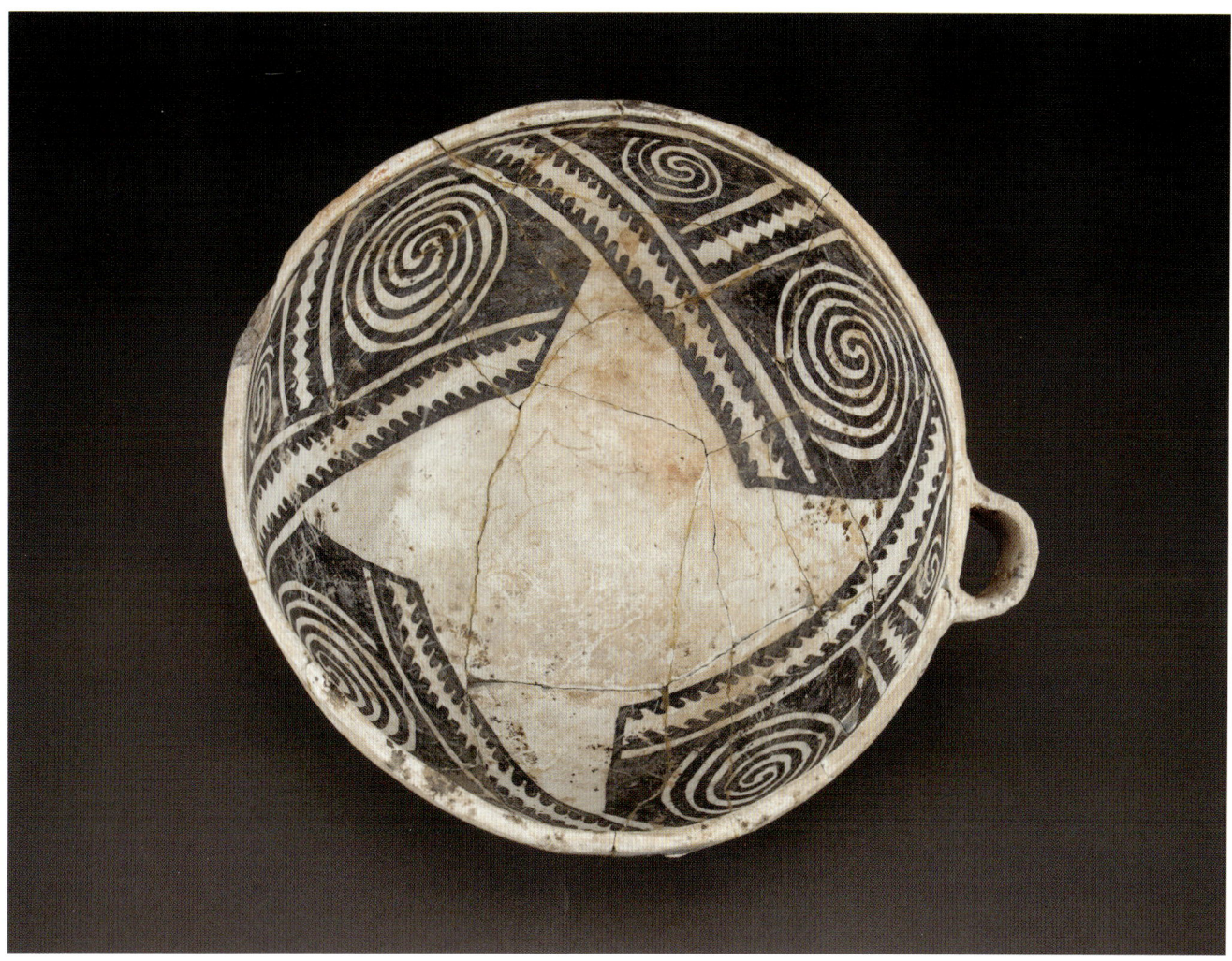

PLATE 40. TUSAYAN BLACK-ON-WHITE BOWL
1200–1300 CE, 3 15/16 × 8 IN. DIA., MIAC/LOA 47394

The four painted quadrants of the design on this bowl produce a star motif in the center of the vessel, an image that dominates the design. Each quadrant contains two interlocked spirals separated by a liminal space. The ticked forms allude to basketry textures and create border-contrast phenomena through dynamic zigzags. Perceptually the design flips between painted and unpainted elements, and between the star form and painted friezes.

Design strategies: liminal-space isomers
Optical phenomena: figure–ground spatial reversals, border-contrast phenomena, law of simplicity

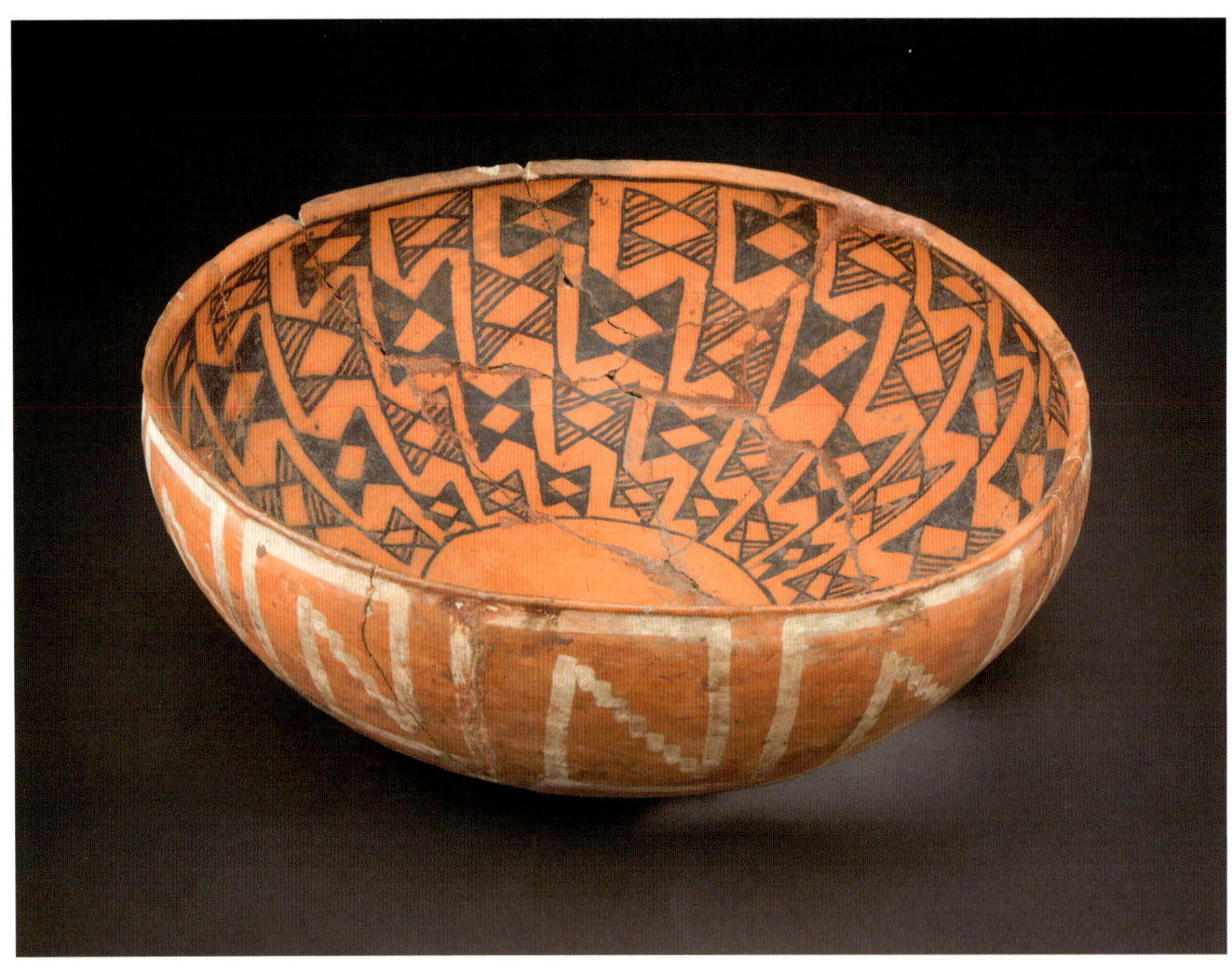

PLATE 41. ST. JOHNS POLYCHROME BOWL
1150–1300 CE, 4 ⅝ × 11 9/16 IN. DIA., MIAC/LOA 8764/11

The interior design of this bowl presents alternating patterns of solid and hachured shapes, all painted within Z-shaped outlines. The unpainted areas create meandering liminal spaces radiating out from the center of the bowl. The stepped motifs on the exterior were created by two sets of Z-shaped lines; one set of Zs defines the outline while another Z connects the outlines.

Design strategies: liminal-space isomers, tessellated isomers
Optical phenomena: figure–ground spatial reversals, border-contrast phenomena, law of simplicity

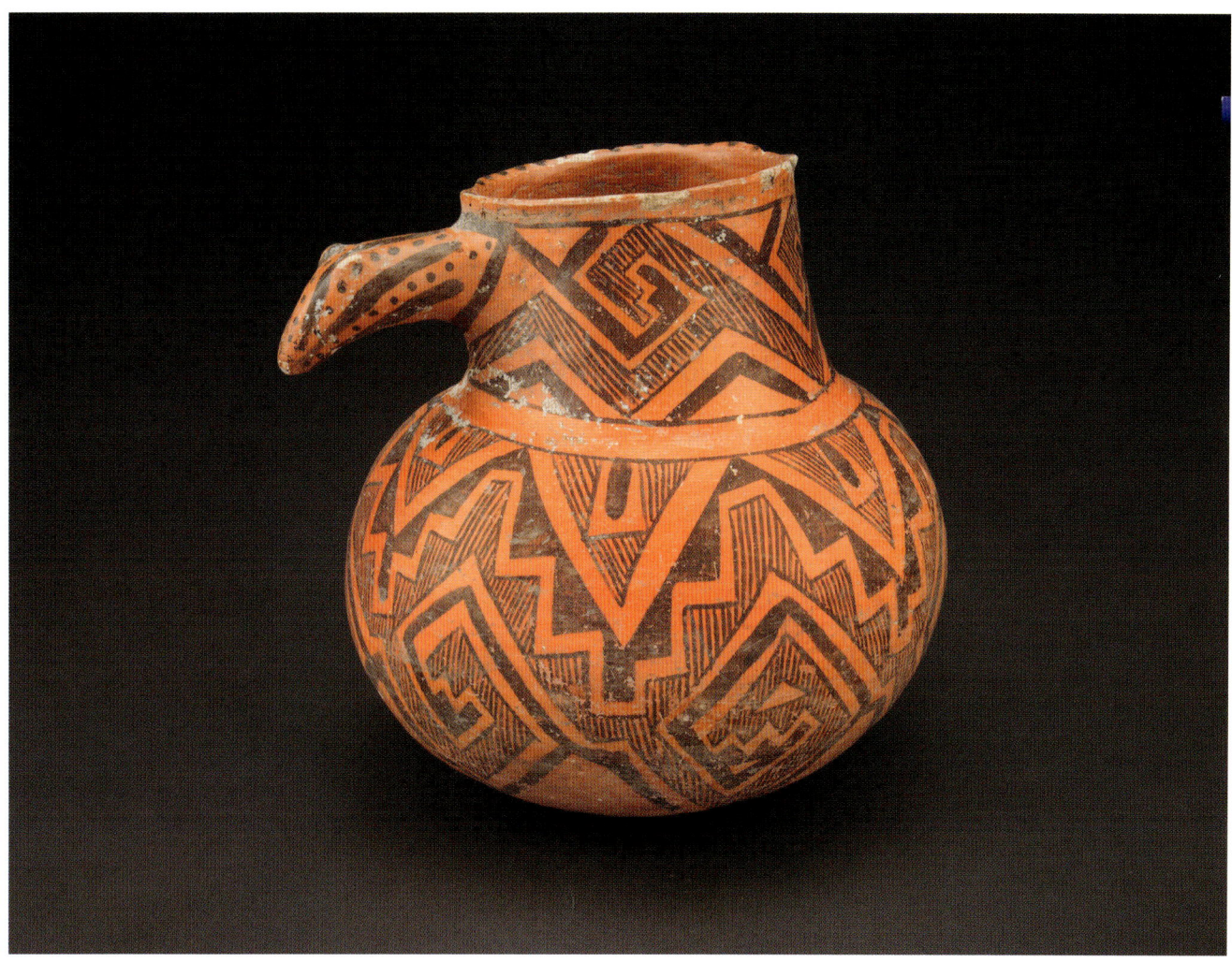

PLATE 42. ST. JOHNS BLACK-ON-RED PITCHER

1150–1300 CE, 6 ½ × 7 IN. DIA., Honorable Dan H. McMillan Collection, MIAC/LOA 8871/11

The frieze painted on the body of this vessel presents interlocked, rectilinear spirals composed of solid and hatchured elements. The triangular spaces between these spirals at the juncture of the body and neck are filled with stepped elements also painted as solid and hachured elements. The artist painted the frieze on the neck also as interlocked, rectilinear spirals composed of solid and hatchured elements. The handle appears as an animal effigy in the shape of a head.

Design Strategies: liminal-space isomers, tessellated isomers
Optical phenomena: figure–ground spatial reversals, border-contrast phenomena

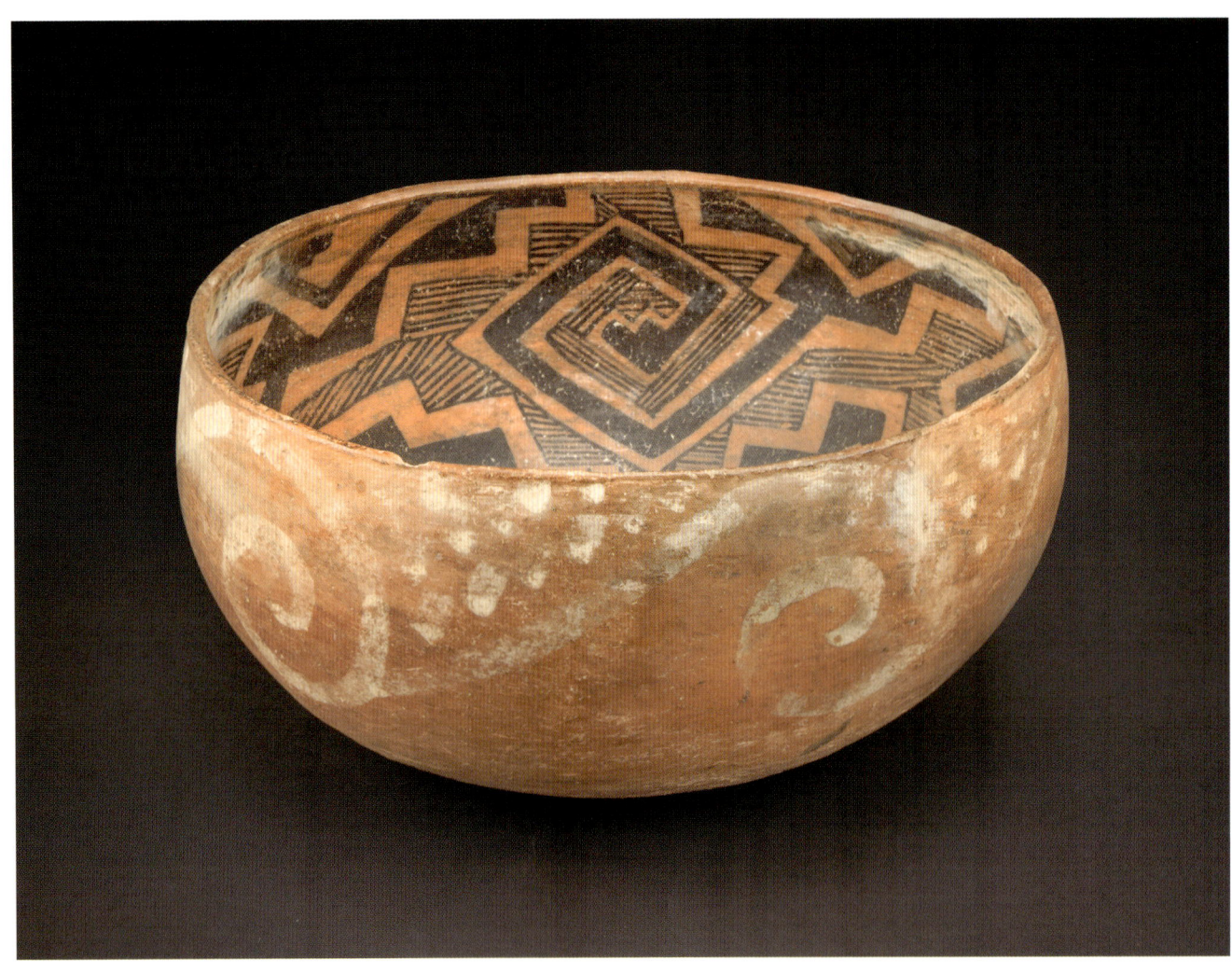

PLATE 43. ST. JOHNS POLYCHROME BOWL
1150–1300 CE, 5 ¾ × 10 ¾ IN. DIA., MIAC/LOA 45818

This St. Johns Polychrome bowl combines rectilinear spirals with stepped motifs on the interior of the bowl. The close hachures and solid elements combine into positive spaces, but these dark motifs cause the red slip to pop spatially against the painted areas. On the exterior, the interlocked dual spirals form a tessellated frieze painted in white kaolin.

Design strategies: liminal-space isomers, tessellated isomers
Optical phenomena: figure–ground spatial reversals, border-contrast phenomena, law of simplicity

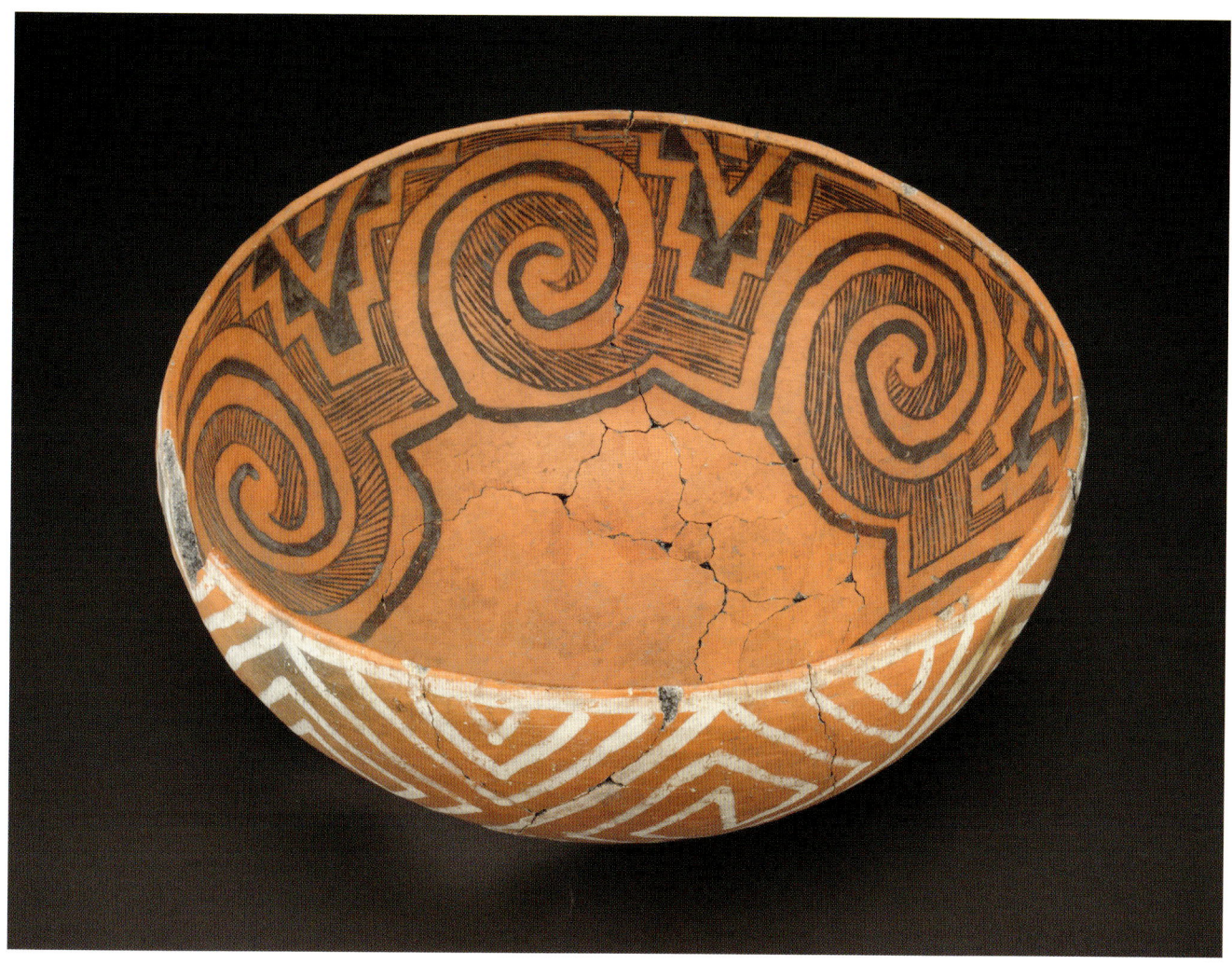

PLATE 44. ST. JOHNS POLYCHROME BOWL

1150–1300 CE, 5 ½ × 12 IN. DIA., MIAC/LOA 46361/11, LA 4988,
Collections from the Gila National Forest at MIAC

Liminal-space isomers are depicted on this bowl as curvilinear spirals on the interior of the vessel, and as rectilinear spirals on the exterior. The hachured shapes on the interior of this bowl link spirals together. The triangular areas between spirals are filled with stepped motifs. On the exterior the frieze defines rectilinear spirals with chevron spacers. Optically the interior presents a reversible figure-and-ground relationship, while the fine white lines on the exterior appear spatially fixed in front of the slip.

Design strategies: liminal-space isomers, tessellated isomers
Optical phenomena: figure–ground spatial reversals, border-contrast phenomena, law of simplicity

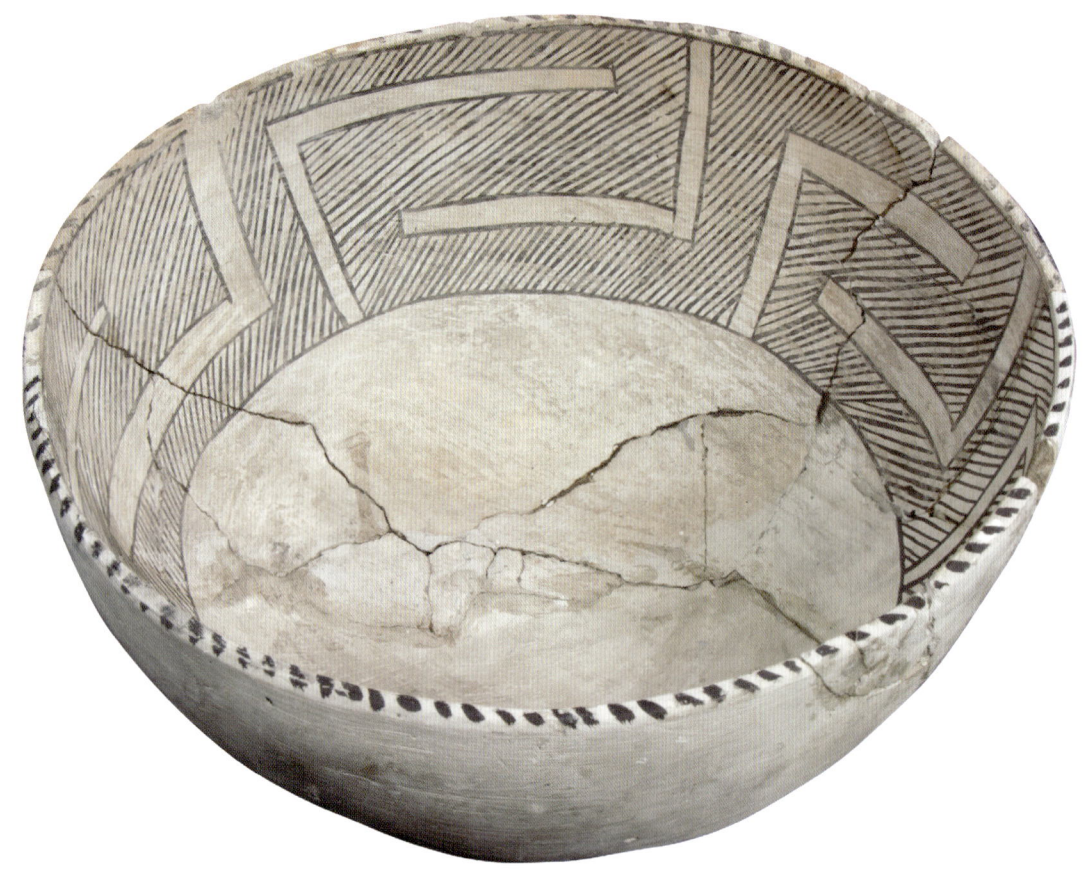

PLATE 47. McELMO BLACK-ON-WHITE BOWL
1200–1300 CE, 4 ½ × 8 ½ IN. DIA., UCB 00141

The hachured design frieze on this bowl is the liminal space separating pairs of unpainted, L-shaped isomers. Optically these unpainted, negative forms emerge as the intended figures in front of the painted liminal space. This spatial illusion is accentuated by border-contrast phenomena where the diagonal hachures intersect with the unpainted isomers.

Design strategies: liminal-space isomers
Optical phenomena: figure–ground spatial reversals, border-contrast phenomena, law of simplicity, size-based optical illusion

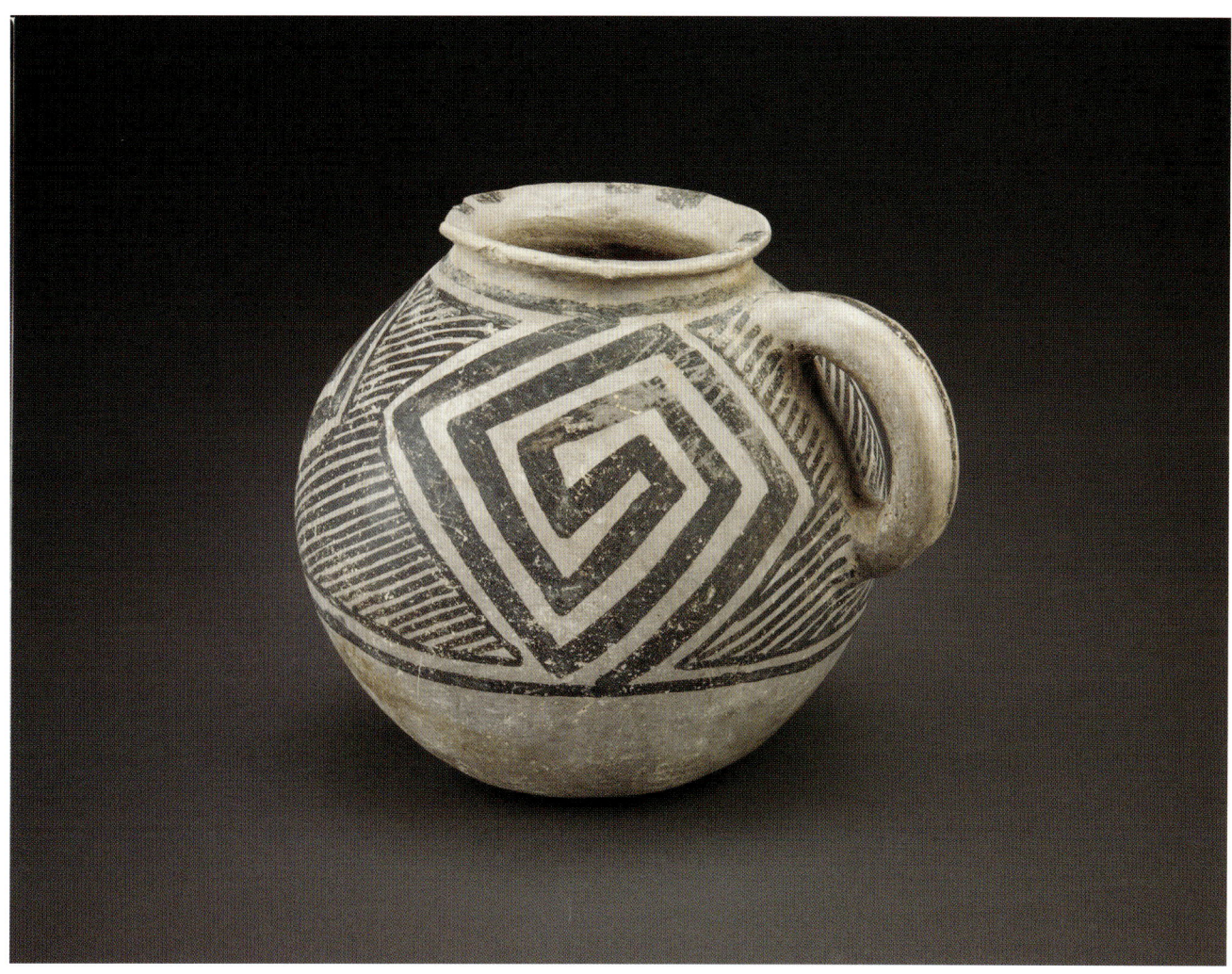

PLATE 48. MESA VERDE BLACK-ON-WHITE MUG
1200–1300 CE, 4 ½ × 5 IN. DIA., MIAC/LOA 43357

As the two painted lines of this interlocked spiral reach the center of the motif on this mug, a Z-shaped line connects the two into a unified emblem. The equal width of painted and liminal spaces creates ambiguous spatial situations allowing the motif to be perceived as both a black-on-white and a white-on-black design. The hachured areas between spiral motifs cause the spiral motifs to act as background for the spiral emblem.

Design strategies: liminal-space isomers, painted-and-unpainted isomers
Optical phenomena: figure–ground spatial reversals, border-contrast phenomena, law of simplicity, size–based optical reversals

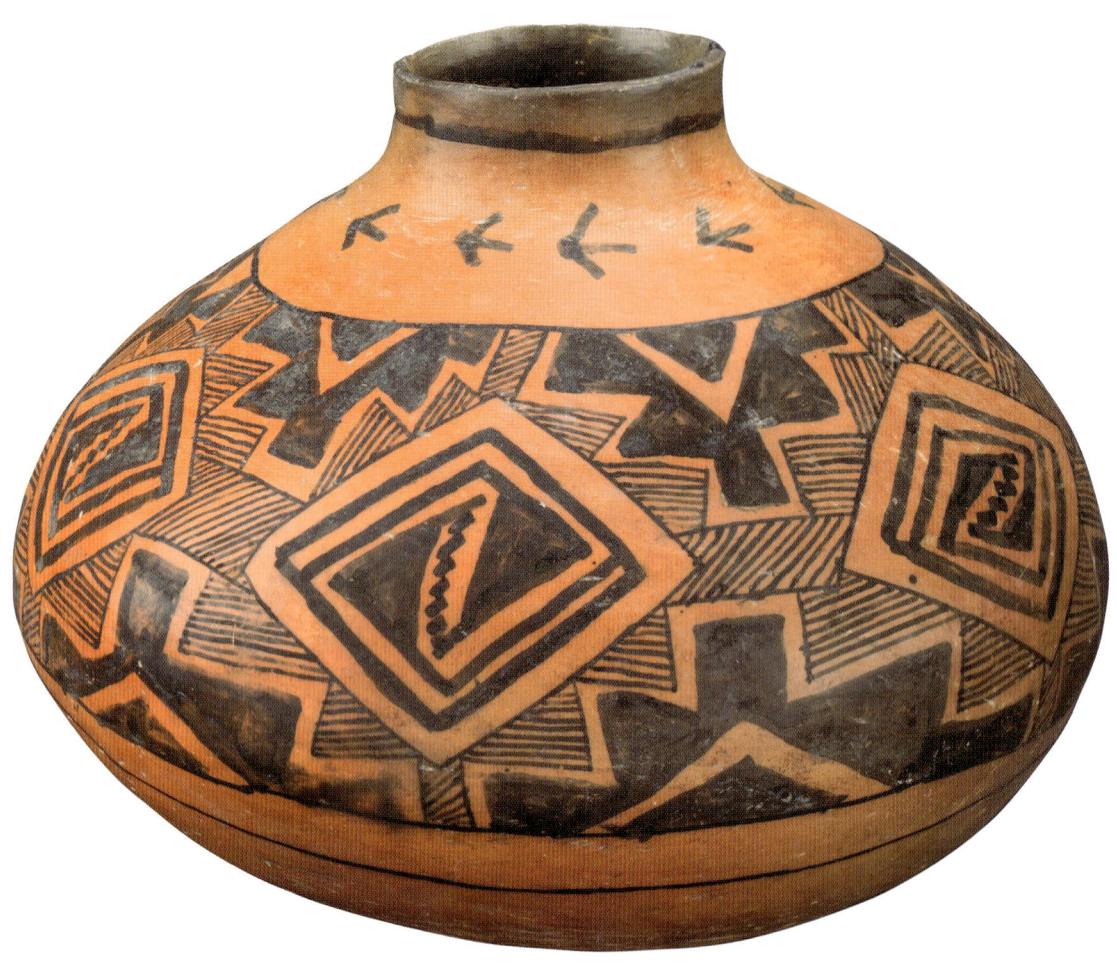

PLATE 49. PINEDALE BLACK-ON-RED JAR
1275–1325 CE, 9 ⅝ × 10 IN. DIA., MIAC/LOA 8169

The design frieze on this jar repeats a version of a St. Johns Polychrome composition. Created as the painting of liminal-space isomers comes to a close, the sloppy painting appears as a caricature of the earlier style. The diamond medallions have lost most of their elegance, and the vessel seems awkwardly molded.

Design strategies: liminal-space isomers
Optical phenomena: figure–ground spatial reversals, border-contrast phenomena, tessellated isomers, law of simplicity

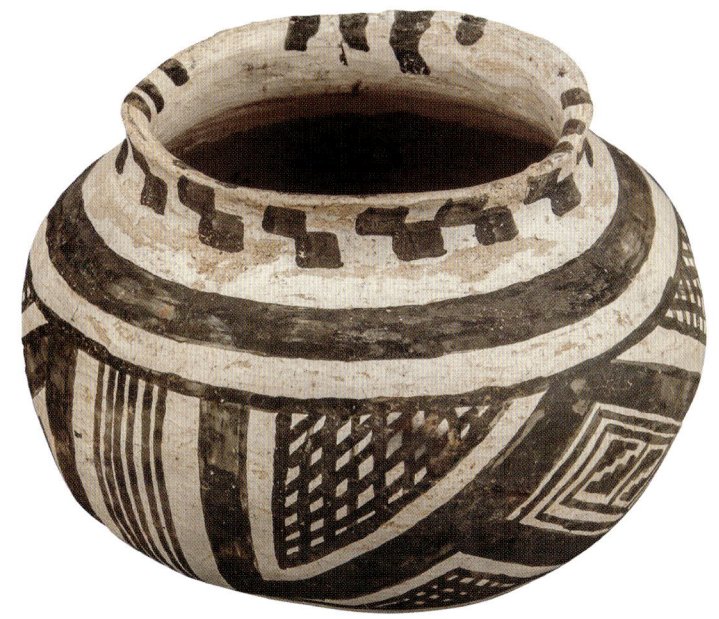

PLATE 50. PINEDALE BLACK-ON-WHITE JAR
1250–1325 CE, 3 ½ × 4 ⅞ IN. DIA., Honorable Dan H. McMillan Collection, MIAC/LOA 21171

The interlocked stepped motifs on this Pinedale bowl appear as minor elements, almost as afterthoughts against overly bold framing lines. This design alludes to the impending disappearance of isomeric designs and the rise of asymmetrical designs early in the fourteenth century.

Design strategies: painted-and-unpainted isomers, tessellated isomers, incomplete-element isomers

Optical phenomena: figure–ground spatial reversals, border-contrast phenomena

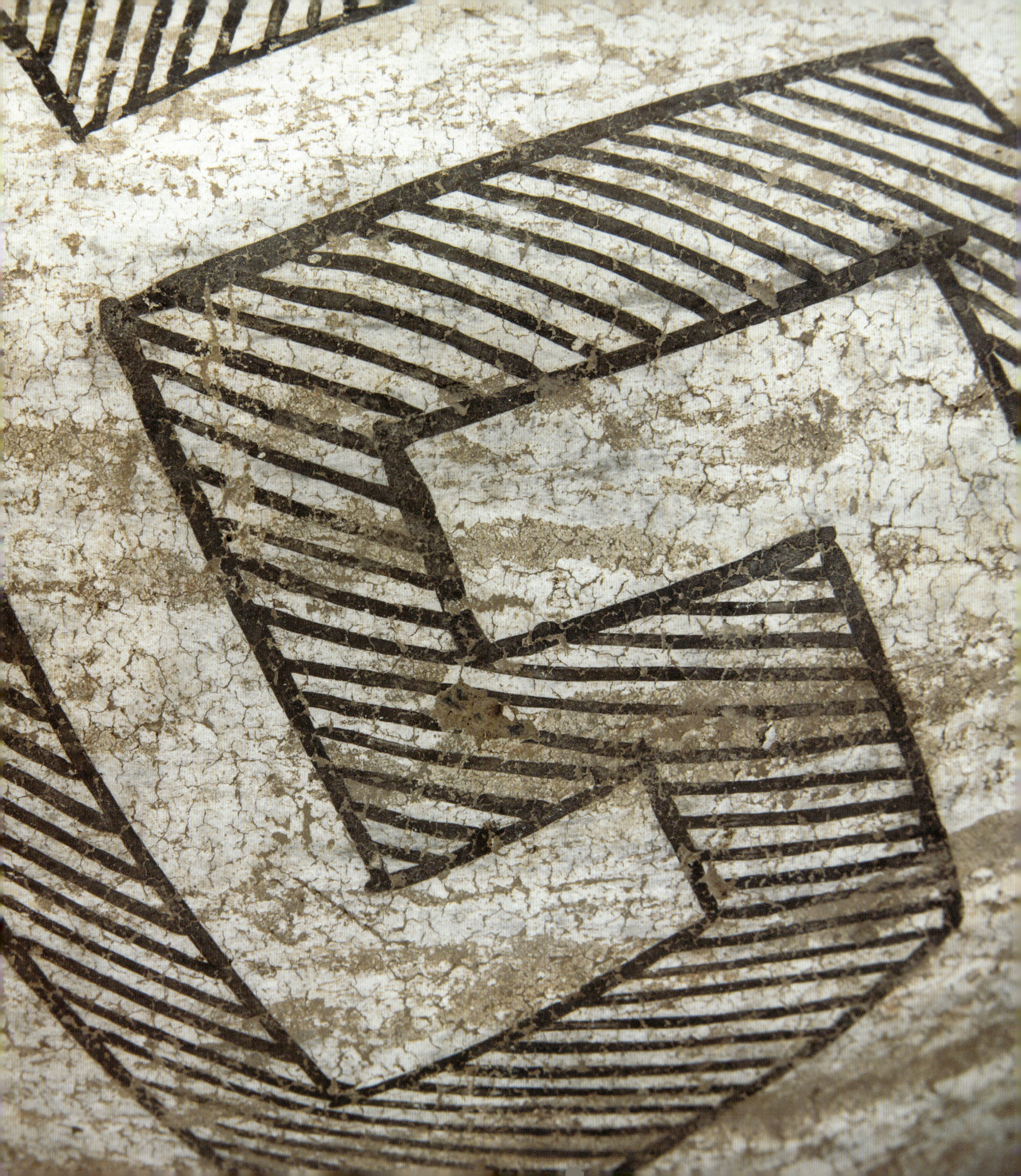

FURTHER READING

Albers, Josef
1971 *Interaction of Color* (first paperback). New Haven, CT: Yale University Press.

Armstrong, Robert Plant
1971 *The Affecting Presence: An Essay in Humanistic Anthropology.*
Urbana: University of Illinois Press.

Bloomer, Carolyn M.
1976 *Principles of Visual Perception.* New York: Van Nostrand Reinhold Co.

Brody, J. J.
1991 *Anasazi and Pueblo Painting.* Albuquerque: University of New Mexico Press.

Brody, J. J., and Rina Swentzell
1996 *To Touch the Past: The Painted Pottery of the Mimbres People.*
New York: Hudson Hills Press.

Bunzel, Ruth
1972 *The Pueblo Potter: A Study of Creative Imagination in Primitive Art.* New York:
Dover Publications. Originally published 1929, Contributions to Anthropology, no. 8,
Columbia University, New York.

Cornsweet, Tom N.
1970 *Visual Perception.* New York: Academic Press.

Dittert, Alfred E., Jr., and Fred Plog
1980 *Generations in Clay: Pueblo Pottery of the American Southwest.*
Flagstaff, AZ: Northland.

Donald, Merlin
1991 *Origins of the Modern Mind: Three Stages in the Evolution of Culture and Cognition.*
Cambridge: Harvard University Press.

Edwards, Betty
1999 *The New Drawing on the Right Side of the Brain.* New York: Tarcher.

Hucko, Bruce
1999 *Art on the Rocks: Rock Art of the Southwest.* Mariposa, CA: Sierra Press.

Kuhn, Thomas S.
1977 *The Essential Tension: Selected Studies in Scientific Tradition and Change.*
Chicago: University of Chicago Press.

Lakoff, George, and Mark Johnson
1980   *Metaphors We Live By*. Chicago: University of Chicago Press.

Lauer, David A., and Stephen Pentak
2007   *Design Basics*. Belmont, CA: Wadsworth.

Lekson, Stephen H., ed.
2006   *The Archaeology of Chaco Canyon: An Eleventh-Century Pueblo Regional Center*. Santa Fe, NM: School of American Research Press.

Malville, J. McKim, and Claudia Putnam
1989   *Prehistoric Astronomy in the Southwest*. Boulder, CO: Johnson Books.

Martin, Paul Sidney, and Fred Plog
1973   *The Archaeology of Arizona: A Study of the Southwest Region*. Garden City, NY: Doubleday.

Morris, Earl H.
1927   *The Beginnings of Pottery Making in the San Juan Area: Unfired Prototypes and Wares of the Earliest Ceramic Period*. New York: American Museum of Natural History

Moulard, Barbara L.
2002   *Re-creating the Word: Painted Ceramics of the Prehistoric Southwest*. Santa Fe, NM: Schenck Southwest Publishing.

Norenzayan, Ara
2013   *Big Gods: How Religion Transformed Cooperation and Conflict*. Princeton, NJ: Princeton University Press.

Ortman, Scott G.
2000   Conceptual Metaphor in the Archaeological Record: Methods and an Example from the American Southwest. *American Antiquity* 65(4):613–45.

2012   *Winds from the North: Tewa Origins and Historical Anthropology*. Salt Lake City: University of Utah Press.

Parsons, Elsie Clews
1994[1926]   *Tewa Tales*. Tucson: University of Arizona Press.

Peckham, Stewart
1990   *From This Earth: The Ancient Art of Pueblo Pottery*. Santa Fe: Museum of New Mexico Press.

Pierce, Christopher
2005   Reverse Engineering the Ceramic Cooking Pot: Cost and Performance Properties of Plain and Textured Vessels. *Journal of Archaeological Method and Theory* June 2005 12(2): 117–157. https://doi.org/10.1007/s10816-005-5665-5.

Seckel, Al
2004   *Masters of Deception: Escher, Dalí and the Artists of Optical Illusion.* New York: Sterling.

Sekaquaptewa, Emory, Kenneth C. Hill, and Dorothy K. Washburn
2015   *Hopi Katsina Songs.* Lincoln: University of Nebraska Press.

Sofaer, Anna, and contributors to the Solstice Project
2008   *Chaco Astronomy: An Ancient American Cosmology.*
Santa Fe, NM: Ocean Tree Books.

Stephens, Pam, and Jim McNeil
2001   *Tessellations: The History and Making of Symmetrical Designs.*
Carpinteria, CA: Crystal Productions.

Swentzell, Rina
1990   Pueblo Space, Form and Mythology. In *Pueblo Style and Regional Architecture,* edited by N. C. Markovich, W. F. E. Preiser, and F. G. Sturm, pp. 23–30. New York: Van Nostrand Reinhold Co.

Traugott, Joseph
2012   *New Mexico Art Through Time: Prehistory to the Present.*
Santa Fe: Museum of New Mexico Press.

Van Dyke, Ruth M.
2008   *The Chaco Experience: Landscape and Ideology at the Center Place.*
Santa Fe, NM: School for Advanced Research Press.

White, Alex W.
2002   *The Elements of Graphic Design.* New York: Allworth Press.

Wilson, C. Dean, and Eric Blinman
1995   Ceramic Types of the Mesa Verde Region. In *Archaeological Pottery of Colorado: Ceramic Clues to the Prehistoric and Protohistoric Lives of the State's Native Peoples,* edited by R. H. Brunswig Jr., B. Bradley, and S. Chandler, pp. 33–64. Occasional Papers, no. 2. Colorado Council of Professional Archaeologists, Denver.

Young, M. Jane
1988   *Signs from the Ancestors.* Albuquerque: University of New Mexico Press.

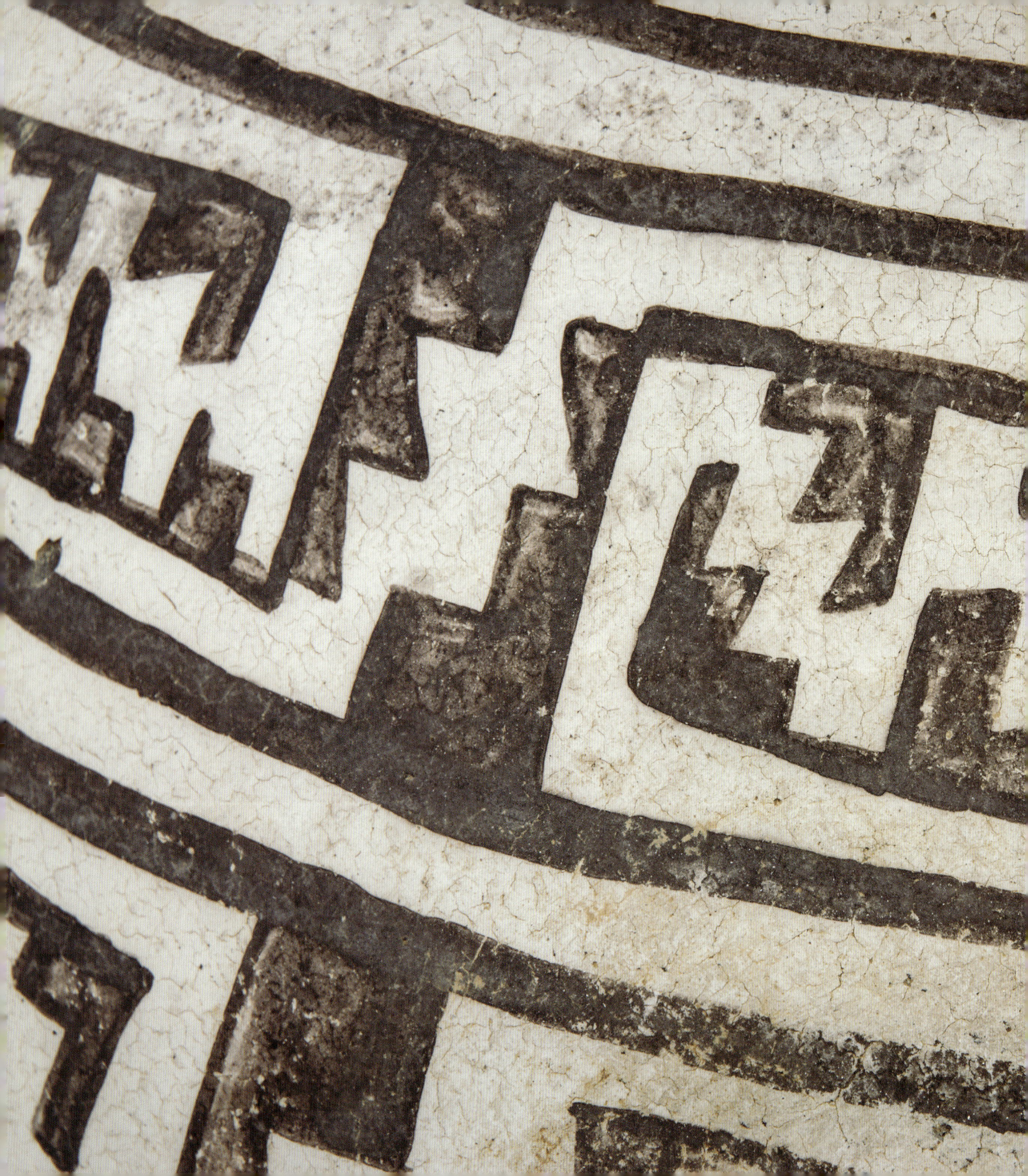

ACKNOWLEDGMENTS

This book would not have been possible without creative support from the Museum of New Mexico Press: Anna Gallegos, Lisa Pacheco, and David Skolkin. In addition, Beth Hadas carefully edited our manuscript and smoothed out the awkward parts. Michael Motley transformed our draft into an elegant synthesis of art and anthropology. MNMP produces beautiful books that bring art, culture, and scholarship from the American Southwest to broad audiences of book lovers.

We have discussed our thoughts on Pueblo pottery designs and their cultural implications with friends and colleagues, including artist Nick Abdalla; Bruce Bernstein, Pueblo of Pojoaque; Eric Blinman and C. Dean Wilson, Office of Archaeological Studies; J.J. Brody; Catherine Cameron, Gerardo Gutierrez, and Arthur Joyce, University of Colorado Boulder; Tony Chavarria and Maxine McBrinn, Museum of Indian Arts and Culture; Linda S. Cordell; Severin Fowles, Barnard College and Columbia University; Mary Jebsen; Steve Lekson, University of Colorado Museum of Natural History; Signa Larralde, Bureau of Land Management; Diana F. Pardue, Heard Museum; Elysia Poon, Indian Arts Research Center, School for Advanced Research; Landis Smith, Conservation, Museum Resources Division; and Porter Swentzel, Institute of American Indian Arts.

We especially wish to thank Peter Briggs, Texas Tech University Museum; Douglas H. Erwin, National Museum of Natural History; and Bill Gilbert, Department of Art and Art History, University of New Mexico, for many helpful comments on previous versions of the text.

Thanks to Cindy Abel Morris, Center for Southwest Research; Melissa Lawton, History Colorado; David A. Phillips and Diane Tyink, Maxwell Museum of Anthropology; Diane Bird, Allison Colborne, and Valerie Verzuh, Museum of Indian Arts and Culture/Laboratory of Anthropology; Shawn San Roman and Anthony Thibodeau, Museum of Northern Arizona; Tammy Legler, New Mexico Museum of Mining; Mark Stiger, Western State Colorado University; and Christina Cain, University of Colorado Museum of Natural History.

The photographers who worked on this project made it possible to bring these works of art to you. Blair Clark photographed the collections at the Museum of Indian Arts and Culture and the Maxwell Museum, Emma Noffsinger at the University of Colorado Museum of Natural History, and Jennifer Day at the School for Advanced Research. In addition, Ronald Costell and Laurie Webster lent their own photographs.

Finally, we thank our respective spouses, Gigi Schwartz and Laurel Wallace, for putting up with us as we pursued this lengthy project. We are truly grateful.

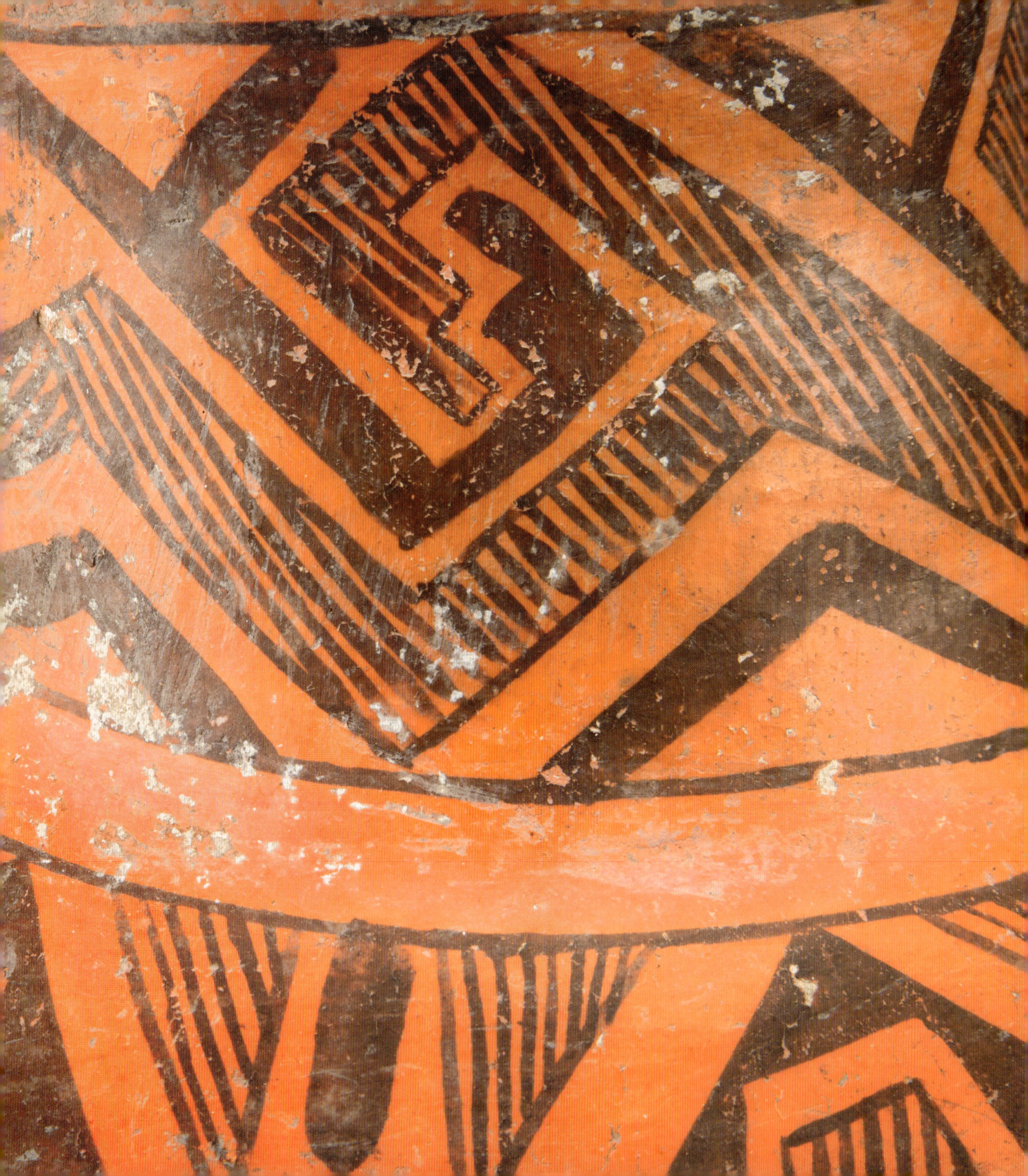

INDEX

Page numbers in *italics* refer to illustrations.

aerial perspective, 18, *19*
affecting presence, 14, 20
afterimages, 14, 73
agriculture, 13, 49–50, 58–59, 69–70
Albers, Josef, 14
Allen Canyon, Utah, *48*, 49
American Southwest, 11, 25, 43, 47, 75, 77
Ancestral Pueblo: architecture, 66, *68*; art, 76; artists, 22, 25, 26, 27, 46; communities, 74; culture, 63, 65; design, 18, 21, 22, 23, 27, 31, 66, 76; kivas, 57; life, 49, 65; people, 12, 52, 58, 59, 63, 69, 73; potters, 15, 52, 53, 76, 77; pottery, 7, 11, 12, 13, 14, 15, 17, 18, 27, *28*, 41, 70, 75; ritual, 73; society, 13, 71, 73, 77; weavers, 53; world, 38, 51, 75
architecture, 66, *67*, *68*, 74–76. *See also* kivas
Armstrong, Robert Plant, 14
art, role of, 12, 73, 76
astronomical events, 47, 58–59, *60–62*, 63, 73
asymmetrical designs, 129

Basketmaker Period, 52, 57
basketry, 39, 46, 65; coiled, 13, *48*, 49–50, 53, *54–56*, 58, 98–99; influences pottery forms/designs, 13, 49–53, *54–56*, 73, *98–99*, 119; and kivas, *57*, 58, 59; and links to pottery, 58, 63; plaited, *51*, 52, 53, 55, 81

beans, 13, 49–50, 52
Black-on-red pottery: Pinedale jars, *38, 128*; Puerco bowl, *34–35, 45*, 68, *108*; St. Johns pitcher, *45, 121*
Black-on-white pottery: Black Mesa bowls, *85, 102*; Chuska bowl, *29, 101*; Cortez effigy pitcher, *124*; Dogoszhi jars, *106–7*; Escavada bowls, *28*, 34, 35, *95*; Escavada jar, *46–47, 96*; Flagstaff bowls, *36–37, 112, 118*; Kana-a pitcher, *24*, 25, *50–51*; Kayenta jar, 43; Kiatuthlana gourd-shaped jar, 34, *82*; Kiatuthlana/Red Mesa bowl, 44, *81*; Klagetoh canteen, 31, *117*; La Plata bowl, *26*; Leupp jar, 34, *38, 110*, 111; Mancos bowl, 28, *36, 125*; Mangas bowl, 38, *55, 80*; Newcomb bowl, 36, *90*; Pinedale jars, 38, *39, 129*; Puerco bowl, 44; Red Mesa bowl, *84*; Red Mesa pitcher, 36, 44, *83*; Reserve bowl, 26, 27, *45*; Snowflake jar, 57; Socorro bowl, *88*; Tusayan/Betatakin bowls, 31, 56, 72, *98–99*; Tusayan bowls, 21, *103, 119*; Walnut jar, *100*. *See also* Gallup pottery; McElmo pottery; Mesa Verde pottery; Mimbres pottery; Tularosa pottery
Blinman, Eric, 13

Bloomer, Carolyn M., 17–18, 23
border-contrast phenomena: examples of, *19, 80–129*; explanation of, 19–20, 22, 25, 27, 30, 36–37, 39, 44, 46, 73, 75
Brody, J. J., 11
Bunzel, Ruth, 75

Chaco Canyon (New Mexico), 12, 17, 46, 59–61, *62–63*, 71, 74
checkerboard motif, 20, 31–33, 41, 56, 73, 89, *93*
Chetro Ketl (Chaco Canyon), 17
chevrons, 53, *58*, 87, *123*
Cibola region, 46
Classic times, 11
clothing, 52, 65
Cochiti Pueblo (New Mexico), *64*, 65
Colorado Plateau, 52
containers: baskets as, 13, *48*, 49–52; of clay, 13, 49–52; and kiva murals, 57; of organic materials, *48*, 49–52
cooking vessels, 13, 49, 50–51, 52
Cornsweet illusion, 20
Cornsweet, Tom, 20
corrugated vessels, *51*, 52, 55
cultural: context, 13–15, 20, 63, 65, 73; knowledge, 22, *23*, 71; metaphor, 55; significance, 11, 49, 76–77

Dance, Pueblo of Cochiti, NM (Lummis), *64*, 65

dualities, concept of, 11, 14–15, 73–74. *See also* isomeric design: perceptual dualities of

economic activity, 59, 74–75
Edwards, Betty, 27
effigy vessels, 66, *67*, *116*, *121*, *124*
Elements of Graphic Design, The (White), 21
Escher, M. C., 31

figure-and-ground relationships: ambiguous, 22, 74, *83*, *124*; examples of, *21–23*, *30*, *37*, *56*, *103*; explanation of, 17–18, 21–23, 25, 27, 36, 39, 46, 75
figure-and-ground reversals: examples of, 79, *80–129*; explanation of, 14–15, 22, 37, 44, 47, 73
firing process, 13, 17, 25–26, 49
food acquisition/preparation, 74. *See also* agriculture; cooking vessels
Four Corners Region, 12
frieze designs: examples of, *32*, *35*, *43*, *84–85*, *87*, *90*, *98–100*, *105*, *107*, *109*, *115–19*, *121–24*, *126*, *128*; explanation of, 20, 32, 35, 37, 39; in kiva murals, *58*, *59*; mimic basket designs, 55, *56*
From This Earth (Peckham), 17

Gallup, New Mexico, 16–17
Gallup pottery: bowls, *16*, *17*, *28*, *29*, *30*, *35*, *45*, *46*, *47*, *89*, *92*; jars, *29*, *32–33*, *35*, *93–94*, *97*; pitcher, *28*, *31*, *91*
gender divisions, 12, 74–76

gourds/gourd vessels, 13, 25, *34*, 49–51, 82
Grayware pottery, *50*
Great Pueblo Period, 12, 15, 25, *39*, 41, 46, 50–51, 57, 67, 69, 71, 73–74, 79
grid understructure, 26, *27*, *28–31*, *32*, 35–36, *38–39*, 52, 55, *56*

hachured elements, 26, *27*, *30*, 31, *32*, *35*, 36, 68, *87–89*, *91*, *93–94*, *97*, *101*, *106*, *108*, *114–15*, *120–23*, *126–27*
Hohokam region, 74
Holly House (Hovenweep), 63
Hovenweep National Monument (Colorado/Utah), 63
hunters and gatherers, 69

iconographic content, 76
iconology, 13–14, 74
incomplete-element isomers: examples of, *28*, *36–37*, *42*, *44*, *81*, *83*, *85*, *90*, *100*, *109*, *112*, *118*, *124–25*, *129*; explanation of, 27–28, 36–37, 39, 41, 68, 73
Interaction of Color (Albers), 14
isomeric design: changes in, 38–39; decline of, 38, *39*, 71, 129; emergence of, 13, 52–53, *54*, 70–71, 74; four strategies for, 27, *28*, 39, 41, *42*, 43, 74–75, 79; introduction to, 11–15; meanings of, 65, 73–74; perceptual dualities of, 27, *28*, 39, 73–74; popularity of, 68–69, 76; prototypes of, 25, 49–51, 53; significance of, 11, 49, 63, 65, 74–77

kaolin, 43, 57, *58*, *122*
katsinas, 70–71
kivas, 57, 74–75; ceremonies in, 71; murals in, *57–58*, *59*, *61*, *63*, 73; roofs of, 58, 59, 66; and spirit world, 65–67, 69

L-shaped elements, *35*, *37*, *94*, *113*, *126*
Lakoff, George, 14
law of simplicity: examples of, *20*, *81–90*, *92–96*, *98–101*, *103–9*, *111–20*, *122–28*; explanation of, 20–21, 25, 36–37, 39, 73
light-and-dark patterns/illusions: and basketry, *48*, *49*; examples of, *19*, *48*, *49*, *80*, *96*; explanation of, 11–12, 18–19, 21–22, 30, 75. *See also* sunlight and shadow
liminal-space isomers: examples of, *28*, *34–35*, *42*, *80–90*, *94–95*, *100–103*, *107–8*, *110–28*; explanation of, 27–28, 33, 35, 37–38, 41, 44, 68
Little Colorado drainage, 71
Lowry Ruin (Colorado), 57, 58
Lummis, Charles, *64*, 65

McElmo pottery: bowls, *28*, *31*, *36*, *47*, *125*, *126*; dipper, *45–46*, *111*
Mesa Verde pottery, 74; bowls, 26, *27*, *29*, *34*, *47*, *109*, *113*; dipper, *38*; mugs, *29*, *32*, *33–34*, *45*, *58*, *66*, *67*, *105*, *127*; pitcher, *104*
Mesa Verde region, 46
metaphors, 14–15, 47, 55, 58, 63, 73–74

Mexico, 69
Mimbres pottery, 11, 38, *55*, 74, *80*, *86–87*
mirror-image reflection, *64*, 65–68, 70, 73
motifs, 79; abstractions of, 21, 37, 39, *112*, *116*; on basketry, 53; common ones, *40*, 41, 43–44; conventional, 22, *23*; painting of, 25–27, 37–39, 41, 43, 46–47; repeated, 27, 31, *32*, 39, 41, *42–43*, 73, *116*; visually active, 12, 14. *See also* specific types
mural paintings, *57–58*, 63, 71, 73

optical: ambiguity, 38–39; dualities, 27, *28*, 30; illusions, 14–15, 22, *23*, 25, 68, 73, 79; phenomena, 41, 46; principles, 17–21
optical reversals: examples of, *22*, *30*, *56*, *79*, *85*, *95*, *102*, *109*; explanation of, 11–12, 14, 17, 21–22, 29, 39, 73; size-based, 18, *99*, *103*, *105*, *124–25*, *127*
organizational understructures, 15, 25, *26–27*, 29, *30*, *33–35*, 37, 38–39, *125*. *See also* grid understructure

painted-and-unpainted isomers: and basketry, 53; examples of, *28–30*, *42*, *79*, *81–82*, *84*, *86–87*, *91–93*, *96–102*, *104–9*, *112*, *114*, *124*, *127*, *129*; explanation of, 17–18, 27–32, 39, 41, 53, 68
painted versus unpainted forms, 11, 22, 25
Panofsky, Erwin, 13–14

Parsons, Elsie Clews, 66
Peckham, Stewart, 17
petroglyphs, 59, *60–62*, 63
physical world, 65–68, *69*, 70–71, 73, 76
Pierce, Christopher, 51–52
Polychrome pottery. *See* St. Johns Polychrome
population changes, 12–13, 38, 71
positive-and-negative spaces: examples of, *35*, *36*, *56*, *103*, *116*, *122*, *124*; explanation of, 11, 17–18, 21, 27, 68, 73
potters, skills of, 15, 25, 38–39, 55–56, 74–77, *114*
pottery technology, 55, 65; emergence/development of, 13, 49–52; experimentation in, 25–26, 50, 52; nomenclature for, 17; and painting motifs, 37–38, 46, 50, 74–75; and the potters, 15, 74–75, 77. *See also* firing process
Principles of Visual Perception (Bloomer), 18
pronged motifs, *16*, 17, 29, *30*, *46–47*, *54*, 73, *92*, *96*, *107*, *109*
Pueblo Bonito (Chaco Canyon), *59*, 63
Pueblo III period, *54*
Pueblo people: communal nature of, 13, 70–71, 73–74; emergence of, 12, 57, 66; and material inequalities, 71; migrations of, 71; "opposites" essential to, 12; regional systems of, 12, 17, 63, 74–75; technological developments of, 65, 71, 77; villages of, 12–13, 25, 69, 74

Pueblo philosophy, 12, 15, 65–71, 75, 77
Pueblo Potter, The (Bunzel), 75
Pueblo pottery: advantages of, 39, 46, 49–50, 52; classification of, 17; emergence of, 13, 49–51; production of, 74–75, 77; significance of, 49, 63
Pueblo pottery design: from bowls to jars, 37, *38*; complexity of, 18, 26–27, 33, 35, 75, *93*; dualism in, 74; experimentation in, 25, 50; and links to basketry, 58, 63; meanings of, 13–15, 47, 66, 76; mimics baskets, 50, *51*, 52–53, *54–56*, 73, *98–99*, *119*; painting of, 11, 50, 55, 74–75, *110*; pre-isomeric, 25; and Pueblo history, 12–13, 25, 47, 57, 63; visually active, 12, 14, *118*
Pueblo society, 12–13, 17, 47, 50, 65, 69–71, 73–77

Rio Grande drainage, 71
ritual knowledge, 73–76
rituals, 58–59, 61–62, *64*, 65–66, 70–71, 75. *See also* kivas
rock art, 71. *See also* petroglyphs
Rubin diagrams, *22–23*
Rubin, Edgar, 22

San Juan drainage (New Mexico), 13, 57
San Ysidro, New Mexico, *62*
Sand Canyon Pueblo (Colorado), 74
Santa Clara Pueblo, 12
Sofaer, Anna, 61